Wild Women

Edited by Melissa Mia Hall

Illustrations by Jill Karla Schwarz

Carroll & Graf Publishers Inc.
New York

Collection and headnotes © 1997 by Melissa Mia Hall and Tekno Books

All rights reserved

First Carroll & Graf edition 1997

Carroll & Graf Publishers Inc.
260 Fifth Avenue
New York, NY 10001

Wild women / compiled by Melissa Mia Hall ; illustrations by Jill
    Karla Schwarz. — 1st Carroll & Graf ed.
        p. cm.
    ISBN 0-7867-0415-2 (cloth)
    1. American literature—20th century. 2. Women—Literary
collections. 3. Wild women—Literary collections. I. Hall,
Melissa Mia. II. Schwarz, Jill Karla.
PS509.W6W55 1997
810.8'09287'0904—dc21   97-9874
                                                                   CIP

Manufactured in the United States of America

Thanks to my mother, Mary Mason Ray,
who gave me the courage to find my path,
and to Clarissa Pinkola Estés,
whose words helped in a dark time.
I also wish to express gratitude to my contributors,
especially Jill, Nancy, Carole, Lisa, Jane, and
Margaret (there at the beginning, here at the
end) who helped me turn this
dream into a reality.

and then there's Marty and John, Katie,
Cheryl, Westwind, Michele, Melody,
and Ted, again, thanks.

Contents

■

Introduction

■

Wild women know their own power.

Whether mother, wife, sister, daughter, or lover, many women have had their primal selves stifled by restrictive societies. This anthology celebrates women who have reconnected to their wildish selves, who have not been buried by the expectations and denials of a patriarchal society.

Both male and female authors deliver these fictional wild women. Some visons are disturbing, others triumphant, all depict women who are in tune with their own needs.

Clarissa Pinkola Estés, Ph.D., in *Women Who Run with the Wolves* states boldly, "Stories are medicine." She writes, "They have such power; they do not require that we do, be, act anything—we need only listen. The remedies for repair or reclamation of any lost psychic drive are contained in stories. Stories engender the excitement, sadness, questions, longings and understandings that spontaneously bring the Archetype, in this case Wild Woman, back to the surface."*

In today's world we have been inundated with images of stereotyp-

*Estés, Clarissa Pinkola Ph.D., *Women Who Run With the Wolves*. Ballantine Books, New York © 1992, 1995 (p. 15).

ical wild women that frighten and dismay: the woman with the knife, the angry macho woman, the strident radical, the demonically successful businesswoman who crushes anyone in her path. To address that vision, I included some stories that dissected violence against women and/or by women. It intrigued me to include stories by male authors that portray wild women dealing with violence as well as those by female authors. But that's just the tip of the proverbial iceberg.

Also included are gentle stories about women suddenly recovering the hope that they may find their wild selves. The humorous, mysterious, fantastical, sexual, and haunting aspects of wild women are also explored. Poetry about wild women is also included. Indeed, wild women are living poems. Margaret Atwood's "Half-Hanged Mary," about a woman who refuses to die, became my mantra as I worked on this project for quite a long time, often wondering if it would ever bear fruition.

I chose to focus on contemporary living writers not usually thrown together (with the exception of Fritz Lieber, whose "The Girl with the Hungry Eyes" is timeless and seems required reading for anyone contemplating the contemporary fear shown the wild woman) for this volume, to provide a provocative mix.

In my search, I discovered that despite a somewhat innate fear of the strength displayed so freely by wild women, there's a basic respect and even love for the diva/goddess/wild woman. We stand in awe of her. It is not easy being in tune with the primal self, comfortable in your own skin.

Some years back, Karen Durbin wrote an article in *Mirabella* titled "Psychofemmes." She noted that it's shame that keeps women "good," that keeps them silent, docile, and powerless. Are wild women shameless? It's something I've pondered. At one time I considered calling this anthology *Psychofemmes* or *Crazy Women* and then discovered Dr. Estés landmark book, *Women Who Run With the Wolves* and decided my ideal wild women is merely empowered, in touch with her primal self.

If wild women go over the edge, they usually have been pushed there and must defend their territory. They are angels who don't have to have wings or halos to fly under their own power.

I was asked by one contributor if a child can be a wild woman. It sounds impossible; then I realized wild women begin as children and so included stories about very young girls taking their first steps on the wildish path. I was also asked by this same contributor if a wild woman can kill others or if a wild woman could kill herself. Then other questions from family and friends surfaced. Everyone I spoke to had a question. Everyone had an idea on what a wild woman is or can be. I hope these stories are helpful in creating your own answers.

Regarding "stories as medicine", remember, sometimes medicine may not taste good going down. Still, I hope you agree these stories have power, a healing power.

Be brave. Read on.

—Melissa Mia Hall
January 1997
Fort Worth, Texas

Half-Hanged Mary

■

MARGARET ATWOOD

("Half-hanged Mary" was Mary Webster, who was accused of witchcraft in the 1680s in a Puritan town in Massachusetts and hanged from a tree— where she stayed all night, by one account. When cut down she was still alive. She lived another fourteen years.)

7 P.M.

Rumor was loose in the air,
hunting for some neck to land on.
I was milking the cow,
the barn door open to the sunset.

I didn't feel the aimed word hit
and go in like a soft bullet.
I didn't feel the smashed flesh
closing over it like water
over a thrown stone.

I was hanged for living alone,
for having blue eyes and a dark skin,
tattered skirts, few buttons,
a weedy farm in my own name,
and a surefire cure for warts;

Oh yes, and breasts,
and a sweet pear hidden in my body.
Whenever there's talk of demons
these come in handy.

8 P.M.

The rope was an improvisation.
With time they'd have thought of axes.

Up I go like a windfall in reverse,
a blackened apple stuck back onto the tree.

Trussed hands, rag in my mouth,
a flag raised to salute the moon,

old bone-faced goddess, old original,
who once took blood in return for food.

The men of the town stalk homeward,
excited by their show of hate,

their own evil turned inside out like a glove
and me wearing it.

9 P.M.

The bonnets come to stare,
the dark skirts also,
the upturned faces in between,
mouths closed so tight they're lipless.
I can see down into their eyeholes
and nostrils. I can see their fear.

You were my friend, you too.
I cured your baby, Mrs.,
and flushed yours out of you,
Non-wife, to save your life.

Help me down? You don't dare.
I might rub off on you,
like soot or gossip. Birds
of a feather burn together
though as a rule ravens are singular.

In a gathering like this one
the safe place is the background,
pretending you can't dance,
the safe stance pointing a finger.

I understand. You can't spare
anything, a hand, a piece of bread, a shawl
against the cold,
a good word. Lord
knows there isn't much
to go around. You need it all.

10 P.M.

Well God, now that I'm up here
with maybe some time to spare
away from the daily
fingerwork, legwork, work
at the hen level,
we can continue our quarrel,
the one about free will.

Is it my choice that I'm dangling
like a turkey's wattles from this
more than indifferent tree?
If Nature is Your alphabet,
what letter is this rope?
Does my twisting body spell out Grace?
I hurt, therefore I am.
Faith, Charity, and Hope
are three dead angels
falling like meteors or
burning owls across
the profound blank sky of Your face.

11 P.M.

Passing by me in the wavering moonlight
you would not see anything unusual.
A limp silhouette, hardly worth spitting at.
A woman in poor clothing
depending by the neck from a tree,
her bared legs a scandal.

A piece of extra darkness unhooks
itself from the forest and watches me.
Could be a bear, but I'm up here
where travelers string meat to keep it
safe. Sorry, my carnivores,
come back tomorrow,

I'm busy being
static between earth and sky.
Holding my breath, what's left of it.
No signs of life. No action.
My best chance is to counterfeit death,
as certain snakes do, birds also.

Stay as still as possible.
Don't provoke the tree.
Imitate ice
in complete lucidity.

12 MIDNIGHT

My throat is taut against the rope
choking off words and air;
I'm reduced to knotted muscle.
Blood bulges in my skull,
my clenched teeth hold it in;
I bite down on despair.

Death sits on my shoulder like a crow
waiting for my squeezed beet
of a heart to burst
so he can eat my eyes

or like a judge
muttering about sluts and punishment
and licking his lips
or like a dark angel
insidious in his glossy feathers
whispering to me to be easy
on myself. To breathe out finally.
Trust me, he says, caressing
me. *Why suffer?*

A temptation, to sink down
into these definitions.
To become a martyr in reverse,
or food, or trash;

To give up my own words for myself,
my own refusals.
To give up knowing.
To give up pain.
To let go.

1 P.M.

Over there by the skyline
there's young thunder
beginning to push itself out.
Lightning slow as asparagus growing,
the thick shoot, then the delicate branching.
Small veins on eyelids,
cracks in black marble.
Each fission lasts an hour:
time shuts down when you're dying.
Then a long tumble of stones,
huge thrown-down boulders of air coming nearer.

I think, How tall is this tree?
I think, Don't let it hit me!
I think this between one torn
last breath and another.

2 P.M.

Out of my mouth is coming, at some
distance from me, a thin gnawing sound
which you could confuse with prayer except that
praying is not constrained.

Or is it, Lord?
Maybe it's more like being strangled
than I once thought. Maybe it's
a gasp for air, prayer.
Did those men at Pentecost
want flames to shoot out of their heads?
Did they ask to be tossed
on the ground, gabbling like holy poultry,
eyeballs bulging?

As mine are, as mine are.
There is only one prayer; it is not
the knees in the clean nightgown
on the hooked rug,
I want this, I want that.
Oh far beyond.
Call it *Please.* Call it *Mercy.*
Call it *Not yet, not yet,*
as Heaven threatens to explode
inwards in fire and shredded flesh, and the angels caw.

3 P.M.

Wind seethes in the leaves around
me the trees exude night
birds night birds yell inside
my ears like stabbed hearts my heart
stutters in my fluttering cloth
body I dangle with strength
going out of me the wind seethes
in my body tattering
the words I clench
my fists hold No
talisman or silver disk my lungs
flail as if drowning I call
on you as witness I did
no crime I was born I have born I
bear I will be born this is
a crime I will not
acknowledge leaves and wind
hold on to me
I will not give in

6 A.M.

Sun comes up, huge and blaring,
no longer a simile for God.
Wrong address. I've been out there.

Time is relative, let me tell you
I have lived a millennium.
I would like to say my hair turned white
overnight, but it didn't.
Instead it was my heart:
bleached out like meat in water.

Also, I'm about three inches taller.
This is what happens when you drift in space
listening to the gospel
of the redhot stars.
Pinpoints of infinity riddle my brain,
a revelation of deafness.

At the end of my rope
I testify to silence.
Don't say I'm not grateful.

Most will have only one death.
I will have two.

8 A.M.

When they came to harvest my corpse
(open your mouth, close your eyes)
cut my body from the rope,
surprise, surprise:
I was still alive.

Tough luck, folks,
I know the law:
you can't execute me twice
for the same thing. How nice.

I fell to the clover, breathed it in,
and bared my teeth at them
in a filthy grin.
You can imagine how that went over.

Now I only need to look
out at them through my skyblue eyes.
They see their own ill will
staring them in the forehead
and turn tail.

Before, I was not a witch.
But now I am one.

7 P.M.

I am a practical person.
I use the rope for a belt.
I milk the cow.
I have a surefire cure for warts
and for love too if you want one.

There are few buyers.
They fear whatever malice
got seeded in me
by spending twelve hours
as a flesh decoration strung on a tree.

Rumor has it
I've got the town penises
like so many dried morels
threaded on a leather thong
I wear as a necklace.
I could, if I wanted.

But revenge doesn't interest me.
I have other things to do,
the crops and stars to attend to.

MIDNIGHT

My body of skin waxes and wanes
around my true body,
a tender nimbus.
I skitter over the paths and fields
mumbling to myself like crazy,
mouth full of juicy adjectives
and purple berries.
The townsfolk dive headfirst into the bushes
to get out of my way.

My first death orbits my head,
an ambiguous halo,
medallion of my ordeal.
No one crosses that circle.

Having been hanged for something
I never said,
I can now say anything I can say.

Holiness gleams on my dirty fingers,
I eat flowers and dung,
two forms of the same thing, I eat mice
and give thanks, blasphemies
gleam and burst in my wake
like lovely bubbles.
I speak in tongues,
my audience is owls.

My audience is God,
because who the hell else could understand me?
Who else has been dead twice?

The words boil out of me,
coil after coil of sinuous possibility.
The cosmos unravels from my mouth,
all fullness, all vacancy.

Going North

■

LUCY TAYLOR

"Why do you want to go to the North Pole?" asked Aunt Gish as she and Pruitt waited in line at the Galleria Mall to see Santa Claus.

Pruitt shrugged, wishing she'd never said anything about the North Pole. She didn't know if she could trust Aunt Gish with something so important. In her seven years, Pruitt had learned not to trust anyone, to play along with what the adults wanted when she had to, but better yet, to stay out of their way.

Pruitt wasn't even sure if it was okay to talk to Santa, but she figured she had to take the chance. Even a mall Santa was more than just an ordinary grown-up. He was someone who might be able to help her.

The Galleria Mall in Fort Lauderdale was crowded with shoppers, adults carrying packages and scurrying around so frantically they reminded Pruitt of roach bugs carrying off crumbs when you turned on the light in the kitchen at night, and little kids, some excited, some shy, one or two bawling like babies, who were standing in line to see Santa.

Pruitt Nelson and her Aunt Gish were near the middle of a line that stretched from Santa's big, star-dusted throne all the way to the

Wal-Marts at the bend in the "L" of the mall. They'd been waiting almost an hour already and Pruitt was worried: Was Aunt Gish going to become impatient and drag her out of there before she had a chance to talk to Santa? Especially since Aunt Gish hadn't even gone to the ladies' room to do a joint or a line or anything. Neither Miriam nor Daddy could have put up with the mall for five minutes without a smoke or a snort.

Aunt Gish seemed to be doing just fine, though, and Pruitt was grateful, if a little surprised. She'd already heard Daddy telling Miriam that Aunt Gish was crazy, that the reason she hadn't come to Mom's funeral two years ago was that she was locked up in the loony bin in New York City after getting hysterical and threatening to shoot herself right there in the principal's office of the school where she used to teach second grade.

The line inched forward. Pruitt could see the shine on Santa's nose, the fake snow on his knee-high black boots. *Help me,* she thought. *Please help me.*

"It's real cold at the North Pole," Aunt Gish said long after Pruitt had assumed the subject was dropped. "Why would you want to leave Florida, where it's warm and sunny, to go live in a place that's so cold?"

"Because I *hate* it here," said Pruitt, crowding up behind a fat toddler with a lollipop stick protruding from his mouth like a very thick hypodermic syringe. "I hate the Palmetto bugs and the hot weather, and I hate . . ." Pruitt started to say "Daddy and Kenny and Miriam" but decided against it. Aunt Gish was Momma's older sister, after all, and she might repeat what Pruitt was getting ready to say, and Pruitt might get smacked around.

"And what makes you think the North Pole would be better?"

Pruitt didn't answer. She just clamped her lips shut tight against her teeth and waited while the line crept forward, inch by inch, toward Santa.

Pruitt knew perfectly well that this red-suited, lumpy-looking man with the white beard and the crinkly brown eyes wasn't the real, the one and only, Santa Claus. She'd already seen one Santa ringing a bell next to a kettle outside the Sears store on Federal Highway and still another waiting at a bus stop, leaning up against a lamppost, looking puffy-eyed and hung over. She figured, however, that these assistant Santas probably reported back to the *real* one at the North Pole and that they probably filed their information (which Pruitt imagined like a kind of police report) with the Big Man himself.

So when she was settled on Santa's lap and he asked her what she wanted most for Christmas, Pruitt told him, and Santa laughed and said that wasn't possible and Pruitt, who didn't think what she'd asked for was the least bit funny, punched Santa in the eye with her small, knobby fist and then burst into frustrated howls.

"Are you gonna beat the crap out of me?" asked Pruitt as she and Aunt Gish drove out Sunrise Boulevard toward the subdivision in Lake of the Pines where she lived with her father and his girlfriend Miriam. It was the first time that she'd spoken since the disaster with Santa Claus, when Aunt Gish had come swooping down like an enraged falcon and snatched Pruitt away, demanding to know what Santa had said or done to so distress the child.

"No, of course, I'm not going to beat you," Aunt Gish said. "Why would you ask such a thing?"

"When I'm bad, Miriam always says she's gonna beat the crap out of me and that she wishes I was dead."

Aunt Gish fumbled in her purse on the seat between her and Pruitt, pulled out a Bic and a pack of Winstons, and lit a cigarette. Pruitt noticed that her fingernails were so badly bitten they looked red and infected, and her hands were trembling. She figured that must be because Aunt Gish hadn't gone to the ladies' room to smoke or snort or inject anything during the whole time that she and Pruitt were out.

"Pruitt, I need to ask you something. When you hit Santa Claus, was it because he did something to you? Did he touch you where he shouldn't have? Your private parts, I mean."

"Between my legs?" asked Pruitt.

"That's right."

"You mean the way Daddy and Kenny touch me when Miriam's not around?"

A delivery van was backing out of the driveway of a Furniture Warehouse and Aunt Gish almost broadsided it, swerving out of the way just at the last second and making the tires of her Plymouth squeal. She pulled into the parking lot of a convenience store at the next corner and shut the motor off.

"What do you mean, Pruitt? Who's Kenny? What do he and your daddy do?"

Pruitt realized that she'd said too much, but Aunt Gish kept asking questions, so finally Pruitt told her a little bit, that Kenny was one of Daddy's customers who came around a couple of times a week with lots of cash, but she left some things out because Aunt Gish got very white and started biting on her lower lip and a drop of blood leaked out that she didn't even seem to feel. Pruitt thought what Aunt Gish probably needed was a very stiff drink, as Miriam would say, but she was scared to suggest it.

"Santa didn't hurt me like Daddy and Kenny do," said Pruitt, deciding it was time to change the subject. "I hit him cause he laughed at me when I said I wanted to go to the North Pole."

Aunt Gish poked at her weepy eyes with a Kleenex and lit another cigarette, holding it outside the window so the smoke didn't get in the car.

"You want to go to the North Pole really bad, don't you?"

"Yeah," said Pruitt. "I have to."

Aunt Gish started up the motor again. "It's still light. We can't go to the North Pole, but do you want to go to the beach?"

"What about Daddy and Miriam?"

"Fuck 'em," said Aunt Gish.

Pruitt was impressed that her geeky-looking aunt would use such a word and thought maybe she'd been wrong to think Aunt Gish was just a nerd and a weirdo. It was an easy mistake, though. Aunt Gish was enormously fat and looked frumpy and old in a candy-cane blouse that was meant to look Christmasy but really just looked dumb, and a brown polyester skirt and ugly brown shoes, and her hair (which was the same color as the shoes except for a thick streak of white at the top) tucked up like a huge mushroom that was sprouting out of the top of her head. She'd seen Miriam snicker when Aunt Gish first waddled in the front door and Daddy had muttered to Miriam that Aunt Gish's clothes must be "loony-bin chic" and that maybe it was the shock treatments that had caused part of her hair to go white.

"Yeah, fuck 'em," whispered Pruitt under her breath, and if Aunt Gish heard, she pretended not to.

They drove over one of the bridges crossing the Intercoastal Waterway and parked in the lot of a motel across the street from the ocean. Aunt Gish took off her clunky shoes and her hose and Pruitt took off her Keds and they walked down onto the sand, which was still warm even though the sun was now almost down, the light slanting off the waves so fiercely that it looked like someone had tossed a million silver coins onto the water.

Aunt Gish was very quiet and after a while, Pruitt looked up and said, "Are you mad at me?"

Aunt Gish looked surprised. "Of course not. Why would you think that?"

"You're crying."

"Because I'm sad," said Aunt Gish, "and I'm angry. Oh, Pruitt, I'm so angry I could . . . I'm just very angry, but not at you. You haven't done anything."

They continued up the beach together, passing beneath a pier where people were casting poles off into the silvery water and pelicans swooped and rose against the glitter of the sea. At one point Aunt Gish reached to take Pruitt's hand and lead her around a jellyfish, but Pruitt pulled her hand away and stepped around the jellyfish herself. She didn't want to hold hands with Aunt Gish or anyone else. It made her feel trapped, like her hand was being molded into a part of the adult's body and no longer belonged to her. Of all the scary feelings that Pruitt had known in her short life, the feeling of not belonging to herself was the scariest of all.

After they'd walked in silence for a while, Pruitt got her nerve up to ask the question she'd been wondering about ever since Daddy first told her that Momma had had an older sister who'd moved to Florida and bought a house trailer in Delray Beach.

"Daddy says you were locked up in a place for crazy people. Were you *really*? Or was Daddy just making it up because he doesn't like you?"

Aunt Gish laughed and almost reached for Pruitt's hand. Then she must have remembered that this was something Pruitt didn't seem to like, and she let her hand fall back by her side.

"Your Daddy's right. I had what they used to call a nervous breakdown, but really that just means I cried all the time and couldn't eat or sleep or work and I didn't want to live."

Pruitt remembered when her mother was alive and acted that way every time she couldn't get her crack. She'd gone out one night, leaving Pruitt with her father, and she never came back. There'd been a stabbing, said the policeman who came to the door the next day. Something about a drug deal gone bad that Pruitt's mother got in the middle of.

"When you didn't want to live no more, was it because you couldn't get drugs?" asked Pruitt, kicking at what looked like long strands of foamy spit hawked up by the ocean.

"No, nothing like that," Aunt Gish said. "I used to teach school, and a few years ago there was a little boy in my class, a wonderful little boy named Timmy Anderson, and he kept coming to school with bruises so I called the people who're supposed to look out for children like Timmy and said I thought someone was hurting him. Someone in his home. But those people were very overworked and they didn't really have time to visit Timmy's house more than once and, well, one of his parents beat Timmy very badly soon after that and he died. And then a year later there was a little girl named Angie Myers and she had blood in her underpants one day, and I reported it to the same people who were supposed to help Timmy and you know what? They were still really busy, and somebody misplaced Angie's file and one day she didn't come to school at all and—"

"She got killed, didn't she?"

"Oh, honey, I'm sorry. I shouldn't be telling you such awful things. It's just that, after Angie, that was when I didn't want to live anymore. It just seemed like there wasn't any point, like children were dying right under my nose and all I was doing was making stupid phone calls. I felt so bad, I bought a gun and decided to shoot myself. But then I thought, maybe I wasn't ready to die, maybe that was too easy a solution, so I went to a hospital for a while and then when I got better, I decided to come down here to Florida. Take what they call early retirement. Because I couldn't stand to see any more Timmys or Angies. I just thought it would kill me to see anything like that again."

"Come to the North Pole with me."

"Why the North Pole, honey?"

"It's safe there," said Pruitt, kicking the water ahead of her in long silver arcs. "It's cold and quiet and empty so you can just walk for miles and not run into anybody else. And the sun shines and the ice sparkles all the time and it's . . . safe."

She kicked at the water. A long time ago, back when her mother was still alive, she remembered seeing a cartoon about a pair of children who went to the North Pole to visit Santa. She remembered cliffs of white ice rising straight up into a cold, sunny sky and herds of reindeer moving across frozen, empty plains where you could run forever and no one would ever see you or hear you or hurt you or cause you pain, and when Daddy or Kenny were hurting her or when Miriam was screaming at her, she would go to that cold, clear place of endless, empty space and she would roam among the ice castles and watch the polar bears play and she would be safe, so safe . . . and free . . . and she would belong to herself. . . .

"The North Pole is a long way off," Aunt Gish was saying. "You'd need a map to get there."

"No, I won't," said Pruitt, and she told Aunt Gish her plan.

The beach was brown with shadows, the horizon just a purple streak, like grape jelly smeared over silk, when Aunt Gish said they'd better turn back.

"I could stay with you at your trailer tonight," Pruitt said, and Aunt Gish told a deep breath and said, "Oh, honey, I wish you could. But your dad and Miriam were expecting us back a long time ago. I have to take you home now."

"Please?" said Pruitt. "Don't make me go back there."

"I can't," Aunt Gish said. "I'm sorry, Pruitt, I can't help you. I can't do anything at all."

She shook another cigarette out of the pack, but her hands were shaking so badly now she couldn't light it and finally she said a long string of bad words and threw the cigarette into the sea.

The pink house where Pruitt lived was in the middle of a block of two-story stucco houses in various pastel shades. All the houses had chimneys, built more for looks than for function, but useful during South Florida's occasional winter cold snaps. Pruitt's house had the additional decoration of a trellis extending up one side of the house to roof level. When Pruitt's mother was alive the trellis had been covered with morning glory vines. Now it resembled empty scaffolding, badly worn and in need of a paint job.

A man was knocking on the front door when Aunt Gish and Pruitt drove up. Pruitt's heart sank as she recognized Kenny. He was darkly tanned with very short, baby-fine blond hair and skin the color and texture of alligator hide, and he drove a silver Jag with New Jersey license plates.

"That's Kenny," Pruitt whispered. "The one who touches me."

When Kenny saw Pruitt and Aunt Gish approaching, he stared at Pruitt, at her bare feet, the wet legs of her jeans, and a very pale, sickly glow seemed to shine behind the dark brown of his tan that reminded Pruitt of the yellow eyes in a battery-powered Triceratops she'd once seen.

Aunt Gish guided Pruitt ahead of her as if they were crossing a very dangerous intersection.

"Pretty kid," Kenny said to Aunt Gish as they came up on the porch, although his eyes never left Pruitt. "Gonna be a real looker someday."

The silence following that remark was the loudest Pruitt had ever heard.

Kenny reached down as if to ruffle Pruitt's hair.

Aunt Gish snatched Pruitt backward out of his reach. She put her red, fatty face an inch away from Kenny's tanned, plastic-looking skin and said, in a voice so close to a whisper that Pruitt could barely hear her, "You ever lay a hand on this child again and you'll be in prison buying your drugs with blow jobs, you fucking pervert."

Kenny took a step back, almost stumbling off the top step of the porch, just as Pruitt's father opened the door. He was a short, wiry man with a boxer's build and blue eyes iced over with perpetual rage.

"Who is this bitch?" Kenny asked with a hiss. "What does she mean calling me a pervert and accusing me of buying drugs? Who the hell *is* she?"

Pruitt's father apologized to Kenny, who smirked and went inside the house. Then he started screaming at Aunt Gish.

"Go back to New York or the funny farm or wherever the hell you wanna go, but don't you ever come back here, you fat, fucked-up bitch." He smacked Aunt Gish hard across the face and she fell backward onto the grass with a loud thump. "Don't you come 'round here makin' trouble for me, insultin' my friends. You ain't no family of mine. Now get the fuck outta here! Go!"

Pruitt got a glimpse of Aunt Gish before Daddy shoved her ahead of him into the house. She was getting to her feet and her candy-cane blouse was all streaked with dirt and her eyes looked like little black dots sunken into the centers of soft, doughy rolls with a splotch of clown red on each cheek.

"Don't make her go," Pruitt said. "She didn't do anything."

Daddy slapped Pruitt and then picked her up off the floor and slapped her again and gave her a kick in the butt for good measure.

"Get your ass upstairs. You'll prob'ly grow up to be as crazy as she is."

Pruitt ran upstairs and threw herself across the bed and cried and after she finished crying she prayed for help. She prayed for Christmas Eve to come and she prayed to Santa Claus.

On Christmas Eve, Pruitt was allowed to play outside until it got dark. Then Miriam called her inside and fed her pizza and orange juice in the kitchen.

Around nine o'clock Kenny came over with some coke and a fifth of Jack Daniels and Pruitt went up to bed. "I'll be up later," Daddy said, and Pruitt felt her stomach constrict into a sharp little fist.

In her room, she opened the window wide and climbed out onto the ledge. The trellis, which was only a few inches away, suddenly looked very distant, the wooden slats rickety and spindly. Pruitt got a foothold and then grabbed it with her hands. The wood made cracking sounds, but it held her weight. She put the other leg up and started to climb.

Climbing up to the roof wasn't so bad. Getting over the edge was the hard part. She had to get her feet up as high on the trellis as possible and then throw herself forward onto the roof and kind of snake-shimmy onto the roof and then she had to take care to avoid the skylight that looked down over the living room.

But finally she made it to the very top and sat with her back against the chimney, listening to the cars pass on the street below, waiting. The air was warm and muggy, humid with the promise of rain. Presently Pruitt's head lolled and she slept and dreamed . . . of ice palaces and bright, clean cold.

When she awoke, the night seemed much darker and starless. Pruitt felt the soft stirrings of panic. She wondered if Santa Claus had come and gone already, if she'd missed her one chance.

Downstairs she could hear voices. Peering through the skylight, she saw Daddy and Miriam and Kenny. They were gathered around the card table, playing poker. For some reason, Miriam had taken off her clothes and was sitting there stark naked, but neither Daddy nor Kenny seemed to notice this. They just kept on playing cards.

From below, Pruitt heard footsteps. She looked up the block and was astonished to see Santa Claus approaching. He wasn't riding in his sleigh and landing on the roof like he was supposed to. The pack that was slung over his shoulder looked lumpy and not very full. Once Santa glanced up, almost like he was looking at the roof, and Pruitt waved her hand wildly—*up here, take me with you*—but he didn't seem to see.

When he got closer, Santa turned and marched straight up the walk. Pruitt heard the doorbell chime. She couldn't believe it. Santa was ringing the bell and coming in the front door. He had it all wrong. He should be on the roof, so she could ask him to let her go with him. He'd fucked up. Santa Claus had fucked up!

Angry tears filled Pruitt's eyes. Frantically she lowered herself over the edge of the roof and started to climb down the trellis.

She heard Daddy answer the door. His voice was slurry and he had that don't-fuck-with-me growl to it, but then he shouted back into the house to Kenny and Miriam, "Hey, look what we got here! Santa Claus says we won some kinda Christmas lottery. Hey, Miriam, did you . . . ?"

The popping started just about the time Pruitt reached the window and was climbing back into her room. She thought: Daddy and Kenny are killing Santa Claus, and then she was running down the hall toward the stairs, and she heard the popping sounds again and again and then everything got very still.

The first one she saw was Miriam, leaning up against the TV. She was still naked, but now she looked like she was wearing a red blouse. Daddy lay in the hall. His face looked like it was made of Silly Putty that squashed with their fists.

Pruitt's mouth dropped open and she uttered a soundless "O," but she felt neither grief nor fear, just a strange, fluttery sickness in her stomach.

She crept into the kitchen, where Kenny lay with a row of what looked like bright red buttons across his back. A cigarette still burned between his fingers.

From the bathroom, Pruitt heard someone throwing up and a toilet flushing. Then Santa came out of the bathroom wiping his beard and carrying what Pruitt recognized to be a semi-automatic pistol.

"Don't be afraid," said Santa, but even before she heard the voice, Pruitt recognized the small white hands with the fingernails chewed away.

Aunt Gish tucked the pistol back into her sack, which was stuffed with what looked like foam rubber. "Come with me?" she said.

Pruitt looked at the bodies all around her and at Santa/Aunt Gish and she knew Daddy might have been right about one thing, that Aunt Gish might just be crazy as hell, but maybe that was okay, maybe crazy was the best way anybody could be.

Aunt Gish squatted down and looked into Pruitt's face.

"Listen to me, honey. I shot three people tonight, so the police will be looking for me. For you, too. If they find us, they'll take care of you, but they won't let you see me anymore. You'll have to find your way to the North Pole alone. Do you think you can do that?"

Pruitt thought about the dangers and possibilities ahead: the chance to find a place to be free, to be safe, a place to belong to herself.

She reached up and took Aunt Gish's hand.

They left the house and walked up the street to where Aunt Gish had hidden the Plymouth behind some Dumpsters.

"It's not easy getting to the North Pole," said Aunt Gish. "It may take years and years and all your courage. Not many people get there. I didn't, Pruitt, I never did, but I want you to have a chance."

Pruitt nodded, believing that it could be done, knowing that, with Aunt Gish or without her, she would find her way to the North Pole someday, even if she had to make the map herself.

How I Got to Be Queen

■

GREG SARRIS

I watched Justine across the street. I seen her from the window. Even with Sheldon and Jeffrey asking for lunch, I seen clear enough to know she was up to her old tricks. I said to myself, that queen, she's up to it again. This time it was a boy, a black boy whose name I'd learn in a matter of hours. Justine wastes no time. But just then I pulled away from the window, in case the two little guys might see what I did. Kids have a way of telling things, after all.

Nothing was unpacked. Not even the kitchen this time. I pulled a towel from boxes on the floor and dusted the paper plates left from breakfast. What food we had was on the table. Half loaf of Wonder Bread. Two large jars of peanut butter. Two cans of pie filling. Justine went for another loaf of bread, jam, and a packet of lemonade mix. She got far as the store, which is kitty-corner, just down the street, in plain view from the window.

She stood on one side of the bicycle rack, by the newspaper stand. She stood with a hand on her hip, her head lifted and tilted to the side. Like she was taking a dare, or fixing on some scheme. It makes people notice her. She draws them in that way. She looked black as the boy straddling a bike on the other side of the rack.

I wondered what Mom would do if she seen her there. That's if

Mom wasn't at the cannery with Auntie. I think it's bad the way Justine and Mom talk to each other when there's trouble. "Damned
black-neck squaw," Mom says. "Dirty fat Indian," Justine says. "You
don't even know which Filipino in that apple orchard is my father."
On and on it goes. Of course, Mom don't say much any other time.
And if Justine goes on long enough, Mom goes out or watches TV.
Like nothing was ever started. Like she does with just about anything
else.

I took the longest time setting two pieces of bread on each plate. I
found things to look for: the aluminum pie tins, the plastic cups left
over from Cousin Jeanne's party, the rolling pin. "I'm going to make
a pie," I said to the boys standing at the table. "We'll have a party
with pie and lemonade." They shifted on their feet with no patience.
"All right," I said. "You act like starved rats and you look worse than
pigs. Now wash up." I spread peanut butter on the bread, then sprin-
kled on some sugar. "I don't want no complaining," I told them when
they came back.

Justine came in about four, an hour before Mom.

"Now what good's that?" I asked. She put the bag of groceries on
the table. "You might as well go back and get the burger and torts
for dinner. And get flour. I got canned pumpkin for pies."

"Don't give me no shit, Alice," she said. Times like this she played
older sister. She wasn't listening to me. She just shook that silky hair
and said, "I'm in love. And he is fine. Ou wee, sis, the boy is fine."

She was talking like a black person. It's one of her things. I don't
mean talking like a black person. Justine does things so you notice.
She goes for a response. Like what she started with Jack, the boys'
father. Which is behind us coming to Santa Rosa. Mom said it's Justine's fault. I said Jack was old and his family would come for him
sooner or later, anyway. Giving Justine credit just fed the fire.

It started with a Social Security check that wandered to the bottom
of Mom's purse and stuck itself into something or other. Since a week
went by and it didn't come up for air, Jack started to get edgy. "My
money, where is it?" he kept asking. He was at the point if his dinner
wasn't on time, you was trying to starve him. If a door or window was
left open, you wanted him to die of pneumonia. It didn't surprise me
he called Clifford, his son.

"What do you mean, you lost it?" Clifford said to Mom.

I heard Jack make the call, so I figured trouble. Clifford and Mom have a history, and Clifford was all along dead against Mom being conservator and signing for Jack. True, Jack wasn't in his right mind half the time, and his insides was shot. Like a sponge that doesn't suck water is what the clinic doctor said. But Mom wasn't no crook. I opened my huckleberry jam. I made toast and set the table. But Clifford, who's more stubborn than a ass and looks worse, seen none of it.

"What's the matter, Mollie, you start on the bottle again?" he asked Mom.

Mom was sitting next to Jack. I looked at the place mats and the food. Anyone could see the old man was cared for and fed.

"Cliff," I said. "Why not put a stop on the check? Go to the Social Security." I felt funny saying Cliff. For a while it was Dad.

"Yeah, and what's my father supposed to eat in the meantime? You kids is using up his money." Then he looked at Mom. "I'm telling you, Mollie, I'm sick of what's going on here."

He brushed past Justine, who stood in the doorway. I said the check would turn up. Justine said, "Who cares?"

But Justine seen how to use the situation to her end. She never liked Jack. "He nags Mom," she said. I said, "How can he give anybody else attention when he's half dead?" Justine didn't see my point. And it was Easter vacation, no school and no work in the orchards, which means you had nothing to do, no one to see. Or, in Justine's case, nowhere else to pull her stunts. So there was time for thinking.

All of a sudden Justine was dressed up. I mean dressed up every day. She found clothes I never knowed existed in that house. She mixed skirts and blouses in different ways. She wore down her eyeliner pencil in a week. Each morning she worked her hair into a hive the size of Sheldon's basketball. And when that was done, she sat at the kitchen table painting her nails the color of a red jelly bean. Then, when Mom went to register at the cannery, she started on how she was going to buy a stereo. "I put down fifty dollars at the Golden Ear," she said.

That got Justine a response.

Clifford made it from the reservation in one hour. And he wasn't alone. His white woman was with him, the woman who opens her mouth only when her nose is plugged and she can't breathe. Her I wasn't afraid of. It was Evangeline, his sister, who just as soon spit than say hello. She hated Mom. She looked at me like I was Mom's bare foot and she wanted to smash it under her work boots.

I knowed the old man went into the bedroom and called someone. I figured one of his kids. I just never put two and two together. And neither did Justine. She never got the pleasure of being falsely accused of stealing.

Clifford left his woman and sister guard. Like we would lift the last penny from Jack's pockets. Then he came back with suitcases and boxes. "Come on, Dad," he said, "Evangeline is going to take care of you. She won't spend the money on *her* kids. Not like this lot of swine."

Mom wasn't legal with Jack. There was nothing she could do. It was agreed about the checks only because he lived with us. Since the car was Jack's, it was gone now, too. Even so, she walked to town, then took the bus to Santa Rosa, and canceled the check at the Social Security. Of course, three days later it floats up from the mess in her purse.

Auntie drove Mom to the res, but it was no use. Evangeline wouldn't let her see Jack. She didn't care about the check. I know what Evangeline said. I heard it before. "You screwed my brother, then went for my father. Dirty whore. I don't believe those two kids are my father's. Now get." I reminded Mom that we are from Lake County. "We're not from that res," I said.

Justine unloaded what I first sent her for, then tore off for the dinner stuff. This time she was back right away. She kept the boys out of my hair. I got busy. My nerves pushed me. Rolling dough for pies, I thought of things. Which is a way I calm my nerves when working won't do it alone. I didn't like what I seen at the store and my imagination started to get the best of me. I thought of Jack. I guess because I hadn't made a pie since we left Healdsburg and came here. I thought how he'd settle down his griping when I cooked. Mom called me whenever he started screeching. He acted drunk, though the hardest thing he took those days was ginger ale. I rolled pie dough and didn't notice when he picked berries or apples or whatever it was out of the bowl. He was quiet. I thought that's what a grandfather would be like.

I set the pies in the oven. Then I got to work on dinner. I turned meat in one skillet and warmed torts in the other. I sent Justine to the store again, this time for cheese and chili sauce. The skillet of meat, a plate of warmed torts, sliced cheese and toast was on the table when Mom got home. Her place was at the head. It's where I put things, like the cheese and chili sauce which she likes on her meat, so you know.

She didn't say nothing. She was tired, I know. She finished eating, then cleaned up and went to play cards with Auntie like she did every night. "Tomorrow, we'll start on the boxes," she told me before she left. She was standing in the kitchen then, combing back her washed hair with Sheldon's pink comb. I kept on with the dishes. It has been two weeks, I thought to myself. Then, with my hands in the greasy water, I resolved to start unpacking myself, no matter what she said. We couldn't wait to see if we was going to stay here or not. Tomorrow, I told myself, first thing. I heard the front door slam.

I was still scrubbing, finishing the damned skillets, when I turned to tell the boys to take a bath before I gave them pie, which I had cooling on the sink. I thought Justine was behind me, seated at the table. But she wasn't. She was standing there with her friend.

"This is Ducker," she said.

First thing I noticed, the boys wasn't there. "They're taking baths," Justine said, seeing how I was looking at the empty seats.

She was referring to them not seeing Ducker. I never heard the door open since it slammed behind Mom. My ears pick up on those things. So I was caught off guard. Justine didn't have to embarrass me. "Close your mouth," she said. "You look like Clifford's wife."

I thought of the boys again. The bathroom door was shut. Then I thought this Ducker might think I'm stupid, or prejudice on account of him being black. My mind was going in several directions at once. I said what made no sense given the circumstances.

"Here, Mister Ducker, sit down and have some pie." I put a pie on the table.

Justine started laughing. I knowed she thought I was in shock seeing this black person in our house.

"It ain't *Mister Ducker*," she said. "It's Ducker. Ducker Peoples."

"Well . . ."

"We don't want pie," she said. She looked toward the bathroom, then to Ducker. "We're going for a walk."

"Nice to meet you . . ." he said, stopping when he got to my name.

"Alice," Justine said.

"Alice," he said.

I was still standing in the same place after they went out the front door. I tore to the window. Then I seen what he looked like. When they was across the street, almost to the store, I remembered who it was in front of me two minutes before. Funny thing about Ducker, he wasn't a man. Well, I mean grown. He was a kid, looked like. Bony arms hanging from flapping short sleeves. His face, shiny smooth, no hair. Like he should be chewing bubble gum and keeping baseball cards. Not holding on to Justine, who was sixteen and looked it.

"Who was here?"

I jumped around, half scared to death. It was Sheldon and Jeffrey out of the bathtub, drying their naked bodies.

"Now dry off in the bathroom," I said.

"Sound like a nigger."

"Hush up, Sheldon."

"Who was here?"

"Nobody."

Next day something concerned me. Mom was in the kitchen, putting things in cupboards. I heard her even before I got up. Even then I didn't think she'd make a day of it.

"It's Tuesday," she said. "Day off."

She finished with the kitchen before I started breakfast. I had to open cupboards to find things. She was in the bedroom by the time I could help her. Her things she put in the closet first. I seen her red dress from where I was standing, opening the boys' boxes. It's crinoline with ruffles. She wears it with her black patent leather shoes with the sides busted out. Like at Great-Auntie's funeral. Or when she came home with Clifford. Same thing with Jack.

"I guess this means we're staying here," I said.

This move was a trail. Ever since we came to Santa Rosa seemed nothing worked for very long. First that house on West Seventh we couldn't afford. Then the one by the freeway that no one told us they was going to tear down for development. Got two months rent from us, anyway. And now this, which Auntie, whose idea it was for us to come here, got from the landlord she knows.

"What choice do we have?" she asked.

The way she said that matched her business putting things away. Like it was nothing. Seemed to me just then, anyway. Like I said, it concerned me. I was the one who most of the time put things away, after all. No matter what she said before or after. It was just this time she made such a big deal about the neighborhood. Then I guess we moved so much. Just three months in Santa Rosa, and three times already.

"Well," I said. "I like it here. It's a change."

"A lot of blacks," Mom said. "Auntie didn't say so much about that."

"Not everybody can be a Pomo Indian," I said. Since Mom had her stuff on the bed, I spread the boys' things on their sleeping bags, which I hadn't rolled up yet. I sorted underwear on my knees. I thought of reminding her that Justine is part Filipino, and that I'm part Mexican. But that is what Justine would do.

"It's nice having Auntie up the street," I said. I liked the way Mom called her cousin "Auntie," which she did for us kids. "I like hearing Auntie tell stories."

"Ah, don't listen to that old Indian stuff."

Auntie cooks good. She's got recipes. And she's classy. Slender-bodied, not like me and Mom. She knows how to talk to social workers, those kind of people.

I got up and put the folded things in the boys' drawers. Mom was hanging up me and Justine's clothes. "Is this okay?" I asked, seeing how she was putting things where she wanted.

"Your sister, I don't know what she'll do here. Run with them kids out there. Niggers, anything."

That made it click. My worries took form in a picture. Justine and Ducker. Still, I wasn't certain, I mean about Mom just then. Did Sheldon or Jeffrey see last night and tell? It's how Mom says things by not saying them. It puts you in a place where you don't know if she's saying something or not. That's far as she'll go. Unless it's with Justine in a fight.

I was caught, trapped, and bothered just the same. Mom kept working, her back to me.

"Don't worry about Justine," I said.

* * *

We had a normal family dinner that night. I fixed chops and fried potatoes. I cut celery sticks and carrots. People need greens. But this family don't eat them. Which is one reason there's so much crabbing. They're stopped up.

Mom stayed and helped with the dishes before she went to Auntie's. Of course while things looked peaceful I imagined a disaster. Like Ducker knocking on the door. I wondered if Mom was hanging around in case that happened. I saw loudmouth Sheldon saying, "It's him. It's him." But nothing happened. Even after Mom left.

The boys opened drawers, looking to find where I put their clothes. They kept bugging me about getting the TV fixed and hooked up. Justine moved stuff in the closet to her liking. Me, I only wanted a long enough couch in the living room. I was sleeping on the floor with the boys. I can't sleep in the bed with Mom and Justine. No rest, even with them out like a light.

Next day Mom went fishing to the coast with Auntie. Auntie's mom and uncle, they sat in the car when Auntie came in for Mom. The old lady stuck her white head out and said for me to come along. I stood on the front porch to say hello. "I can't," I said. Then she said to me in Indian what men used to say in the old days when they set out fishing. "Get the grill ready, then."

"Damn cannery's so cheap. Got illegals instead of working us extra days," Mom said when she came out.

"Don't think of work, Mollie," Auntie said.

Justine padded up and stood with me to wave good-bye. She was still waving after the car left. I thought she was nuts until I seen it was Ducker she was waving forward. Bold as daylight. He walked right up the front porch.

"Morning, Alice," he said.

I thought of my mouth this time. I kept it closed, not shocked. And I thought what to do. Already the boys seen everything. I got some bread in a plastic bag and headed for the park. I carried Jeffrey part of the way. Sheldon, I just about dragged by the hair.

"What's so big about seeing goldfish?" he said, whining like he does. A sure trait of his father. Proof I would have for Evangeline.

"Shut up," I said. "You damn ass brat."

"You just don't want us there with that—"

I slapped his face. Then he started crying like I tied him to a stake and burned him. Which I wanted to do. We was at the park by then. I put bread in the water for the fish. But nothing worked. Sheldon screamed so the whole park could hear. "I'm telling Mom," he said. Then I thought of the opposite of fire. Water. And I had it right there.

"Shut up," I said, "before I rub your face in dog shit. Now shut up, damn you." Then Jeffrey started crying. "Now see," I said. "Stop it, Sheldon. Please."

I threatened the police. Sheldon quit some, but I knowed what weapon he was harboring, that he'd use against me the minute he seen Mom. I looked at the soggy bread floating on the empty water.

"I'll get the TV fixed," I said. "But not if you act like that, Sheldon."

So I spent what was left in the tobacco tin. It's how I kept Ducker in the house and the boys quiet.

Ducker got to be a regular thing. And more—his friends. The only break I had was Mom's days off. Every night the party was on like clockwork. Soon as Mom was gone to Auntie's ten minutes. Then a worse deal. If Mom went fishing on a day off, the party was all day. I was never one for school, but I wanted this summer over.

Ducker brought his radio. I seen every latest dance. Imagine Justine. She was in her element. She knowed the dances best of anybody and showed it. The boys clapped. It was just boys coming to the house. "Why should girls come here?" Justine said when I asked. "We're the girls."

We had talks, Justine and me. I told her how we couldn't go on like this. She told me not to be so shy. "Don't be afraid to smile," she said. "Don't be worried about your weight."

Then she said how she had a plan for when school started. "I'll show them snobby white girls," she said. "I'll show them Indians from Jack's res, too." She pictured herself walking down the hall with Ducker. She was going to lose fifteen pounds. She was going to wear all kinds of makeup on her face. People would be shocked. They'd be scared of her.

"You already done that plan at Healdsburg," I said, reminding her of how it got her a white boy and a hassle with his family so she hit the mother, knocking her tooth out, and had the cops come and take her to juvee and tell the welfare to take us from Mom.

"Well, everything turned out okay," she said. "You have to see who you are, Alice. Look around and see what you see. See what you can do. How you can be queen. The queen is the baddest. She knows it all. That's how she's queen. Like how I walk at school. Don't be worried about your weight. Some boys like it."

Only thing I was worried about was her plan. I couldn't see the outcome to this one yet. I wasn't a queen. She tried to get certain of Ducker's friends with me. "The kids won't tell, if that's what you're worried about," she said.

This was true. It's not just the TV keeping the boys quiet now. It was Ducker. He took them to the school yard. He showed them all his basketball stuff. After that, I might as well disappear into thin air far as Sheldon cared. I had to get Ducker to make Sheldon mind.

If it was Mom's day off and she went fishing, I took Jeffrey to the park and left Sheldon with Justine. Not that I felt right about it. Another thing I must say, I had a friend. Anthony. Not a boyfriend, not in my mind. Anthony just made himself useful tagging along. "Now don't forget bread for the fish," he said, if we was going to the park. Sometimes we did that, on Mom's day off, all of us. What else Anthony and me talked about I don't know. I got used to him. I didn't even think of him being black. Until we run into Auntie's mom and uncle in the park.

I couldn't get out of it. The two old ones sitting on the park bench seen me five minutes before I seen them. The old lady was looking away the Indian style of looking away. Like you know she seen you and looked away so you don't have to see her. In them situations it's a sign to help yourself and keep walking.

I was hardly fifty feet from them. Anthony with me. He was carrying Jeffrey on his shoulders. I knowed the picture they seen. I took the old lady's cue. I turned straight around, in the direction we came, and went behind the tall cypress trees, out of sight. It wasn't just that Anthony was black. I don't even think it was black people that bothered Mom so much. It was anything disturbing. It was what nobody talked about.

I found the sheets that day. I remember. I had my senses. After what happened in the park, I was thinking. I knowed if I tried to wash the sheets in the sink anybody might see the blood. Anybody could walk in. So I burned them out back in the garbage can. Justine never mentioned a thing, even when I was cleaning up. "Me and Ducker had the most fun," she said, after Mom went to Auntie's that night.

Indians say blood is a sign of the devil. Where it spills will be poison everlasting. That's how a place gets taboo. Auntie told me a story once. It was at Great-Auntie's funeral. It was to explain why Mom didn't cry, why Mom didn't like Great-Auntie who raised Mom and didn't like having to raise her. Great-Auntie got stuck with Mom and her sisters after some man poisoned Mom's mom. But here's what I think of. How Mom and her sisters found their mom in a puddle of salamander eggs and blood.

With Justine the expected worried me much as the unexpected. The expected, I worried when. The unexpected, what. When came like a straight shot, now that I look back at things. Mom came home early from Auntie's that same night. After the park, Justine's episode, and all my cleaning the floors and bed. Why that night? Why at all? I can't believe Mom didn't know what was going on before. Maybe she didn't want us to think she was dumb. Maybe she had to keep face for Auntie, if the old lady said something to Auntie. I don't know.

By this time our house was party central. It was Justine's party. She was queen. That's what the boys called her. Dance, Justine, dance. The neighborhood knowed Justine. She was dressing again. She was dressed up every day. Mom saw the party. She stood in the doorway half a minute, then turned around and left.

I unplugged Ducker's radio. I told everyone to get out. Must've been ten guys there. Something came over me so I was fierce. Justine said to shut up. The older sister, again. Usually, I ignored her, kept on about my business. Like Mom with most things. But this time I was Justine and more. I was going to floor her with the weight of my body. She must've seen because she was stopped cold. She tore out the front door with the guys.

Sheldon and Jeffrey, I put in the tub. Sheldon, I slapped in the mouth for no reason. He never made a peep. Neither one of them did. I put them to bed. No TV.

I finished the dishes and put them away. I wiped down the stove and refrigerator with Windex. I did the kitchen table too. Then I put together flour and water for torts. Torts by scratch. Mom's favorite. I was plopping them when Justine snuck past to the bedroom.

I finished. I set the torts on the clean table. I placed a fresh kitchen towel over the pile to keep in the warmth. Then next to a place mat made of paper towels I put a half cube of butter and the sugar bowl with a spoon next to it. Finally, I filled a glass with ice cubes and put it to the left of the place mat, opposite the butter and sugar.

Mom didn't come home until late. Around midnight. I was in the front room. I must've been dozing in the chair because when I opened my eyes, half startled, Mom was past me, turning into the bedroom. I thought of Justine and Mom in that bed together. I didn't hear a sound. Then I dozed again.

It was early morning I heard it. Like two roosters woke up and found themselves in the same pen. It started low in the bedroom, then came at full blast to the kitchen. Really loud. I thought of the boys. I pictured them hiding their heads for cover in their sleeping bags. I didn't move from the chair where I'd been all night.

Mom was hollering. "You're the lowest dirty, black-neck squaw. Chink . . ." And Justine. "Which one is my father? Tell me, you drunk slob, low-life Indian. Prove you're not the whore everyone says you are."

Then I heard the cupboard and something slam on the kitchen table. I couldn't believe my ears. I knowed without seeing what it was. Still, I didn't move. I don't know, it was strange. Then Mom comes out, her hair all wild from sleeping, and takes off, out the front door.

"Look how stupid," Justine said, nodding to the shotgun on the table. It was Jack's, what he forgot. I was still rubbing my eyes, just standing there. I picked it up and put it away.

"Fat bitch thought she was going to scare me with that," Justine said.

"Shut up," I said. "Just shut up."

I turned on the oven and warmed the untouched torts for breakfast.

Mom might as well moved to Auntie's. We hardly seen her, except when she came back to sleep. She put so much money in the tobacco tin for me to spend. Like when she was drinking, only now we never seen her, and I didn't have to keep the money in my pockets for fear she'd take it out of the tin. Once, when she was drinking, she accused me of stealing the money. I'd spent it, of course, and gave her what

I had left. Five dollars. She went berserk, hollering in the backyard. Just screaming, no words. Someone called the police. She stopped when they got there, then locked herself in the bathroom and cried herself to sleep. Later, to bug Mom, Justine said she called the police.

Mom strayed, like I said. It was me and Justine and the boys. And Ducker and Anthony and whoever else. Seemed nothing I could do.

We walked together, all of us. Who I mentioned. Justine didn't hang back at the house with Ducker so much anymore. She didn't say it, but I knowed she was anxious to try out with other boys what she tried out with Ducker. Certain things she said. The ways she talked to Ducker's friends and looked at them. Especially Kolvey, who was bigger, more grown, like a man. Signs Justine was up to something.

Anyway, I fixed the lunches. Most days we went to the park. Sometimes we walked other places. Like the fairgrounds where they was putting up the rides. Once we took a bus to the mall. Anthony would help me with things. He carried the Koolmate so we'd have cold pop. Another thing he did was the shopping. "What do you need?" he asked me. Like we was a pair. But there was nothing between us. In fact, lots of times at the park I went off by myself. I left him where Justine was pulling her stunts and where the two old ones sat and seen whatever they wanted. I took Jeffrey and went behind the cypress trees. He was the only one obeyed me. "Time to take a nap," I told him. It was cool there, away from everyone, and I pulled him close and slept.

It was Anthony who got me up. He told me something was going on with Justine. I was dead asleep on the grass there, and I felt Jeffrey slip from my arms.

"What?" I asked.

But by this time both Jeffrey and Anthony was looking through the trees. Then I seen it, too. Some skinny black girl and a couple of her friends, small and skinny like her, stood about twenty yards from Justine. Far enough so they was shouting and I could hear. The black girl was sticking out her hand, curling her finger like a caterpillar walking. "Miss Doris say for Mister Ducker Peoples to come right this minute," she was saying.

The boys was still on the ground, setting there. Justine was standing in all her clothes and makeup. Red lips. Nails. "What's this Miss Doris shit?" she said.

The girl shifted her weight to one side and put her hand on her hip. "Miss Doris say for Ducker to come right this minute if he knows what's good for him."

"Justine say Miss Doris eat shit," Justine said.

Then I grabbed Jeffrey. It happened fast. Justine crossed the line. She was face-to-face with that girl, and, with no words, just popped her one upside the head. The girl went over, like she flopped, hitting the ground on her side. Her two friends jumped back, like Justine would go after them next.

"Justine say to eat shit, Miss Doris," Justine said, looking down at that girl who was setting up now holding her face.

"I'm telling you, your sister shouldn't done that," Anthony said.

Something in the way he said that scared me. Like I knowed he told the truth.

"There's your grandparents," he said.

I looked to where Anthony was looking. With the commotion I hadn't seen the old ones on the bench, if they was ever sitting there. They was walking in the opposite direction, away.

"They ain't my grandparents," I said.

It was in the air. Justine's doings filled the rooms of our house, in every cupboard I opened, every potato I sliced. Like you seen the white of the potato and seen Justine when you was doing everything not to. And it was outside. Like fog settling in the streets. It was between the houses, across at the store. You seen it in the way a bird sat still on the telephone wire.

I made macaroni and cheese and potato salad. Macaroni and cheese is easy. Just boil macaroni and melt the cheese. Potato salad, that takes time. Boiling the potatoes, chopping celery and onions. Mayonnaise. All that. I did it. And more. Two pies from scratch. And a cake, even if that was from a box. You'd think we was still on the reservation and I was putting up food for a funeral.

Mom knowed, too. After dinner, she didn't go to Auntie's. How could she explain herself being there when Auntie and them knowed about the trouble here?

I never sat, not once while the others ate. The pies and all that. And I started right in with the dishes. I frosted the cake and set it on the table with a knife and new paper plates. I folded paper towels to make napkins at each place. I put a plastic fork on top of each napkin. I thought of candles and ice cream, but it was too late for that.

I was scrubbing the pots when I heard the first noises and looked over my shoulder and seen the crowd collecting outside on the street. From the sink, if you turned around, you could look through the kitchen door and the front door to the street. I wanted to close the front door, but I didn't move. I mean I kept on in the kitchen. Mom was at the table, kind of peeking out. She had her hands on her knees. Straight arms, like she does when she's going to get up. The boys looked at the cake like they was waiting for me to cut it. I was just about to do that. I thought, what am I doing forgetting about the cake.

Then Justine came out from the bedroom.

She was in Mom's red dress. That's no getup for the occasion, I thought. Not that I lingered on that thought just then. Mom got up and went into the bedroom and the boys followed her. The bedroom door closed.

"Don't do it," I said to Justine.

I guess someone outside seen her, too, because the yelling and name-calling rose up. "Dirty whore. Come out and pick on someone your own size. Slut." All that. I looked once then, and the street was filled with people. Some was near the steps. Young people, old people, kids, filling the air. Shouting.

"You don't have to do it, Justine," I told her again. "Just tell them you didn't mean for them guys to go and say yes."

She looked at me straight. Not like she was mad, or even scared. Kind of like she had a plan. Like she does when she tilts her head and half smiles at you. "I told them, 'yes, I would fight that Miss Doris's sisters,' because I ain't scared of nobody. Not three big-ass mean nigger bitches, nobody. They'll see. I'm the queen, remember?"

That's when I took inventory of her getup. The red dress, too big for Justine, was cinched with a black belt, which matched her pump shoes. And she had nylons on and the delicate gold necklace she found in the girls' gym. Her hair was done up just so. Her face, it was a movie star's. This I was focusing on all the while the people outside came closer and louder. The house was surrounded. I thought girls fight in old clothes. Like the times in Healdsburg when Justine met in the park to fight someone.

"Anyway," I said, "you can't fight in them clothes."

She was still looking at me the same way. Half smiling like I didn't know a thing. And she kept that smiling and looking straight at me when she reached to the table and picked up the knife. She tucked it in the front dress pocket, her hand on the handle, and walked out.

When that many people is surrounding the house and screaming, everything is clattering. The walls, windows. It's like things was going to cave in or blow wide apart. It's where the first rip is you look. And I seen it. A rock through the front window. Glass shattering. A hole wide as a fist.

I was in the doorway between the kitchen and front room. That was far as I got, and when I looked out for Justine, after seeing that rock come through the window, she was gone. Just the crowd screaming and the empty house. Like the boys and Mom wasn't even there. Like they was rolling away, around the corner, out of reach. Everybody. It all just went so fast. The whole place blowing apart. Then I seen the hole again. I was in shock by this time, I guess. I turned around and started putting dishes away. I don't know what. I opened cupboards, and seen the gun. Jack's shotgun. I ran to the front porch and shot it.

I didn't know nothing after that. Just colors. Everybody moving. Voices. People talking to me.

"Dumb ass, bitch. What'd you do that for?"

"Alice, you're the queen now. Nobody's going to mess with you, girl."

"Dumb ass, bitch."

"Hey, Alice. You're bad, girl. Justine never got a lick in."

"Stupid, crazy bitch. Now the cops'll come. Dumb ass, bitch."

They said I just stood there with that gun. Like a statue or something. Like I been there a hundred years.

I thought of that and the other things I heard after, when I started to gain my senses. I was standing in the kitchen, against the sink. Auntie was there by that time, and a good thing. She was talking to two cops in our kitchen. She said the blast wasn't a gun. Some kids who throwed a cherry bomb at our window and made a hole. They believed her, because they never searched the house. She was in official's clothes, the kind that match her voice when she talks to social workers.

"It's a single-parent family," she was saying. "It's an Indian family just moved to town."

I looked at Justine. She was lifting a neat piece of chocolate cake to her mouth with a plastic fork. Her I'd have to reckon with on account I upset her show. I looked at Mom and the boys. They was eating cake, too. Auntie was still talking, painting that picture of us not capable of nothing. I seen the cops looking at the table while she talked. I seen what they seen, what Auntie was saying. But I seen more. I seen everything.

Haunted

■

JOYCE CAROL OATES

*H*aunted houses, forbidden houses. The old Medlock farm. The Erlich farm. The Minton farm on Elk Creek. NO TRESPASSING the signs said but we trespassed at will. NO TRESPASSING NO HUNTING NO FISHING UNDER PENALTY OF LAW but we did what we pleased because who was there to stop us?

Our parents warned us against exploring these abandoned properties: The old houses and barns were dangerous, they said. We could get hurt, they said. I asked my mother if the houses were haunted and she said, Of course not, there aren't such things as ghosts, you know that. She was irritated with me; she guessed how I pretended to believe things I didn't believe, things I'd grown out of years before. It was a habit of childhood—pretending I was younger, more childish, than in fact I was. Opening my eyes wide and looking puzzled, worried. Girls are prone to such trickery, it's a form of camouflage, when every other thought you think is a forbidden thought and with your eyes open staring sightless you can sink into dreams that leave your skin clammy and your heart pounding—dreams that don't seem to belong to you that must have come to you from somewhere else from someone you don't know who knows *you*.

There weren't such things as ghosts, they told us. That was just superstition. But we could injure ourselves tramping around where we weren't wanted—the floorboards and the staircases in old houses were likely to be rotted, the roofs ready to collapse, we could cut ourselves on nails and broken glass, we could fall into uncovered wells—and you never knew who you might meet up with, in an old house or barn that's supposed to be empty. "You mean a bum?—like somebody hitchhiking along the road?" I asked. "It could be a bum, or it could be somebody you know," Mother told me evasively. "A man, or a boy— somebody you know . . ." Her voice trailed off in embarrassment and I knew enough not to ask another question.

There were things you didn't talk about, back then. I never talked about them with my own children, there weren't the words to say them.

We listened to what our parents said, we nearly always agreed with what they said, but we went off on the sly and did what we wanted to do. When we were little girls: my neighbor Mary Lou Siskin and me. And when we were older, ten, eleven years old, tomboys, roughhouses our mothers called us. We liked to hike in the woods and along the creek for miles, we'd cut through farmers' fields, spy on their houses— on people we knew, kids we knew from school—most of all we liked to explore abandoned houses, boarded-up houses if we could break in, we'd scare ourselves thinking the houses might be haunted though really we knew they weren't haunted, there weren't such things as ghosts. Except . . .

I am writing in a dime-store notebook with lined pages and a speckled cover, a notebook of the sort we used in grade school. *Once upon a time* as I used to tell my children when they were tucked safely into bed and drifting off to sleep. *Once upon a time* I'd begin, reading from a book because it was safest so: The several times I told them my own stories they were frightened by my voice and couldn't sleep and afterward I couldn't sleep either and my husband would ask what was wrong and I'd say, Nothing, hiding my face from him so he wouldn't see my look of contempt.

I write in pencil, so that I can erase easily, and I find that I am constantly erasing, wearing holes in the paper. Mrs. Harding, our fifth-grade teacher, disciplined us for handing in messy notebooks: She was a heavy, toad-faced woman, her voice was deep and husky and gleeful when she said, "You, Melissa, what have you to say for yourself?" and I stood there mute, my knees trembling. My friend Mary Lou laughed behind her hand, wriggled in her seat she thought I was so funny. Tell the old witch to go to hell, she'd say, she'll respect you then, but of course no one would ever say such a thing to Mrs. Harding. Not even Mary Lou. "What have you to say for yourself, Melissa? Handing in a notebook with a ripped page?" My grade for the homework assignment was lowered from A to B, Mrs. Harding grunted with satisfaction as she made the mark, a big swooping B in red ink, creasing the page. "More is expected of you, Melissa, so you disappoint me more," Mrs. Harding always said. So many years ago and I remember those words more clearly than words I heard the other day.

One morning there was a pretty substitute teacher in Mrs. Harding's classroom. "Mrs. Harding is unwell, I'll be taking her place today," she said, and we saw the nervousness in her face, we guessed there was a secret she wouldn't tell and we waited and a few days later the principal himself came to tell us that Mrs. Harding would not be back, she had died of a stroke. He spoke carefully as if we were much younger children and might be upset and Mary Lou caught my eye and winked and I sat there at my desk feeling the strangest sensation, something flowing into the top of my head, honey-rich and warm making its way down my spine. *Our Father, Who art in Heaven* I whispered in the prayer with the others my head bowed and my hands clasped tight together but my thoughts were somewhere else leaping wild and crazy somewhere else and I knew Mary Lou's were too.

On the school bus going home she whispered in my ear, "That was because of us, wasn't it!—what happened to that old bag Harding. But we won't tell anybody."

Once upon a time there were two sisters, and one was very pretty and one was very ugly.... Though Mary Lou Siskin wasn't my sister. And I wasn't ugly, really: just sallow-skinned, with a small pinched ferrety face. With dark almost lashless eyes that were set too close together and a nose that didn't look right. A look of yearning, and disappointment.

But Mary Lou *was* pretty, even rough and clumsy as she sometimes behaved. That long silky blond hair everybody remembered her for afterward, years afterward.... How, when she had to be identified, it was the long silky white-blond hair that was unmistakable....

Sleepless nights but I love them. I write during the nighttime hours and sleep during the day; I am of an age when you don't require more than a few hours' sleep. My husband has been dead for nearly a year and my children are scattered and busily absorbed in their own selfish lives like all children and there is no one to interrupt me no one to pry into my business no one in the neighborhood who dares come knocking at my door to see if I am all right. Sometimes out of a mirror floats an unexpected face, a strange face, lined, ravaged, with deep-socketed eyes always damp, always blinking in shock or dismay or simple bewilderment—but I adroitly look away. I have no need to stare.

It's true, all you have heard of the vanity of the old. Believing ourselves young, still, behind our aged faces—mere children, and so very innocent!

Once when I was a young bride and almost pretty my color up when I was happy and my eyes shining we drove out into the country for a Sunday's excursion and he wanted to make love I knew, he was shy and fumbling as I but he wanted to make love and I ran into a cornfield in my stockings and high heels, I was playing at being a woman I never could be, Mary Lou Siskin maybe, Mary Lou whom my husband never knew, but I got out of breath and frightened, it was the wind in the cornstalks, that dry rustling sound, that dry terrible rustling sound like whispering like voices you can't quite identify and he caught me and tried to hold me and I pushed him away sobbing and he said, What's wrong? My God what's wrong? as if he really loved me as if his life was focused on me and I knew I could never be equal to it, that love, that importance, I knew I was only Melissa the ugly one the one the boys wouldn't give a second glance, and one day he'd understand and know how he'd been cheated. I pushed him away, I said, Leave me alone! don't touch me! You disgust me! I said.

He backed off and I hid my face, sobbing.

But later on I got pregnant just the same. Only a few weeks later.

Always there were stories behind the abandoned houses and always the stories were sad. Because farmers went bankrupt and had to move away. Because somebody died and the farm couldn't be kept up and nobody wanted to buy it—like the Medlock farm across the creek. Mr.

Medlock died aged seventy-nine and Mrs. Medlock refused to sell the farm and lived there alone until someone from the county health agency came to get her. Isn't it a shame, my parents said. The poor woman, they said. They told us never, never to poke around in the Medlocks' barns or house—the buildings were ready to cave in, they'd been in terrible repair even when the Medlocks were living there.

It was said that Mrs. Medlock had gone off her head after she'd found her husband dead in one of the barns, lying flat on his back his eyes open and bulging, his mouth open, tongue protruding, she'd gone to look for him and found him like that and she'd never gotten over it they said, never got over the shock. They had to commit her to the state hospital for her own good (they said) and the house and the barns were boarded up, everywhere tall grass and thistles grew wild, dandelions in the spring, tiger lilies in the summer, and when we drove by I stared and stared narrowing my eyes so I wouldn't see someone looking out one of the windows—a face there, pale and quick—or a dark figure scrambling up the roof to hide behind the chimney . . .

Mary Lou and I wondered was the house haunted, was the barn haunted where the old man had died, we crept around to spy, we couldn't stay away, coming closer and closer each time until something scared us and we ran away back through the woods clutching and pushing at each other until one day finally we went right up to the house to the back door and peeked in one of the windows. Mary Lou led the way, Mary Lou said not to be afraid, nobody lived there anymore and nobody would catch us, it didn't matter that the land was posted, the police didn't arrest kids our ages.

We explored the barns, we dragged the wooden cover off the well and dropped stones inside. We called the cats but they wouldn't come close enough to be petted. They were barn cats, skinny and diseased-looking, they'd said at the county bureau that Mrs. Medlock had let a dozen cats live in the house with her so that the house was filthy from their messes. When the cats wouldn't come we got mad and threw stones at them and they ran away hissing—nasty dirty things, Mary Lou said. Once we crawled up on the tar-paper roof over the Medlocks' kitchen, just for fun, Mary Lou wanted to climb up the big roof too to the very top but I got frightened and said, No, No please don't, no Mary Lou please, and I sounded so strange Mary Lou looked at me and didn't tease or mock as she usually did. The roof was so steep, I'd known she would hurt herself. I could see her losing her footing and slipping, falling, I could see her astonished face and her flying hair as she fell, knowing nothing could save her. You're no fun, Mary Lou said, giving me a hard little pinch. But she didn't go climbing up the big roof.

Later we ran through the barns screaming at the top of our lungs just for fun for the hell of it as Mary Lou said, we tossed things in a heap, broken-off parts of farm implements, leather things from the horses' gear, handfuls of straw. The farm animals had been gone for years but their smell was still strong. Dried horse and cow droppings that looked like mud. Mary Lou said, "You know what—I'd like to burn this place down." And she looked at me and I said, "Okay—go on and do it, burn it down." And Mary Lou said, "You think I wouldn't?—just give me a match." And I said, "You know I don't have any match." And a look passed between us. And I felt something flooding at the top of my head, my throat tickled as if I didn't know would I laugh or cry and I said, "You're crazy—" and Mary Lou said with a sneering little laugh, *"You're* crazy, dumbbell—I was just testing you."

By the time Mary Lou was twelve years old Mother had got to hate her, was always trying to turn me against her so I'd make friends with other girls. Mary Lou had a fresh mouth, she said. Mary Lou didn't respect her elders—not even her own parents. Mother guessed that Mary Lou laughed at her behind her back, said things about all of us. She was mean and snippy and a smart-ass, rough sometimes as her brothers. Why didn't I make other friends? Why did I always go running when she stood out in the yard and called me? The Siskins weren't a whole lot better than white trash, the way Mr. Siskin worked that land of his.

In town, in school, Mary Lou sometimes ignored me when other girls were around, girls who lived in town, whose fathers weren't farmers like ours. But when it was time to ride home on the bus she'd sit with me as if nothing was wrong and I'd help her with her homework if she needed help, I hated her sometimes but then I'd forgive her as soon as she smiled at me, she'd say, "Hey 'Lissa are you mad at me?" and I'd make a face and say no as if it was an insult, being asked.

Mary Lou was my sister I sometimes pretended, I told myself a story about us being sisters and looking alike, and Mary Lou said sometimes she'd like to leave her family her goddamned family and come live with me. Then the next day or the next hour she'd get moody and be nasty to me and get me almost crying. All the Siskins had mean streaks, bad tempers, she'd tell people. As if she was proud.

Her hair was a light blond, almost white in the sunshine, and when I first knew her she had to wear it braided tight around her head—her grandmother braided it for her, and she hated it. Like Gretel or Snow White in one of those damn dumb picture books for children, Mary Lou said. When she was older she wore it down and let it grow long so that it fell almost to her hips. It was very beautiful—silky and shimmering. I dreamed of Mary Lou's hair sometimes but the dreams were confused and I couldn't remember when I woke up whether I was the one with the long blond silky hair, or someone else. It took me a while to get my thoughts clear lying there in bed and then I'd remember Mary Lou, who was my best friend.

She was ten months older than I was, and an inch or so taller, a bit heavier, not fat but fleshy, solid and fleshy, with hard little muscles in her upper arms like a boy. Her eyes were blue like washed glass, her eyebrows and lashes were almost white, she had a snubbed nose and Slavic cheekbones and a mouth that could be sweet or twisty and smirky depending upon her mood. But she didn't like her face because it was round—a moon-face she called it, staring at herself in the mirror though she knew damned well she was pretty—didn't older boys whistle at her, didn't the bus driver flirt with her?—calling her "Blondie" while he never called me anything at all.

Mother didn't like Mary Lou visiting with me when no one else was home in our house: She didn't trust her, she said. Thought she might steal something, or poke her nose into parts of the house where she wasn't welcome. That girl is a bad influence on you, she said. But it was all the same old crap I heard again and again so I didn't even listen. I'd have told her she was crazy except that would only make things worse.

Mary Lou said, "Don't you just hate them?—your mother, and mine? Sometimes I wish—"

I put my hands over my ears and didn't hear.

*   *   *

The Siskins lived two miles away from us, farther back the road where it got narrower. Those days, it was unpaved, and never got plowed in the winter. I remember their barn with the yellow silo, I remember the muddy pond where the dairy cows came to drink, the muck they churned up in the spring. I remember Mary Lou saying she wished all the cows would die—they were always sick with something—so her father would give up and sell the farm and they could live in town in a nice house. I was hurt, her saying those things as if she'd forgotten about me and would leave me behind. Damn you to hell, I whispered under my breath.

I remember smoke rising from the Siskins' kitchen chimney, from their wood-burning stove, straight up into the winter sky like a breath you draw inside you deeper and deeper until you begin to feel faint.

Later on, that house was empty too. But boarded up only for a few months—the bank sold it at auction. (It turned out the bank owned most of the Siskin farm, even the dairy cows. So Mary Lou had been wrong about that all along and never knew.)

As I write I can hear the sound of glass breaking, I can feel glass underfoot. *Once upon a time there were two little princesses, two sisters, who did forbidden things.* That brittle terrible sensation under my shoes— slippery like water—"Anybody home? Hey—anybody home?" and there's an old calendar tacked to a kitchen wall, a faded picture of Jesus Christ in a long white gown stained with scarlet, thorns fitted to His bowed head. Mary Lou is going to scare me in another minute making me think that someone is in the house and the two of us will scream with laughter and run outside where it's safe. Wild frightened laughter and I never knew afterward what was funny or why we did these things. Smashing what remained of windows, wrenching at stair- way railings to break them loose, running with our heads ducked so we wouldn't get cobwebs in our faces.

One of us found a dead bird, a starling, in what had been the parlor of the house. Turned it over with a foot—there's the open eye looking right up calm and matter-of-fact. *Melissa*, that eye tells me, silent and terrible, *I see you.*

That was the old Minton place, the stone house with the caved-in roof and the broken steps, like something in a picture book from long ago. From the road the house looked as if it might be big but when we explored it we were disappointed to see that it wasn't much bigger than my own house, just four narrow rooms downstairs, another four upstairs, an attic with a steep ceiling, the roof partly caved in. The barns had collapsed in upon themselves; only their stone foundations remained solid. The land had been sold off over the years to other farmers, nobody had lived in the house for a long time. The old Minton house, people called it. On Elk Creek where Mary Lou's body was eventually found.

In seventh grade Mary Lou had a boy friend she wasn't supposed to have and no one knew about it but me—an older boy who'd dropped out of school and worked as a farmhand. I thought he was a little slow—not in his speech which was fast enough, normal enough, but in his way of thinking. He was sixteen or seventeen years old. His name was Hans; he had crisp blond hair like the bristles of a brush, a coarse blemished face, derisive eyes. Mary Lou was crazy for him she said, aping the older girls in town who said they were "crazy for" certain boys or young men. Hans and Mary Lou kissed when they didn't think I was watching, in an old ruin of a cemetery behind the Minton house, on the creekbank, in the tall marsh grass by the end of the Siskins' driveway. Hans had a car borrowed from one of his brothers, a battered old Ford, the front bumper held up by wire, the running board scraping the ground. We'd be out walking on the road and Hans would come along tapping the horn and stop and Mary Lou would cimb in but I'd hang back knowing they didn't want me and the hell with them: I preferred to be alone.

"You're just jealous of Hans and me," Mary Lou said, unforgivably, and I hadn't any reply. "Hans is sweet. Hans is nice. He isn't like people say," Mary Lou said in a quick bright false voice she'd picked up from one of the older, popular girls in town. "He's . . ." And she stared at me blinking and smiling not knowing what to say as if in fact she didn't know Hans at all. "He isn't *simple,*" she said angrily, "—he just doesn't like to talk a whole lot."

When I try to remember Hans Meunzer after so many decades I can see only a muscular boy with short-trimmed blond hair and protuberant ears, blemished skin, the shadow of a mustache on his upper lip—he's looking at me, eyes narrowed, crinkled, as if he understands

how I fear him, how I wish him dead and gone, and he'd hate me too
if he took me that seriously. But he doesn't take me that seriously,
his gaze just slides right through me as if nobody's standing where I
stand.

There were stories about all the abandoned houses but the worst story
was about the Minton house over on the Elk Creek Road about three
miles from where we lived. For no reason anybody ever discovered Mr.
Minton had beaten his wife to death and afterward killed himself with
a .12-gauge shotgun. He hadn't even been drinking, people said. And
his farm hadn't been doing at all badly, considering how others were
doing.

Looking at the ruin from the outside, overgrown with trumpet vine
and wild rose, it seemed hard to believe that anything like that had
happened. Things in the world even those things built by man are so
quiet left to themselves. . . .

The house had been deserted for years, as long as I could remember. Most of the land had been sold off but the heirs didn't want to
deal with the house. They didn't want to sell it and they didn't want
to raze it and they certainly didn't want to live in it so it stood empty.
The property was posted with NO TRESPASSING signs layered one atop
another but nobody took them seriously. Vandals had broken into the
house and caused damage, the McFarlane boys had tried to burn down
the old hay barn one Halloween night. The summer Mary Lou started
seeing Hans she and I climbed in the house through a rear window—
the boards guarding it had long since been yanked away—and walked
through the rooms slow as sleepwalkers our arms around each other's
waist our eyes staring waiting to see Mr. Minton's ghost as we turned
each corner. The inside smelled of mouse droppings, mildrew, rot, old
sorrow. Strips of wallpaper torn from the walls, plasterboard exposed,
old furniture overturned and smashed, old yellowed sheets of newspaper underfoot, and broken glass, everywhere broken glass. Through
the ravaged windows sunlight spilled in tremulous quivering bands.
The air was afloat, alive: dancing dust atoms. "I'm afraid," Mary Lou
whispered. She squeezed my waist and I felt my mouth go dry for
hadn't I been hearing something upstairs, a low persistent murmuring
like quarreling like one person trying to convince another going on
and on and on but when I stood very still to listen the sound vanished

and there were only the comforting summer sounds of birds, crickets, cicadas.

I knew how Mr. Minton had died: He'd placed the barrel of the shotgun beneath his chin and pulled the trigger with his big toe. They found him in the bedroom upstairs, most of his head blown off. They found his wife's body in the cistern in the cellar where he'd tried to hide her. "Do you think we should go upstairs?" Mary Lou asked, worried. Her fingers felt cold; but I could see tiny sweat beads on her forehead. Her mother had braided her hair in one thick clumsy braid, the way she wore it most of the summer, but the bands of hair were loosening. "No," I said, frightened. "I don't know." We hesitated at the bottom of the stairs—just stood there for a long time. "Maybe not," Mary Lou said. "Damn stairs'd fall in on us."

In the parlor there were bloodstains on the floor and on the wall—I could see them. Mary Lou said in derision, "They're just waterstains, dummy."

I could hear the voices overhead, or was it a single droning persistent voice. I waited for Mary Lou to hear it but she never did.

Now we were safe, now we were retreating, Mary Lou said as if repentant, "Yeah—this house *is* special."

We looked through the debris in the kitchen hoping to find something of value but there wasn't anything—just smashed chinaware, old battered pots and pans, more old yellowed newspaper. But through the window we saw a garter snake sunning itself on a rusted water tank, stretched out to a length of two feet. It was a lovely coppery color, the scales gleaming like perspiration on a man's arm; it seemed to be asleep. Neither one of us screamed, or wanted to throw something—we just stood there watching it for the longest time.

Mary Lou didn't have a boy friend any longer, Hans had stopped coming around. We saw him driving the old Ford now and then but he didn't seem to see us. Mr. Siskin had found out about him and Mary Lou and he'd been upset—acting like a damn crazy man Mary Lou said, asking her every kind of nasty question then interrupting her and not believing her anyway, then he'd put her to terrible shame by going over to see Hans and carrying on with him. "I hate them all," Mary Lou said, her face darkening with blood. "I wish . . ."

We rode our bicycles over to the Minton farm, or tramped through the fields to get there. It was the place we liked best. Sometimes we brought things to eat, cookies, bananas, candy bars, sitting on the broken stone steps out front, as if we lived in the house really, we were sisters who lived here having a picnic lunch out front. There were bees, flies, mosquitoes, but we brushed them away. We had to sit in the shade because the sun was so fierce and direct, a whitish heat pouring down from overhead.

"Would you ever like to run away from home?" Mary Lou said. "I don't know," I said uneasily. Mary Lou wiped at her mouth and gave me a mean narrow look. " 'I don't know,' " she said in a falsetto voice, mimicking me. At an upstairs window someone was watching us—was it a man or was it a woman—someone stood there listening hard and I couldn't move feeling so slow and dreamy in the heat like a fly caught on a sticky petal that's going to fold in on itself and swallow him up. Mary Lou crumpled up some wax paper and threw it into the weeds. She was dreamy too, slow and yawning. She said, "Shit—they'd just find me. Then everything would be worse."

I was covered in a thin film of sweat but I'd begun to shiver. Goose bumps were raised on my arms. I could see us sitting on the stone steps the way we'd look from the second floor of the house, Mary Lou sprawled with her legs apart, her braided hair slung over her shoulder, me sitting with my arms hugging my knees my backbone tight and straight knowing I was being watched. Mary Lou said, lowering her voice, "Did you ever touch yourself in a certain place, Melissa?" "No," I said, pretending I didn't know what she meant. "Hans wanted to do that," Mary Lou said. She sounded disgusted. Then she started to giggle. "I wouldn't let him, then he wanted to do something else— started unbuttoning his pants—wanted me to touch *him*. And—"

I wanted to hush her, to clap my hand over her mouth. But she just went on and I never said a word until we both started giggling together and couldn't stop. Afterward I didn't remember most of it or why I'd been so excited my face burning and my eyes seared as if I'd been staring into the sun.

On the way home Mary Lou said, "Some things are so sad you can't say them." But I pretended not to hear.

* * *

A few days later I came back by myself. Through the ravaged cornfield: the stalks dried and broken, the tassels burned, that rustling whispering sound of the wind I can hear now if I listen closely. My head was aching with excitement. I was telling myself a story that we'd made plans to run away and live in the Minton house. I was carrying a willow switch I'd found on the ground, fallen from a tree but still green and springy, slapping at things with it as if it was a whip. Talking to myself. Laughing aloud. Wondering was I being watched.

I climbed in the house through the back window and brushed my hands on my jeans. My hair was sticking to the back of my neck.

At the foot of the stairs I called up, "Who's here?" in a voice meant to show it was all play, I knew I was alone.

My heart was beating hard and quick, like a bird caught in the hand. It was lonely without Mary Lou so I walked heavy to let them know I was there and wasn't afraid. I started singing, I started whistling. Talking to myself and slapping at things with the willow switch. Laughing aloud, a little angry. Why was I angry, well I didn't know, someone was whispering telling me to come upstairs, to walk on the inside of the stairs so the steps wouldn't collapse.

The house was beautiful inside if you had the right eyes to see it. If you didn't mind the smell. Glass underfoot, broken plaster, stained wallpaper hanging in shreds. Tall narrow windows looking out onto wild weedy patches of green. I heard something in one of the rooms but when I looked I saw nothing much more than an easy chair lying on its side. Vandals had ripped stuffing out of it and tried to set it afire. The material was filthy but I could see that it had been pretty once—a floral design—tiny yellow flowers and green ivy. A woman used to sit in the chair, a big woman with sly staring eyes. Knitting in her lap but she wasn't knitting just staring out the window watching to see who might be coming to visit.

Upstairs the rooms were airless and so hot I felt my skin prickle like shivering. I wasn't afraid!—I slapped at the walls with my springy willow switch. In one of the rooms high in a corner wasps buzzed around a fat wasp's nest. In another room I looked out the window leaning out the window to breathe thinking this was my window, I'd come to live here. She was telling me I had better lie down and rest because I was in danger of heatstroke and I pretended not to know

what heatstroke was but she knew I knew because hadn't a cousin of
mine collapsed haying just last summer, they said his face had gone
blotched and red and he'd begun breathing faster and faster not getting enough oxygen until he collapsed. I was looking out at the overgrown apple orchard, I could smell the rot, a sweet winey smell, the
sky was hazy like something you can't get clear in your vision, pressing
in close and warm. A half-mile away Elk Creek glittered through a
screen of willow trees moving slow glittering with scales like winking.

Come away from that window, someone told me sternly.

But I took my time obeying.

In the biggest of the rooms was an old mattress pulled off rusty
bedsprings and dumped on the floor. They'd torn some of the stuffing
out of this too, there were scorch marks on it from cigarettes. The
fabric was stained with something like rust and I didn't want to look
at it but I had to. Once at Mary Lou's when I'd gone home with her
after school there was a mattress lying out in the yard in the sun and
Mary Lou told me in disgust that it was her youngest brother's mattress—he'd wet his bed again and the mattress had to be aired out.
As if the stink would ever go away, Mary Lou said.

Something moved inside the mattress, a black-glittering thing, it
was a cockroach but I wasn't allowed to jump back. Suppose you have
to lie down on that mattress and sleep, I was told. Suppose you can't
go home until you do. My eyelids were heavy, my head was pounding
with blood. A mosquito buzzed around me but I was too tired to brush
it away. Lie down on that mattress, Melissa, she told me. You know
you must be punished.

I knelt down, not on the mattress, but on the floor beside it. The
smells in the room were close and rank but I didn't mind, my head
was nodding with sleep. Rivulets of sweat ran down my face and sides,
under my arms, but I didn't mind. I saw my hand move out slowly
like a stranger's hand to touch the mattress and a shiny black cockroach scuttled away in fright, and a second cockroach, and a third—
but I couldn't jump up and scream.

Lie down on that mattress and take your punishment.

I looked over my shoulder and there was a woman standing in the
doorway—a woman I'd never seen before.

She was staring at me. Her eyes were shiny and dark. She licked her lips and said in a jeering voice, "What are you doing here in this house, miss?"

I was terrified. I tried to answer but I couldn't speak.

"Have you come to see me?" the woman asked.

She was no age I could guess. Older than my mother but not old-seeming. She wore men's clothes and she was tall as any man, with wide shoulders, and long legs, and big sagging breasts like cows' udders loose inside her shirt not harnessed in a brassiere like other women's. Her thick wiry gray hair was cut short as a man's and stuck up in tufts that looked greasy. Her eyes were small, and black, and set back deep in their sockets; the flesh around them looked bruised. I had never seen anyone like her before—her thighs were enormous, big as my body. There was a ring of loose soft flesh at the waistband of her trousers but she wasn't fat.

"I asked you a question, miss. Why are you here?"

I was so frightened I could feel my bladder contract. I stared at her, cowering by the mattress, and couldn't speak.

It seemed to please her that I was so frightened. She approached me, stooping a little to get through the doorway. She said, in a mock-kindly voice, "You've come to visit with me—is that it?"

"No," I said.

"No!" she said, laughing. "Why, of course you have."

"No. I don't know you."

She leaned over me, touched my forehead with her fingers. I shut my eyes waiting to be hurt but her touch was cool. She brushed my hair off my forehead where it was sticky with sweat. "I've seen you here before, you and that other one," she said. "What is her name? The blond one. The two of you, trespassing."

I couldn't move, my legs were paralyzed. Quick and darting and buzzing my thoughts bounded in every which direction but didn't take hold. "Melissa is *your* name, isn't it," the woman said. "And what is your sister's name?"

"She isn't my sister," I whispered.

"What is her name?"

"I don't know."

"You don't know!"

". . . don't know," I said, cowering.

The woman drew back half sighing half grunting. She looked at me pityingly. "You'll have to be punished, then."

I could smell ashes about her, something cold. I started to whimper, started to say I hadn't done anything wrong, hadn't hurt anything in the house, I had only been exploring—I wouldn't come back again—

She was smiling at me, uncovering her teeth. She could read my thoughts before I could think them.

The skin of her face was in layers like an onion, like she'd been sunburned or had a skin disease. There were patches that had begun to peel. Her look was wet and gloating. Don't hurt me, I wanted to say. Please don't hurt me.

I'd begun to cry. My nose was running like a baby's. I thought I would crawl past the woman I would get to my feet and run past her and escape but the woman stood in my way blocking my way leaning over me breathing damp and warm her breath like a cow's breath in my face. Don't hurt me, I said, and she said, "You know you have to be punished—you and your pretty blond sister."

"She isn't my sister," I said.

"And what is her name?"

The woman was bending over me, quivering with laughter.

"Speak up, miss. What is it?"

"I don't know . . ." I started to say. But my voice said, "Mary Lou."

The woman's big breasts spilled down onto her belly, I could feel her shaking with laughter. But she spoke sternly saying that Mary Lou and I had been very bad girls and we knew it her house was forbidden territory and we knew it hadn't we known all along that others had come to grief beneath its roof?

"No," I started to say. But my voice said, "Yes."

The woman laughed, crouching above me. "Now, miss, 'Melissa' as they call you—your parents don't know where you are at this very moment, do they?"

"I don't know."

"Do they?"

"No."

"They don't know anything about you, do they?—what you do, and what you think? You and 'Mary Lou.' "

"No."

She regarded me for a long moment, smiling. Her smile was wide and friendly.

"You're a spunky little girl, aren't you, with a mind of your own, aren't you, and your pretty little sister. I bet your bottoms have been warmed many a time," the woman said, showing her big tobacco-stained teeth in a grin, ". . . your tender little asses."

I began to giggle. My bladder tightened.

"Hand that here, miss," the woman said. She took the willow switch from my fingers—I had forgotten I was holding it. "I will now administer punishment: take down your jeans. Take down your panties. Lie down on that mattress. Hurry." She spoke briskly now, she was all business. "Hurry, Melissa! *And* your panties! Or do you want me to pull them down for you?"

She was slapping the switch impatiently against the palm of her left hand, making a wet scolding noise with her lips. Scolding and teasing. Her skin shone in patches, stretched tight over the big hard bones of her face. Her eyes were small, crinkling smaller, black and damp. She was so big she had to position herself carefully over me to give herself proper balance and leverage so that she wouldn't fall. I could hear her hoarse eager breathing as it came to me from all sides like the wind.

I had done as she told me. It wasn't me doing these things but they were done. Don't hurt me, I whispered, lying on my stomach on the mattress, my arms stretched above me and my fingernails digging into the floor. The coarse wood with splinters pricking my skin. Don't don't hurt me O please but the woman paid no heed her warm wet breath louder now and the floorboards creaking beneath her weight. "Now, miss, now 'Melissa' as they call you—this will be our secret won't it—"

When it was over she wiped at her mouth and said she would let me go today if I promised never to tell anybody if I sent my pretty little sister to her tomorrow.

She isn't my sister, I said, sobbing. When I could get my breath.

I had lost control of my bladder after all, I'd begun to pee even before the first swipe of the willow switch hit me on the buttocks, peeing in helpless spasms, and sobbing, and afterward the woman scolded me saying wasn't it a poor little baby wetting itself like that. But she sounded repentant too, stood well aside to let me pass. Off you go! Home you go! And don't forget!

And I ran out of the room hearing her laughter behind me and down the stairs running running as if I hadn't any weight my legs just blurry beneath me as if the air was water and I was swimming I ran out of the house and through the cornfield running in the cornfield sobbing as the corn stalks slapped at my face *Off you go! Home you go! And don't forget!*

I told Mary Lou about the Minton house and something that had happened to me there that was a secret and she didn't believe me at first saying with a jeer, "Was it a ghost? Was it Hans?" I said I couldn't tell. Couldn't tell what? she said. Couldn't tell, I said. Why not? she said.

"Because I promised."

"Promised who?" she said. She looked at me with her wide blue eyes like she was trying to hypnotize me. "You're a goddamned liar."

Later she started in again asking me what had happened what was the secret was it something to do with Hans? Did he still like her? Was he mad at her? And I said it didn't have anything to do with Hans not a thing to do with him. Twisting my mouth to show what I thought of him.

"Then who—?" Mary Lou asked.

"I told you it was a secret."

"Oh shit—what kind of a secret?"

"A secret."

"A secret *really?*"

I turned away from Mary Lou, trembling. My mouth kept twisting in a strange hurting smile. "Yes. A secret *really*," I said.

The last time I saw Mary Lou she wouldn't sit with me on the bus, walked past me holding her head high giving me a mean snippy look out of the corner of her eye. Then when she left for her stop she made sure she bumped me going by my seat, she leaned over to say, "I'll find out for myself, I hate you anyway," speaking loud enough for everybody on the bus to hear, "—I always have."

*   *   *

Once upon a time the fairy tales begin. But then they end and often you don't know really what has happened, what was meant to happen, you only know what you've been told, what the words suggest. Now that I have completed my story, filled up half my notebook with my handwriting that disappoints me, it is so shaky and childish—now the story is over I don't understand what it means. I know what happened in my life but I don't know what has happened in these pages.

Mary Lou was found murdered ten days after she said those words to me. Her body had been tossed into Elk Creek a quarter mile from the road and from the old Minton place. Where, it said in the paper, nobody had lived for fifteen years.

It said that Mary Lou had been thirteen years old at the time of her death. She'd been missing for seven days, had been the object of a countywide search.

It said that nobody had lived in the Minton house for years but that derelicts sometimes sheltered there. It said that the body was unclothed and mutilated. There were no details.

This happened a long time ago.

The murderer (or murderers as the newspaper always said) was never found.

Hans Meunzer was arrested of course and kept in the county jail for three days while police questioned him but in the end they had to let him go, insufficient evidence to build a case it was explained in the newspaper though everybody knew he was the one wasn't he the one?—everybody knew. For years afterward they'd be saying that. Long after Hans was gone and the Siskins were gone, moved away nobody knew where.

Hans swore he hadn't done it, hadn't seen Mary Lou for weeks. There were people who testified in his behalf said he couldn't have done it for one thing he didn't have his brother's car any longer and he'd been working all that time. Working hard out in the fields—couldn't have slipped away long enough to do what police were saying he'd done. And Hans said over and over he was innocent. Sure he was innocent. Son of a bitch ought to be hanged my father said, everybody knew Hans was the one unless it was a derelict or a fisherman—fishermen often drove out to Elk Creek to fish for black bass, built fires on the creekbank, and left messes behind—sometimes prowled around the Minton house too looking for things to steal. The police had records of automobile license plates belonging to some of these men, they questioned them but nothing came of it. Then there was that crazy man that old hermit living in a tar-paper shanty near the Shaheen dump that everybody'd said ought to have been committed to the state hospital years ago. But everybody knew really it was Hans and Hans got out as quick as he could, just disappeared and not even his family knew where unless they were lying which probably they were though they claimed not.

Mother rocked me in her arms crying, the two of us crying, she told me that Mary Lou was happy now, Mary Lou was in Heaven now, Jesus Christ had taken her to live with Him and I knew that didn't I? I wanted to laugh but I didn't laugh. Mary Lou shouldn't have gone with boys, not a nasty boy like Hans, Mother said, she shouldn't have been sneaking around the way she did—I knew that didn't I? Mother's words filled my head flooding my head so there was no danger of laughing.

Jesus loves you too you know that don't you Melissa? Mother asked hugging me. I told her yes. I didn't laugh because I was crying.

They wouldn't let me go to the funeral, said it would scare me too much. Even though the casket was closed.

It's said that when you're older you remember things that happened a long time ago better than you remember things that have just happened and I have found that to be so.

For instance I can't remember when I bought this notebook at Woolworth's whether it was last week or last month or just a few days ago. I can't remember why I started writing in it, what purpose I told myself. But I remember Mary Lou stooping to say those words in my ear and I remember when Mary Lou's mother came over to ask us at suppertime a few days later if I had seen Mary Lou that day—I remember the very food on my plate, the mashed potatoes in a dry little mound. I remember hearing Mary Lou call my name standing out in the driveway cupping her hands to her mouth the way Mother hated her to do, it was white trash behavior.

"Lissa!" Mary Lou would call, and I'd call back, "Okay, I'm coming!" *Once upon a time.*

The Dancer

■

PATRICIA PRECIADO MARTIN

*A*ll I ever really wanted to be was a dancer—a ballerina—the kind that gets all dressed up in something white and frothy with feathers and see-through veils and white silk stockings and white satin toe shoes and a paste-jewel crown. A ballerina is always a beautiful, sad princess who has ladies-in-waiting with flowers in their hair dancing around her. She's rescued from the witch in black by a handsome prince who leaps and twirls and throws her in the air and carries her upside down (she doesn't seem to mind), and nobody ever falls down.

The people who come to see you dance the ballet are real fancy. We went to see *Swan Lake* at the Temple of Music and Art on a school field trip once. The men wore tuxedos and top hats, and the ladies wore long dresses with white gloves and ropes of fake pearls. They had stoles made out of dead foxes and rabbits with little staring glass eyes, some with their tails still attached. The concert hall was painted all in gilt, and there was a red velvet curtain with gold tassels and a crystal chandelier as big as our house. It was all very high class.

But when I asked Papá about classical ballet lessons, he said, "No seas simple. They don't give lessons like that on our side of town, and who do you think is going to be chauffeuring you three times a week to the East Side Ballet Academy? Your Mamá doesn't drive, and I'm moonlighting at Blackie's Service Station. Anyway, those kind of dance lessons are for rich *güeritas,* and you'd be out of place."

He gave me a big smile and a hug, but I didn't feel any better.

"Okay, okay," I persisted. "What about tap-dancing lessons? They have classes after school at the "Y" on Third Avenue, and they're real cheap, and I can take the bus. My friend Graciela gets to go, and she says it's real fun. The shoes are neat—black patent leather tied with a ribbon at the ankle, with taps on the heel and toe so you clack-clack whenever you walk, and sometimes they make little sparks when you're dancing."

"No seas ridícula," he countered. "There's no way I'm going to give you permission to take those tap-dancing lessons and wear a skin-tight leotard—*que no tiene vergüenza la juventud*[1]—and those short skirts that when you twirl around *enseñan todo, hasta los calzoncillos y las nalgas.*[2] My *compadre* told me he went to a recital to see his niece, your friend Graciela, and the girls were all wearing pancake makeup and blue eyeshadow and bright red lipstick, and they all looked like you know what. Excuse me, but that's what he said. What would your *abuelita* say? She'd probably have an *ataque* and keel right over from the *susto* and *escándalo.*"

"Okay, okay," I tried. "What about flamenco? Father Estanislao's old aunt is visiting from Spain and is giving lessons in the parish hall after choir practice. It's free, and the girls wear long, flouncy dresses and three petticoats and a mantilla and shawl even. *Abuelita* would like that. There's not much showing off, either; they just stand in one spot and do the *zapateado* and click those castanets."

"Ahora sí," said Papá. "Now you're going to start getting ideas that you're *española.* Stay true to your culture. You're *mexicana* through and through. Besides, I don't want you hanging around those *gachupines* who conquered our fatherland and destroyed our temples and stole our gold and silver, *y que se creen con todo eso de lo gitano y fandango y jota.*"[3]

So, get this. Angel Hernández and Mercedes Guerrero opened up

---

[1]. Young people, they have no shame.
[2]. They show everything, even your undies and your butt.
[3]. Who think they're superior with all those Spanish airs.

El Instituto del Ballet Folklórico Mexicano last year on West Drach-
man Street. What I wouldn't give to wear one of those *trajes de gala*
from Jalisco and dance "La Negra"; or *el traje de jarocha* from Vera
Cruz, a white lace dress with an embroidered apron and silk-fringed
rebozo, and dance "La Bamba"; or a china *poblana* dress from Puebla,
with the eagle and the serpent and the Mexican flag appliquéd in
sequins, and dance "La Espuelas de Amazoc."

But I'm too old—I'm in my early thirties now—and I'd feel ridiculous clomping around with all those *quinceañeras*.[4]

I can remember my great-grandmother Cleofas dancing "El Jarabe
Tapatío" on her saint's day in the back lot at my grandmother's house
in Barrio Hollywood. She'd gather up her long, black, homespun skirt
and dance barefooted in the dusty corral, her wide Indian feet pounding the earth into little explosions of dirt. She'd hum the tune through
the gaps in her teeth, her huge gold filigree *coqueta* earrings weighing
down her earlobes almost to her shoulders, her thin white braids whipping the air. She used to tell me, in her Nahuatl-laced Spanish, her
ancient face wrinkling in delight, how as a young girl she had been a
calentano dancer in her village of Pungarabato and kept time to the
music while her feet tapped out the rhythm on a hollow log called a
tarimba while the *conjunto de Juan Reynoso* played "El Son Guerrense."

So I guess it's in my blood.

Anyway, I'm married now with one kid and another one on the way.
Now don't get me wrong—I'm crazy about my husband and child. But
my *viejo* used to take me dancing all the time when we were *novios*.
I'd get all dressed up in a red lace dress and red high heels, and
tirábamos la chancla[5] every Saturday night at El Casino Ballroom or
Club La Selva on West Congress Street. We'd dance every dance, and
the little circles of light would be going around and around on the
ceiling, and I was so happy that sometimes I felt that I wasn't even
on this earth.

But now he usually says he's too tired, *pobre viejo*, working full time
and going to the university at night; he's got to study. Or there's a

---

[4.] Fifteen-year-old debutantes.
[5.] Danced a lot (literally, "threw our shoes").

football game on TV or a pickup basketball game with his buddies at La Madera Park.

No matter.

It's just that sometimes when the baby is crying and I'm standing at the kitchen sink, my hands chapped from the dishwater, my face sweaty from the steam, my legs achy from standing so long to cashier the afternoon shift at Abco to make ends meet. . . .

I think I'm gonna get those red high heels that I have in a box on the shelf at the back of our bedroom closet, and I'm just going to waltz right out of here . . .

for a little while.

The Girl with the Hungry Eyes

FRITZ LIEBER

*A*ll right, I'll tell you why the Girl gives me the creeps. Why I can't stand to go down town and see the mob slavering up at her on the tower, with that pop bottle or pack of cigarettes or whatever it is beside her. Why I hate to look at magazines anymore because I know she'll turn up somewhere in a brassiere or a bubble bath. Why I don't like to think of millions of Americans drinking in that poisonous half-smile. It's quite a story—more story than you're expecting.

No, I haven't suddenly developed any long-haired indignation at the evils of advertising and the national glamor-girl complex. That'd be a laugh for a man in my racket, wouldn't it? Though I think you'll agree there's something a little perverted about trying to capitalize on sex that way. But it's okay with me. And I know we've had the Face and the Body and the Look and what not else, so why shouldn't someone come along who sums it all up so completely, that we have to call her the Girl and blazon her on all the billboards from Times Square to Telegraph Hill?

But the Girl isn't like any of the others. She's unnatural. She's morbid. She's unholy.

Oh, these are modern times, you say, and the sort of thing I'm hinting at went out with witchcraft. But you see I'm not altogether sure myself what I'm hinting at, beyond a certain point. There are vampires and vampires, and not all of them suck blood.

And there were the murders, if they were murders. Besides, let me ask you this. Why, when America is obsessed with the Girl, don't we find out more about her? Why doesn't she rate a *Time* cover with a droll biography inside? Why hasn't there been a feature in *Life* or *The Post*? A profile in *The New Yorker*? Why hasn't *Charm* or *Mademoiselle* done her career saga? Not ready for it? Nuts!

Why haven't the movies snapped her up? Why hasn't she been on "Information, Please"? Why don't we see her kissing candidates at political rallies? Why isn't she chosen queen of some sort of junk or other at a convention?

Why don't we read about her tastes and hobbies, her views of the Russian situation? Why haven't the columnists interviewed her in a kimono on the top floor of the tallest hotel in Manhattan and told us who her boy friends are?

Finally—and this is the real killer—why hasn't she ever been drawn or painted?

Oh, no she hasn't. If you knew anything about commercial art you'd know that. Every blessed one of those pictures was worked up from a photograph. Expertly? Of course. They've got the top artists on it. But that's how it's done.

And now I'll tell you the why of all that. It's because from the top to the bottom of the whole world of advertising, news, and business, there isn't a solitary soul who knows where the Girl came from, where she lives, what she does, who she is, even what her name is.

You heard me. What's more, not a single solitary soul ever sees her—except one poor damned photographer, who's making more money off her than he ever hoped to in his life and who's scared and miserable as Hell every minute of the day.

No, I haven't the faintest idea who he is or where he has his studio. But I know there has to be such a man and I'm morally certain he feels just like I said.

Yes, I might be able to find her, if I tried. I'm not sure though—by now she probably has other safeguards. Besides, I don't want to.

Oh, I'm off my rocker, am I? That sort of thing can't happen in the

Era of the Atom? People can't keep out of sight that way, not even Garbo?

Well I happen to know they can, because last year I was that poor damned photographer I was telling you about. Yes, last year, when the Girl made her first poisonous splash right here in this big little city of ours.

Yes, I know you weren't here last year and you don't know about it. Even the Girl had to start small. But if you hunted through the files of the local newspapers, you'd find some ads, and I might be able to locate you some of the old displays—I think Lovelybelt is still using one of them. I used to have a mountain of photos myself, until I burned them.

Yes, I made my cut off her. Nothing like what that other photographer must be making, but enough so it still bought this whisky. She was funny about money. I'll tell you about that.

But first picture me then. I had a fourth-floor studio in that rathole the Hauser Building, not far from Ardleigh Park.

I'd been working at the Marsh-Mason studios until I'd gotten my bellyful of it and decided to start in for myself. The Hauser building was awful—I'll never forget how the stairs creaked—but it was cheap and there was a skylight.

Business was lousy. I kept making the rounds of all the advertisers and agencies, and some of them didn't object to me too much personally, but my stuff never clicked. I was pretty near broke. I was behind on my rent. Hell, I didn't even have enough money to have a girl.

It was one of those dark, gray afternoons. The building was very quiet—I'd just finished developing some pix I was doing on speculation for Lovelybelt Girdles and Budford's Pool and Playground. My model had left. A Miss Leon. She was a civics teacher at one of the high schools and modeled for me on the side, just lately on speculation, too. After one look at the prints, I decided that Miss Leon probably wasn't just what Lovelybelt was looking for—or my photography either. I was about to call it a day.

And then the street door slammed four stories down and there were steps on the stairs and she came in.

She was wearing a cheap, shiny black dress. Black pumps. No stockings. And except that she had a gray cloth coat over one of them, those skinny arms of hers were bare. Her arms are pretty skinny, you know, or can't you see things like that anymore?

And then the thin neck, the slightly gaunt, almost prim face, the tumbling mass of dark hair, and looking out from under it the hungriest eyes in the world.

That's the real reason she's plastered all over the country today, you know—those eyes. Nothing vulgar, but just the same they're looking at you with a hunger that's all sex and something more than sex. That's what everybody's been looking for since the Year One—something a little more than sex.

Well, boys, there I was, alone with the Girl, in an office that was getting shadowy, in a nearly empty building. A situation that a million male Americans have undoubtedly pictured to themselves with various lush details. How was I feeling? Scared.

I know sex can be frightening. That cold heart-thumping when you're alone with a girl and feel you're going to touch her. But if it was sex this time, it was overlaid with something else.

At least I wasn't thinking about sex.

I remember that I took a backward step and that my hand jerked so that the photos I was looking at sailed to the floor.

There was the faintest dizzy feeling like something was being drawn out of me. Just a little bit.

That was all. Then she opened her mouth and everything was back to normal for a while.

"I see you're a photographer, mister," she said. "Could you use a model?"

Her voice wasn't very cultivated.

"I doubt it," I told her, picking up the pix. You see, I wasn't impressed. The commercial possibilities of her eyes hadn't registered on me yet, by a long shot. "What have you done?"

Well, she gave me a vague sort of story and I began to check her knowledge of model agencies and studios and rates and what not and pretty soon I said to her, "Look here, you never modeled for a photographer in your life. You just walked in here cold."

Well, she admitted that was more or less so.

All along through our talk I got the idea she was feeling her way, like someone in a strange place. Not that she was uncertain of herself, or of me, but just of the general situation.

"And you think anyone can model?" I asked her pityingly.

"Sure," she said.

"Look," I said, "a photographer can waste a dozen negatives trying to get one halfway human photo of an average woman. How many do you think he'd have to waste before he got a real catchy, glamorous photo of her?"

"I think I could do it," she said.

Well, I should have kicked her out right then. Maybe I admired the cool way she stuck to her dumb little guns. Maybe I was touched by her underfed look. More likely I was feeling mean on account of the way my pictures had been snubbed by everybody and I wanted to take it out on her by showing her up.

"Okay, I'm going to put you on the spot," I told her. "I'm going to try a couple of shots of you. Understand it's strictly on spec. If somebody should ever want to use a photo of you; which is about one chance in two million, I'll pay you regular rates for your time. Not otherwise."

She gave me a smile. The first. "That's swell by me," she said.

Well, I took three or four shots, close-ups of her face since I didn't fancy her cheap dress, and at least she stood up to my sarcasm. Then I remembered I still had the Lovelybelt stuff and I guess the meanness was still working in me because I handed her a girdle and told her to go behind the screen and get into it and she did, without getting flustered as I'd expected, and since we'd gone that far, I figured we might as well shoot the beach scene to round it out, and that was that.

All this time I wasn't feeling anything particular one way or the other, except every once in a while I'd get one of those faint dizzy flashes and wonder if there was something wrong with my stomach or if I could have been a bit careless with my chemicals.

Still, you know, I think the uneasiness was in me all the while.

I tossed her a card and pencil. "Write your name and address and phone," I told her and made for the darkroom.

A little later she walked out. I didn't call any good-byes. I was irked because she hadn't fussed around or seemed anxious about her poses, or even thanked me, except for that one smile.

I finished developing the negatives, made some prints, glanced at them, decided they weren't a great deal worse than Miss Leon. On an impulse I slipped them in with the pictures I was going to take on the rounds next morning.

By now I'd worked long enough, so I was a bit fagged and nervous, but I didn't dare waste enough money on liquor to help that. I wasn't very hungry. I think I went to a cheap movie.

I didn't think of the Girl at all, except maybe to wonder faintly why in my present womanless state I hadn't made a pass at her. She had seemed to belong to a—well, distinctly more approachable social strata than Miss Leon. But then, of course, there were all sorts of arguable reasons for my not doing that.

Next morning I made the rounds. My first step was Munsch's Brewery. They were looking for a "Munsch Girl." Papa Munsch had a sort of affection for me, though he razzed my photography. He had a good natural judgment about that, too. Fifty years ago he might have been one of the shoestring boys who made Hollywood.

Right now he was out in the plant pursuing his favorite occupation. He put down the beaded schooner, smacked his lips, gabbled something technical to someone about hops, wiped his hands on the big apron he was wearing, and grabbed my thin stack of pictures.

He was about halfway through, making noises with his tongue and teeth, when he came to her. I kicked myself for even having stuck her in.

"That's her," he said. "The photography's not so hot, but that's the girl."

It was all decided. I wonder now why Papa Munsch sensed what the Girl had right away, while I didn't. I think it was because I saw her first in the flesh, if that's the right word.

At the time I just felt faint.

"Who is she?" he said.

"One of my new models," I tried to make it casual.

"Bring her out tomorrow morning," he told me. "And your stuff. We'll photograph her here."

"Here, don't look so sick," he added. "Have some beer."

Well, I went away telling myself it was just a fluke, so that she'd probably blow it tomorrow with her inexperience, and so on.

Just the same, when I reverently laid my next stack of pictures on Mr. Fitch, of Lovelybelt's, rose-colored blotter, I had hers on top.

Mr. Fitch went through the motions of being an art critic. He leaned over backward, squinted his eyes, waved his long fingers, and said, "Hmm. What do you think, Miss Willow? Here, in this light, of course, the photograph doesn't show the bias cut. And perhaps we should use the Lovelybelt Imp instead of the Angel. Still, the girl. . . . Come over here, Binns." More finger-waving. "I want a married man's reaction."

He couldn't hide the fact that he was hooked.

Exactly the same thing happened at Budford's Pool and Playground, except that Da Costa didn't need a married man's say-so."

"Hot stuff," he said, sucking his lips. "Oh boy, you photographers!"

I hotfooted it back to the office and grabbed up the card I'd given her to put down her name and address.

It was blank.

I don't mind telling you that the next five days were about the worst I ever went through, in an ordinary way. When next morning rolled around and I still hadn't got hold of her, I had to start stalling.

"She's sick," I told Papa Munsch over the phone.

"She at a hospital?" he asked me.

"Nothing that serious," I told him.

"Get her out here then. What's a little headache?"

"Sorry, I can't."

Papa Munsch got suspicious. "You really got this girl?"

"Of course I have."

"Well, I don't know. I'd think it was some New York model, except I recognized your lousy photography."

I laughed.

"Well look, you get her here tomorrow morning, you hear?"

"I'll try."

"Try nothing. You get her out here."

He didn't know half of what I tried. I went around to all the model and employment agencies. I did some slick detective work at the photographic and art studios. I used up some of my last dimes putting advertisements in all three papers. I looked at high school yearbooks and at employee photos in local house organs. I went to restaurants and drugstores, looking at waitresses, and to dime stores and department stores, looking at clerks. I watched the crowds coming out of movie theaters. I roamed the streets.

Evenings, I spent quite a bit of time along Pick-up Row. Somehow that seemed the right place.

The fifth afternoon I knew I was licked. Papa Munsch's deadline—he'd given me several, but this was it—was due to run out at six o'clock. Mr. Fitch had already canceled.

I was at the studio window, looking out at Ardleigh Park.

She walked in.

I'd gone over this moment so often in my mind that I had no trouble putting on my act. Even the faint dizzy feeling didn't throw me off.

"Hello," I said, hardly looking at her.

"Hello," she said.

"Not discouraged yet?"

"No." It didn't sound uneasy or defiant. It was just a statement.

I snapped a look at my watch, got up, and said curtly, "Look here, I'm going to give you a chance. There's a client of mine looking for a girl your general type. If you do a real good job you might break into the modeling business."

"We can see him this afternoon if we hurry," I said. I picked up my stuff. "Come on. And next time if you expect favors, don't forget to leave your phone number."

"Uh, uh," she said, not moving.

"What do you mean?" I said.

"I'm not going out to see any client of yours."

"The hell you aren't," I said. "You little nut, I'm giving you a break."

She shook her head slowly. "You're not fooling me, baby, you're not fooling me at all. They want me." And she gave me the second smile.

At the time I thought she must have seen my newspaper ad. Now I'm not so sure.

"And now I'll tell you how we're going to work," she went on. "You aren't going to have my name or address or phone number. Nobody is. And we're going to do all the pictures right here. Just you and me."

You can imagine the roar I raised at that. I was everything—angry, sarcastic, patiently explanatory, off my nut, threatening, pleading.

I would have slapped her face off, except it was photographic capital.

In the end all I could do was phone Papa Munsch and tell him her conditions. I knew I didn't have a chance, but I had to take it.

He gave me a really angry bawling out, said "no" several times, and hung up.

It didn't worry her. "We'll start shooting at ten o'clock tomorrow," she said.

It was just like her, using that corny line from the movie magazines. About midnight Papa Munsch called me up.

"I don't know what insane asylum you're renting this girl from," he said, "but I'll take her. Come round tomorrow morning and I'll try to get it through your head just how I want the pictures. And I'm glad I got you out of bed!"

After that it was a breeze. Even Mr. Fitch reconsidered and after taking two days to tell me it was quite impossible, he accepted the conditions too.

Of course you're all under the spell of the Girl, so you can't understand how much self-sacrifice it represented on Mr. Fitch's part when he agreed to forego supervising the photography of my model in the Lovelybelt Imp or Vixen or whatever it was we finally used.

Next morning she turned up on time according to her schedule, and we went to work. I'll say one thing for her, she never got tired and she never kicked at the way I fussed over shots. I got along okay, except I still had that feeling of something being shoved away gently. Maybe you've felt it just a little, looking at her picture.

When we finished I found out there were still more rules. It was about the middle of the afternoon. I started with her to get a sandwich and coffee.

"Uh, uh," she said, "I'm going down alone. And look, baby, if you ever try to follow me, if you ever so much as stick your head out of that window when I go, you can hire yourself another model."

You can imagine how all this crazy stuff strained my temper—and my imagination. I remember opening the window after she was gone—I waited a few minutes first—and standing there getting some fresh air and trying to figure out what could be behind it, whether she was hiding from the police, or was somebody's ruined daughter, or maybe had got the idea it was smart to be temperamental, or more likely Papa Munsch was right and she was partly nuts.

But I had my pictures to finish up.

Looking back it's amazing to think how fast her magic began to take hold of the city after that. Remembering what came after, I'm frightened of what's happening to the whole country—and maybe the world. Yesterday I read something in *Time* about the Girl's picture turning up on billboards in Egypt.

The rest of my story will help show you why I'm frightened in that big, general way. But I have a theory, too, that helps explain, though it's one of those things that's beyond that "certain point." It's about the Girl. I'll give it to you in a few words.

You know how modern advertising gets everybody's mind set in the same direction, wanting the same things, imagining the same things. And you know the psychologists aren't so skeptical of telepathy as they used to be.

Add up the two ideas. Suppose the identical desires of millions of people focused on one telepathic person. Say a girl. Shaped her in their image.

Imagine her knowing the hiddenmost hungers of millions of men. Imagine her seeing deeper into those hungers than the people that had them, seeing the hatred and the wish for death behind the lust. Imagine her shaping herself in that complete image, keeping herself as aloof as marble. Yet imagine the hunger she might feel in answer to their hunger.

But that's getting a long way from the facts of my story. And some of those facts are darn solid. Like money. We made money.

That was the funny thing I was going to tell you. I was afraid the Girl was going to hold me up. She really had me over a barrel, you know.

But she didn't ask for anything but the regular rates. Later on I insisted on pushing more money at her, a whole lot. But she always took it with that same contemptuous look, as if she were going to toss it down the first drain when she got outside.

Maybe she did.

At any rate, I had money. For the first time in months I had money enough to get drunk, buy new clothes, take taxicabs. I could make a play for any girl I wanted to. I only had to pick.

And so of course I had to go and pick. . . .

But first let me tell you about Papa Munsch.

Papa Munsch wasn't the first of the boys to try to meet my model but I think he was the first to really go soft on her. I could watch the change in his eyes as he looked at her pictures. They began to get sentimental, reverent. Mama Munsch had been dead for two years.

He was smart about the way he planned it. He got me to drop some information which told him when she came to work, and then one morning, he came pounding up the stairs a few minutes before.

"I've got to see her, Dave," he told me.

I argued with him, I kidded him, I explained he didn't know just how serious she was about her crazy ideas. I even pointed out he was cutting both our throats. I even amazed myself by bawling him out.

He didn't take any of it in his usual way. He just kept repeating, "But Dave, I've got to see her."

The street door slammed.

"That's her," I said, lowering my voice. "You've got to get out."

He wouldn't, so I shoved him in the darkroom. "And keep quiet," I whispered. "I'll tell her I can't work today."

I knew he'd try to look at her and probably come bustling in, but there wasn't anything else I could do.

The footsteps came to the fourth floor. But she never showed at the door. I got uneasy.

"Get the bum out of here!" she yelled suddenly from beyond the door. Not very loud, but in her commonest voice.

"I'm going up to the next landing," she said. "And if that fat-bellied bum doesn't march straight down to the street, he'll never get another picture of me except spitting in his lousy beer."

Papa Munsch came out of the darkroom. He was white. He didn't look at me as he went out. He never looked at her pictures in front of me again.

That was Papa Munsch. Now it's me I'm telling about. I talked around the subject with her, I hinted, eventually I made my pass.

She lifted my hand off her as if it were a damp rag.

"No, baby," she said. "This is working time."

"But afterward . . ." I pressed.

"The rules still hold." And I got what I think was the fifth smile.

It's hard to believe, but she never budged an inch from that crazy line. I mustn't make a pass at her in the office, because our work was very important and she loved it and there mustn't be any distractions. And I couldn't see her anywhere else, because if I tried to, I'd never snap another picture of her—and all this with more money coming in all the time and me never so stupid as to think my photography had anything to do with it.

Of course I wouldn't have been human if I hadn't made more passes. But they always got the wet-rag treatment and there weren't any more smiles.

I changed. I went sort of crazy and light-headed—only sometimes I felt my head was gong to burst. And I started to talk to her all the time. About myself.

It was like being in a constant delirium that never interfered with business. I didn't pay any attention to the dizzy feeling. It seemed natural.

I'd walk around and for a moment the reflector would look like a sheet of white-hot steel, or the shadows would seem like armies of moths, or the camera would be a big black coal car. But the next instant they'd come all right again.

I think sometimes I was scared to death of her. She'd seem the strangest, most horrible person in the world. But other times . . .

And I talked. It didn't matter what I was doing—lighting her, posing her, fussing with props, snapping my pictures—or where she was—on the platform, behind the screen, relaxing with a magazine—I kept up a steady gab.

I told her everything I knew about myself. I told her about my first girl. I told her about my brother Bob's bicycle. I told her about running away on a freight, and the licking Pa gave me when I came home. I told her about shipping to South America and the blue sky at night. I told her about Betty. I told her about my mother dying of cancer. I told her about being beaten up in a fight in an alley behind a bar. I told her about Mildred. I told her about the first picture I ever sold. I told her how Chicago looked from a sailboat. I told her about the longest drunk I was ever on. I told her about Marsh-Mason. I told her about Gwen. I told her about how I met Papa Munsch. I told her about hunting her. I told her about how I felt now.

She never paid the slightest attention to what I said. I couldn't even tell if she heard me.

It was when we were getting our first nibble from national advertisers that I decided to follow her when she went home.

Wait, I can place it better than that. Something you'll remember from the out-of-town papers—those maybe murders I mentioned. I think there were six.

I say "maybe" because the police could never be sure they weren't heart attacks. But there's bound to be suspicion when attacks happen to people whose hearts have been okay, and always at night when they're alone and away from home and there's a question of what they were doing.

The six deaths created one of those "mystery poisoner" scares. And afterward there was a feeling that they hadn't really stopped, but were being continued in a less suspicious way.

That's one of the things that scares me now.

But at that time my only feeling was relief that I'd decided to follow her.

I made her work until dark one afternoon. I didn't need any excuses, we were snowed under with orders. I waited until the street door slammed, then I ran down. I was wearing rubber-soled shoes. I'd slipped on a dark coat she'd never seen me in, and a dark hat.

I stood in the doorway until I spotted her. She was walking by Ardleigh Park toward the heart of town. It was one of those warm fall nights. I followed her on the other side of the street. My idea for tonight was just to find out where she lived. That would give me a hold on her.

She stopped in front of a display window of Everley's department store, standing back from the flow. She stood there looking in.

I remembered we'd done a big photograph of her for Everley's, to make a flat model for a lingerie display. That was what she was looking at.

At the time it seemed all right to me that she should adore herself, if that was what she was doing.

When people passed she'd turn away a little or drift back farther into the shadows.

Then a man came by alone. I couldn't see his face very well, but he looked middle-aged. He stopped and stood looking in the window.

She came out of the shadows and stepped up beside him.

How would you boys feel if you were looking at a poster of the Girl and suddenly she was there beside you, her arm linked with yours?

This fellow's reaction showed plain as day. A crazy dream had come to life for him.

They talked for a moment. Then he waved a taxi to the curb. They got in and drove off.

I got drunk that night. It was almost as if she'd known I was following her and had picked that way to hurt me. Maybe she had. Maybe this was the finish.

But the next morning she turned up at the usual time and I was back in the delirium, only now with some new angles added.

That night when I followed her she picked a spot under a street lamp, opposite one of the Munsch Girl billboards.

Now it frightens me to think of her lurking that way.

After about twenty minutes a convertible slowed down going past her, backed up, swung into the curb.

I was closer this time. I got a good look at the fellow's face. He was a little younger, about my age.

Next morning the same face looked up at me from the front page of the paper. The convertible had been found parked on a side street. He had been in it. As in the other maybe-murders, the cause of death was uncertain.

All kinds of thoughts were spinning in my head that day, but there were only two things I knew for sure. That I'd got the first real offer from a national advertiser, and that I was going to take the Girl's arm and walk down the stairs with her when we quit work.

She didn't seem surprised. "You know what you're doing?" she said.

"I know."

She smiled. "I was wondering when you'd get around to it."

I began to feel good. I was kissing everything good-bye, but I had my arm around hers.

It was another of those warm fall evenings. We cut across into Ardleigh Park. It was dark there, but all around the sky was a sallow pink from the advertising signs.

We walked for a long time in the park. She didn't say anything and she didn't look at me, but I could see her lips twitching and after a while her hand tightened on my arm.

We stopped. We'd been walking across the grass. She dropped down and pulled me after her. She put her hands on my shoulders. I was looking down at her face. It was the faintest sallow pink from the glow in the sky. The hungry eyes were dark smudges.

I was fumbling with her blouse. She took my hand away, not like she had in the studio. "I don't want that," she said.

First I'll tell you what I did afterward. Then I'll tell you why I did it. Then I'll tell you what she said.

What I did was run away. I don't remember all of that because I was dizzy, and the pink sky was swinging against the dark trees. But after a while I staggered into the lights of the street. The next day I closed up the studio. The telephone was ringing when I locked the door and there were unopened letters on the floor. I never saw the Girl again in the flesh, if that's the right word.

I did it because I didn't want to die. I didn't want the life drawn out of me. There are vampires and vampires, and the ones that suck blood aren't the worst. If it hadn't been for the warning of those dizzy flashes, and Papa Munsch and the face in the morning paper, I'd have gone the way the others did. But I realized what I was up against while there was still time to tear myself away. I realized that wherever she came from, whatever shaped her, she's the quintessence of the horror behind the bright billboard. She's the smile that tricks you into throwing away your money and your life. She's the eyes that lead you on and on, and then show you death. She's the creature you give everything for and never really get. She's the being that takes everything you've got and gives nothing in return. When you yearn toward her face on the billboards, remember that. She's the lure. She's the bait. She's the Girl.

And this is what she said, "I want you. I want your high spots. I want everything that's made you happy and everything that's hurt you bad. I want your first girl. I want that shiny bicycle. I want that licking. I want that pinhole camera. I want Betty's legs. I want the blue sky filled with stars. I want your mother's death. I want your blood on the cobblestones. I want Mildred's mouth. I want the first picture you sold. I want the lights of Chicago. I want the gin. I want Gwen's hands. I want your wanting me. I want your life. Feed me, baby, feed me."

While She Was Out

■

EDWARD BRYANT

*I*t was what her husband said then that was the last straw.

"Christ," muttered Kenneth disgustedly from the family room. He grasped a Bud longneck in one red-knuckled hand, the cable remote tight in the other. This was the time of night when he generally fell into the largest number of stereotypes. "I swear to God you're on the rag three weeks out of every month. PMS, my ass."

Della Myers deliberately bit down on what she wanted to answer. PXMS, she thought. That's what the twins' teacher had called it last week over coffee after the parent-teacher conference Kenneth had skipped. Preholiday syndrome. It took a genuine effort not to pick up the cordless Northwestern Bell phone and brain Kenneth with one savage, cathartic swipe. "I'm going out."

"So?" said her husband. "This is Thursday. Can't be the auto mechanics made simple for wusses. Self-defense?" He shook his head. "That's every other Tuesday. Something new, honey? Maybe a therapy group?"

"I'm going to Southeast Plaza. I need to pick up some things."

"Get the extra-absorbent ones," said her husband. He grinned and thumbed up the volume. ESPN was bringing in wide shots of something that looked vaguely like group tennis from some sweaty-looking Third World country.

"Wrapping paper," she said. "I'm getting some gift wrap and ribbon." Were there Fourth World countries? she wondered. Would they accept political refugees from America? "Will you put the twins to bed by nine?"

"Stallone's on HBO at nine," Kenneth said. "I'll bag 'em out by half-past eight."

"Fine." She didn't argue.

"I'll give them a good bedtime story." He paused. " 'The Princess and the Pea.' "

"Fine." Della shrugged on her long down-filled coat. Any more, she did her best not to swallow the bait. "I told them they could each have a chocolate chip cookie with their milk."

"Christ, Della. Why the hell don't we just adopt the dentist? Maybe give him an automatic monthly debit from the checking account?"

"One cookie apiece," she said, implacable.

Kenneth shrugged, apparently resigned.

She picked up the keys to the Subaru. "I won't be long."

"Just be back by breakfast."

Della stared at him. What if I don't come back at all? She had actually said that once. Kenneth had smiled and asked whether she was going to run away with the Gypsies, or maybe go off to join some pirates. It had been a temptation to say yes, dammit, yes, I'm going. But there were the twins. Della suspected pirates didn't take along their children. "Don't worry," she said. I've got nowhere else to go. But she didn't say that aloud.

Della turned and went upstairs to the twins' room to tell them good night. Naturally they both wanted to go with her to the mall. Each was afraid she wasn't going to get the hottest item in the Christmas doll department—the Little BeeDee Birth Defect Baby. There had been a run on the BeeDees, but Della had shopped for the twins early. "Daddy's going to tell you a story," she promised. The pair wasn't impressed.

"I want to see Santa," Terri said, with dogged, five-year-old insistence.

"You both saw Santa. Remember?"

"I forgot some things. An' I want to tell him again about BeeDee."

"Me, too," said Tammi. With Tammi, it was always "me, too."

"Maybe this weekend," said Della.

"Will Daddy remember our cookies?" said Terri.

Before she exited the front door, Della took the chocolate chip cookies from the kitchen closet and set the sack on the stairstep where Kenneth could not fail to stumble over it.

"So long," she called.

"Bring me back something great from the mall," he said. His only other response was to heighten the crowd noise from Upper Zambo-somewhere-or-other.

Sleety snow was falling, the accumulation beginning to freeze on the streets. Della was glad she had the Subaru. So far this winter, she hadn't needed to use the four-wheel-drive, but tonight the reality of having it reassured her.

Southeast Plaza was a mess. This close to Christmas, the normally spacious parking lots were jammed. Della took a chance and circled the row of spaces nearest to the mall entrances. If she were lucky, she'd be able to react instantly to someone's backup lights and snaffle a parking place within five seconds of its being vacated. That didn't happen. She cruised the second row, the third. Then—there! She reacted without thinking, seeing the vacant spot just beyond a metallic blue van. She swung the Subaru to the left.

And stamped down hard on the brake.

Some moron had parked an enormous barge of an ancient Plymouth so that it overlapped two diagonal spaces.

The Subaru slid to a stop with its nose about half an inch from the Plymouth's dinosaurian bumper. In the midst of her shock and sudden anger, Della saw the chrome was pocked with rust. The Subaru's headlights reflected back at her.

She said something unpleasant, the kind of language she usually only thought in dark silence. Then she backed her car out of the truncated space and resumed the search for parking. What Della eventually found was a free space on the extreme perimeter of the lot. She resigned herself to trudging a quarter mile through the slush. She hadn't worn boots. The icy water crept into her flats, soaked her toes.

"Shit," she said. "Shit shit shit."

Her shortest-distance-between-two-points course took her past the Plymouth hogging the two parking spots. Della stopped a moment, contemplating the darkened behemoth. It was a dirty gold with the remnants of a vinyl roof peeling away like the flaking of a scabrous scalp. In the glare of the mercury vapor lamp, she could see that the rocker panels were riddled with rust holes. Odd. So much corrosion didn't happen in the dry Colorado air. She glanced curiously at the rear license plate. It was obscured with dirty snow.

She stared at the huge old car and realized she was getting angry. Not just irritated. Real, honest-to-god, hard-core pissed off. What kind of imbeciles would take up two parking spaces on a rotten night just two weeks before Christmas?

Ones that drove a vintage, not-terribly-kept-up Plymouth, obviously.

Without even thinking about what she was doing, Della took out the spiral notebook from her handbag. She flipped to the blank page past tomorrow's grocery list and uncapped the fine-tip marker (it was supposed to write across anything—in this snow, it had *better*) and scrawled a message:

DEAR JERK, IT'S GREAT YOU COULD USE UP TWO PARKING SPACES ON A NIGHT LIKE THIS. EVER HEAR OF THE JOY OF SHARING?

She paused, considering; then appended:

—A CONCERNED FRIEND

Della folded the paper as many times as she could, to protect it from the wet, then slipped it under the driver's-side wiper blade.

It wouldn't do any good—she was sure this was the sort of driver who ordinarily would have parked illegally in the handicapped zone—but it made her feel better. Della walked on to the mall entrance and realized she was smiling.

She bought some rolls of foil wrapping paper for the adult gifts—assuming she actually gave Kenneth anything she'd bought for him—and an ample supply of Strawberry Shortcake pattern for the twins' presents. Della decided to splurge—she realized she was getting tired—and selected a package of pretied ribbon bows rather than simply taking a roll. She also bought a package of tampons.

Della wandered the mall for a little while, checking out the shoe stores, looking for something on sale in deep blue, a pair she could wear after Kenneth's office party for staff and spouses. What she *really* wanted were some new boots. Time enough for those after the holiday when the prices went down. Nothing appealed to her. Della knew she should be shopping for Kenneth's family in Nebraska. She couldn't wait forever to mail off their packages.

The hell with it. Della realized she was simply delaying returning home. Maybe she *did* need a therapy group, she thought. There was no relish to the thought of spending another night sleeping beside Kenneth, listening to the snoring that was interrupted only by the grinding of teeth. She thought that the sound of Kenneth's jaws moving against one another must be like hearing a speeded-up recording of continental drift.

She looked at her watch. A little after nine. No use waiting any longer. She did up the front of her coat and joined the flow of shoppers out into the snow.

Della realized, as she passed the rusted old Plymouth, that something wasn't the same. *What's wrong with this picture?* It was the note. It wasn't there. Probably it had slipped out from under the wiper blade with the wind and the water. Maybe the flimsy notebook paper had simply dissolved.

She no longer felt like writing another note. She dismissed the irritating lumber barge from her reality and walked on to her car.

Della let the Subaru warm up for thirty seconds (the consumer auto mechanics class had told her not to let the engine idle for the long minutes she had once believed necessary) and then slipped the shift into reverse.

The passenger compartment flooded with light.

She glanced into the rearview mirror and looked quickly away. A bright, glaring eye had stared back. Another quivered in the side mirror.

"Jesus Christ," she said under her breath. "The crazies are out tonight." She hit the clutch with one foot, the brake with the other, and waited for the car behind her to remove itself. Nothing happened.

The headlights in the mirror flicked to bright. "Dammit." Della left the Subaru in neutral and got out of the car.

She shaded her eyes and squinted. The front of the car behind hers looked familiar. It was the gold Plymouth.

Two unseen car doors clicked open and chunked shut again.

The lights abruptly went out and Della blinked, her eyes trying to adjust to the dim mercury vapor illumination from the pole a few car-lengths away.

She felt a cold thrill of unease in her belly and turned back toward the car.

"I've got a gun," said a voice. "Really." It sounded male and young. "I'll aim at your snatch first."

Someone else giggled, high and shrill.

Della froze in place. This couldn't be happening. It absolutely could not.

Her eyes were adjusting, the glare phantoms drifting out to the limit of her peripheral vision and vanishing. She saw three figures in front of her, then a fourth. She didn't see a gun.

"Just what do you think you're doing?" she said.

"Not doing *nothin'*, yet." That she saw, was the black one. He stood to the left of the white kid who had claimed to have a gun. The pair was bracketed by a boy who looked Chinese or Vietnamese and a young man with dark, Hispanic good looks. All four looked to be in their late teens or very early twenties. Four young men. Four ethnic groups represented. Della repressed a giggle she thought might be the first step toward hysteria.

"So what are you guys? Working on your merit badge in tolerance? Maybe selling magazine subscriptions?" Della immediately regretted saying that. Her husband was always riding her for smarting off.

"Funny lady," said the Hispanic. "We just happen to get along." He glanced to his left. "You laughing, Huey?"

The black shook his head. "Too cold. I'm shiverin' out here. I didn't bring no clothes for this."

"Easy way to fix that, man," said the white boy. To Della, he said, "Vinh, Tomas, Huey, me, we all got similar interests, you know?"

"Listen—" Della started to say.

"Chuckie," said the black Della now assumed was Huey, "let's us just shag out of here, okay?"

"Chuckie?" said Della.

"Shut up!" said Chuckie. To Huey, he said, "Look, we came up here for a vacation, right? The word is fun." He said to Della, "Listen, we were having a good time until we saw you stick the note under the wiper." His eyes glistened in the vapor-lamp glow. "I don't like getting any static from some 'burb-bitch just 'cause she's on the rag."

"For God's sake," said Della disgustedly. She decided he didn't really have a gun. "Screw off!" The exhaust vapor from the Subaru spiraled up around her. "I'm leaving, boys."

"Any trouble here, miss?" said a new voice. Everyone looked. It was one of the mall rent-a-cops, bulky in his fur-trimmed jacket and Russian-style cap. His hand lay casually across the unsnapped holster flap at his hip.

"Not if these underage creeps move their barge so I can back out," said Della.

"How about it, guys?" said the rent-a-cop.

Now there *was* a gun, a dark pistol, in Chuckie's hand, and he pointed it at the rent-a-cop's face. "Naw," Chuckie said. "This was gonna be a vacation, but what the heck. No witnesses, I reckon."

"For God's sake," said the rent-a-cop, starting to back away.

Chuckie grinned and glanced aside at his friends. "Remember the security guy at the mall in Tucson?" To Della, he said, "Most of these rent-a-pig companies don't give their guys any ammo. Liability laws and all that shit. Too bad." He lifted the gun purposefully.

The rent-a-cop went for his pistol anyway. Chuckie shot him in the face. Red pulp sprayed out the back of his skull and stained the slush as the man's body flopped back and forth, spasming.

"For chrissake," said Chuckie in exasperation. "Enough already. Relax, man." He leaned over his victim and deliberately aimed and fired, aimed and fired. The second shot entered the rent-a-cop's left eye. The third shattered his teeth.

Della's eyes recorded everything as though she were a movie camera. Everything was moving in slow motion and she was numb. She tried to make things speed up. Without thinking about the decision, she spun and made for her car door. She knew it was hopeless.

"Chuckie!"

"So? Where's she gonna go? We got her blocked. I'll just put one through her windshield and we can go out and pick up a couple of six-packs, maybe hit the late show at some other mall."

Della heard him fire one more time. Nothing tore through the back of her skull. He was still blowing apart the rent-a-cop's head.

She slammed into the Subaru's driver seat and punched the door-lock switch, for all the good that would do. Della hit the four-wheel-drive switch. *That* was what Chuckie hadn't thought about. She jammed the gearshift into first, gunned the engine, and popped the clutch. The Subaru barely protested as the front tires clawed and bounced over the six-inch concrete row barrier. The barrier screeched along the underside of the frame. Then the rear wheels were over and the Subaru fishtailed momentarily.

Don't over correct, she thought. It was a prayer.

The Subaru straightened out and Della was accelerating down the mall's outer perimeter service road, slush spraying to either side. Now what? she thought. People must have heard the shots. The lot would be crawling with cops.

But in the meantime . . .

The lights, bright and blinding, blasted against her mirrors.

Della stamped the accelerator to the floor.

This was crazy! This didn't happen to people—not to *real* people. The mall security man's blood in the snow had been real enough.

In the rearview, there was a sudden flash just above the left-side headlight, then another. It was a muzzle blast, Della realized. They were shooting at her. It was just like on TV. The scalp on the back of her head itched. Would she feel it when the bullet crashed through?

The twins! Kenneth. She wanted to see them all, to be safely with them. Just be anywhere but here!

Della spun the wheel, ignoring the stop sign and realizing that the access road dead-ended. She could go right or left, so went right. She thought it was the direction of home. Not a good choice. The lights were all behind her now; she could see nothing but darkness ahead. Della tried to remember what lay beyond the mall on this side. There were housing developments, both completed and under construction.

There had to be a 7-Eleven, a filling station, *something*. Anything. But there wasn't, and then the pavement ended. At first the road was suddenly rougher, the potholes yawning deeper. Then the slush-marked asphalt stopped. The Subaru bounced across the gravel;

within thirty yards, the gravel deteriorated to roughly graded dirt. The dirt surface more properly could be called mud.

A wooden barrier loomed ahead, the reflective stripes and lightly falling snow glittering in the headlights.

It *was* like on TV, Della thought. She gunned the engine and ducked sideways, even with the dash, as the Subaru plowed into the barrier. She heard a sickening *crack* and shattered windshield glass sprayed down around her. Della felt the car veer. She tried to sit upright again, but the auto was spinning too fast.

The Subaru swung a final time and smacked firm against a low grove of young pine. The engine coughed and stalled. Della hit the light switch. She smelled the overwhelming tang of crushed pine needles flooding with the snow through the space where the windshield had been. The engine groaned when she twisted the key, didn't start.

Della risked a quick look around. The Plymouth's light were visible, but the car was farther back than she had dared hope. The size of the lights wasn't increasing and the beams pointed up at a steep angle. Probably the heavy Plymouth had slid in the slush, gone off the road, was stuck for good.

She tried the key, and again the engine didn't catch. She heard something else—voices getting closer. Della took the key out of the ignition and glanced around the dark passenger compartment. Was there anything she could use? Anything at all? Not in the glovebox. She knew there was nothing there but the owner's manual and a large pack of sugarless spearmint gum.

The voices neared.

Della reached under the dash and tugged the trunk release. Then she rolled down the window and slipped out into the darkness. She wasn't too stunned to forget that the overhead light would go on if she opened the door.

At least one of the boys had a flashlight. The beam flickered and danced along the snow.

Della stumbled to the rear of the Subaru. By feel, she found the toolbox. With her other hand, she sought out the lug wrench. Then she moved away from the car.

She wished she had a gun. She wished she had learned to *use* a gun. That had been something tagged for a vague future when she'd finished her consumer mechanics course and the self-defense workshop, and had some time again to take another night course. It wasn't, she had reminded herself, that she was paranoid. Della simply wanted to be better prepared for the exigencies of living in the city. The suburbs weren't *the city* to Kenneth, but if you were a girl from rural Montana, they were.

She hadn't expected *this*.

She hunched down. Her nose told her the shelter she had found was a hefty clump of sagebrush. She was perhaps twenty yards from the Subaru now. The boys were making no attempt at stealth. She heard them talking to each other as the flashlight beam bobbed around her stalled car.

"So, she in there chilled with her brains all over the wheel?" said Tomas, the Hispanic kid.

"You an optimist?" said Chuckie. He laughed, a high-pitched giggle. "No, she ain't here, you dumb shit. This one's a tough lady." Then he said, "Hey, lookie there!"

"What you doin'?" said Huey. "We ain't got time for that."

"Don't be too sure. Maybe we can use this."

What had he found? Della wondered.

"Now we do what?" said Vinh. He had a slight accent.

"This be the West," said Huey. "I guess now we're mountain men, just like in the movies."

"Right," said Chuckie. "Track her. There's mud. There's snow. How far can she get?"

"There's the trail," said Tomas. "Shine the light over there. She must be pretty close."

Della turned. Hugging the toolbox, trying not to let it clink or clatter, she fled into the night.

They cornered her a few minutes later.

Or it could have been an hour. There was no way she could read her watch. All Della knew was that she had run; she had run and she had attempted circling around to where she might have a shot at making it to the distant lights of the shopping mall. Along the way, she'd felt the brush clawing at her denim jeans and the mud and slush attempting to suck down her shoes. She tried to make out shapes in the clouded-over dark, evaluating every murky form as a potential hiding place.

"Hey, baby," said Huey from right in front of her.

Della recoiled, feinted to the side, collided painfully with a wooden fence. The boards gave only slightly. She felt a long splinter drive through the down coat and spear into her shoulder. When Della jerked away, she felt the splinter tear away from its board and then break off.

The flashlight snapped on, the beam at first blinding her, then lowering to focus on her upper body. From their voices, she knew all four were there. Della wanted to free a hand to pull the splinter loose from her shoulder. Instead she continued cradling the blue plastic toolbox.

"Hey," said Chuckie, "what's in that thing? Family treasure, maybe?"

Della remained mute. She'd already gotten into trouble enough, wising off.

"Let's see," said Chuckie. "Show us, Della-honey."

She stared at his invisible face.

Chuckie giggled. "Your driver's license, babe. In your purse. In the car."

Shit, she thought.

"Lousy picture." Chuckie. "I think maybe we're gonna make your face match it." Again, that ghastly laugh. "Meantime, let's see what's in the box, okay?"

"Jewels, you think?" said Vinh.

"Naw, I don't think," said his leader. "But maybe she was makin' the bank deposit or something." He addressed Della, "You got enough goodies for us, maybe we can be bought off."

No chance, she thought. They want everything. My money, my rings, my watch. She tried to swallow, but her throat was too dry. My life.

"Open the box," said Chuckie, voice mean now.

"Open the box," said Thomas. Huey echoed him. The four started chanting, "Open the box, open the box, open the box."

"All right," she almost screamed. "I'll do it." They stopped their chorus. Someone snickered. Her hands moving slowly, Della's brain raced. Do it, she thought. But be careful. So careful. She let the lug wrench rest across her palm below the toolbox. With her other hand, she unsnapped the catch and slid up the lid toward the four. She didn't think any of them could see in, though the flashlight beam was focused now on the toolbox lid.

Della reached inside, as deliberately as she could, trying to betray nothing of what she hoped to do. It all depended upon what lay on top. Her bare fingertips touched the cold steel of the crescent wrench. Her fingers curled around the handle.

"This is pretty dull," said Tomas. "Let's just rape her."

Now!

She withdrew the wrench, cocked her wrist back, and hurled the tool about two feet above the flashlight's glare. Della snapped it just like her daddy had taught her to throw a hardball. She hadn't liked baseball all that much. But now—

The wrench crunched something and Chuckie screamed. The flashlight dropped to the snow.

Snapping shut the toolbox, Della sprinted between Chuckie and the one she guessed was Huey.

The black kid lunged for her and slipped in the muck, toppling facefirst into the slush. Della had a peripheral glimpse of Tomas leaping toward her, but his leading foot came down on the back of Huey's head, grinding the boy's face into the mud. Huey's scream bubbled; Tomas cursed and tumbled forward, trying to stop himself with out thrust arms.

All Della could think as she gained the darkness was, I should have grabbed the light.

She heard the one she thought was Vinh, laughing. "Cripes, guys, neat. Just like Moe and Curley and that other one."

"Shut up," said Chuckie's voice. It sounded pinched and in pain. "Shut the fuck up." The timbre squeaked and broke. "Get up, you dorks. Get the bitch."

Sticks and stones—Della thought. Was she getting hysterical? There was no good reason not to.

As she ran—and stumbled—across the nightscape, Della could feel the long splinter moving with the movement of the muscles in her shoulder. The feeling of it, not just the pain, but the sheer, physical sensation of intrusion, nauseated her.

I've got to stop, she thought. I've got to rest. I've got to think.

Della stumbled down the side of a shallow gulch and found she was splashing across a shallow, frigid stream. Water. It triggered something. Disregarding the cold soaking her flats and numbing her feet, she turned and started upstream, attempting to splash as little as possible. This had worked, she seemed to recall, in *Uncle Tom's Cabin*, as well as a lot of bad prison escape movies.

The boys were hardly experienced mountain men. They weren't Indian trackers. This ought to take care of her trail.

After what she estimated to be at least a hundred yards, when her feet felt like blocks of wood and she felt she was losing her balance, Della clambered out of the stream and struggled up the side of the gulch. She found herself in groves of pine, much like the trees where her Subaru had ended its skid. At least the pungent evergreens supplied some shelter against the prairie wind that had started to rise.

She heard noise from down in the gulch. It was music. It made her think of the twins.

"What the *fuck* are you doing?" Chuckie's voice.

"It's a tribute, man. A gesture." Vinh. "It's his blaster."

Della recognized the tape. Rap music. Run DMC, the Beastie Boys, one of those groups.

"Christ, I didn't mean it." Tomas. "It's her fault."

"Well, he's dead," said Chuckie, "and that's it for him. Now turn that shit off. Somebody might hear."

"Who's going to hear?" said Vinh. "Nobody can hear out here. Just us, and her."

"That's the point. She can."

"So what?" said Tomas. "We got the gun, we got the light. She's got nothin' but that stupid box."

"We *had* Huey," said Chuckie. "Now we don't. Shut off the blaster, dammit."

"Okay." Vinh's voice sounded sullen. There was a loud click and the rap echo died.

Della huddled against the rough bark of a pine trunk, hugging the box and herself. The boy's dead, she thought. So? said her common sense. He would have killed you, maybe raped you, tortured you before pulling the trigger. The rest are going to have to die too.

No.

Yes, said her practical side. You have no choice. They started this.

I put the note under the wiper blade.

Get serious. That was harmless. These three are going to kill you. They will hurt you first, then they'll put the gun inside your mouth and—

Della wanted to cry, to scream. She knew she could not. It was absolutely necessary that she not break now.

Terri, she thought, Tammi. I love you. After a while, she remembered Kenneth. Even you. I love you too. Not much, but some.

"Let's look up above," came the voice from the gully. Chuckie. Della heard the wet scrabbling sounds as the trio scratched and pulled their way up from the streambed. As it caught the falling snow, the flashlight looked like the beam from a searchlight at a movie premiere.

Della edged back behind the pine and slowly moved to where the trees were closer together. Boughs laced together, screening her.

"Now what?" said Tomas.

"We split up." Chuckie gestured; the flashlight beam swung wide. "You go through the middle. Vinh and me'll take the sides."

"Then why don't you give me the light?" said Tomas.

"I stole the sucker. It's mine."

"Shit, I could just walk past her."

Chuckie laughed. "Get real, dude. You'll smell her, hear her, somethin'. Trust me."

Tomas said something Della couldn't make out, but the tone was unconvinced.

"Now *do* it," said Chuckie. The light moved off to Della's left. She heard the squelching of wet shoes moving toward her. Evidently Tomas had done some wading in the gully. Either that or the slush was taking its toll.

Tomas couldn't have done better with radar. He came straight for her.

Della guessed the boy was ten feet away from her, five feet, just the other side of the pine. The lug wrench was the spider type, in the shape of a cross. She clutched the black steel of the longest arm and brought her hand back. When she detected movement around the edge of the trunk, she swung with hysterical strength, aiming at his head.

Tomas staggered back. The sharp arm of the lug wrench had caught him under the nose, driving the cartilage back up into his face. About a third of the steel was hidden in flesh. "Unh!" He tried to cry out, but all he could utter was, "Unh, unh!"

"Tomas?" Chuckie was yelling. "What the hell are you doing?"

The flashlight flickered across the grove. Della caught a momentary glimpse of Tomas lurching backward with the lug wrench impaled in his face as though he were wearing some hideous Halloween accessory.

"Unh!" said Tomas once more. He backed into a tree, then slid down the trunk until he was seated in the snow. The flashlight beam jerked across that part of the grove again and Della saw Tomas' eyes stare wide open, dark and blank. Blood was running off the ends of the perpendicular lug wrench arms.

"I see her!" someone yelled. "I think she got Tomas. She's a devil!" Vinh.

"So chill her!"

Della heard branches and brush crashing off to her side. She jerked open the plastic toolbox, but her fingers were frozen and the container crashed to the ground. She tried to catch the contents as they cascaded into the slush and the darkness. Her fingers closed on something, one thing.

The handle felt good. It was the wooden-hafted screwdriver, the sharp one with the slot head. Her auto mechanics teacher had approved. Insulated handle, he'd said. Good forged steel shaft. You could use this hummer to pry a tire off its rim.

She didn't even have time to lift it as Vinh crashed into her. His arms and legs wound around her like eels.

"Got her!" he screamed. "Chuckie, come here and shoot her."

They rolled in the viscid, muddy slush. Della worked an arm free. Her good arm. The one with the screwdriver.

There was no question of asking him nicely to let go, of giving warning, of simply aiming to disable. Her self-defense teacher had drilled into all the students the basic dictum of do what you can, do what you have to do. No rules, no apologies.

With all her strength, Della drove the screwdriver up into the base of his skull. She thrust and twisted the tool until she felt her knuckles dig into his stiff hair. Vinh screamed, a high keening wail that cracked and shattered as blood spurted out of his nose and mouth, splattering against Della's neck. The Vietnamese boy's arms and legs tensed and then let go as his body vibrated spastically in some sort of fit.

Della pushed him away from her and staggered to her feet. Her nose was full of the odor she remembered from the twins' diaper pail.

She knew she should retrieve the screwdriver, grasp the handle tightly, and twist it loose from Vinh's head. She couldn't. All she could do at this point was simply turn and run. Run again. And hope the survivor of the four boys didn't catch her.

But Chuckie had the light, and Chuckie had the gun. She had a feeling Chuckie was in no mood to give up. Chuckie would find her. He would make her pay for the loss of his friends.

But if she had to pay, Della thought, the price would be dear.

Prices, she soon discovered, were subject to change without warning.

With only one remaining pursuer, Della thought she ought to be able to get away. Maybe not easily, but now there was no crossfire of spying eyes, no ganging up of assailants. There was just one boy left, even if he *was* a psychopath carrying a loaded pistol.

Della was shaking. It was fatigue, she realized. The endless epinephrine rush of flight and fight. Probably, too, the letdown from just having killed two other human beings. She didn't want to have to think about the momentary sight of blood flowing off the shining ends of the lug wrench, the sensation of how it *felt* when the slot-headed screwdriver drove up into Vinh's brain. But she couldn't order herself to forget these things. It was akin to someone telling her not, under any circumstances, to think about milking a purple cow.

Della tried. No, she thought. Don't think about it at all. She thought about dismembering the purple cow with a chainsaw. Then she heard Chuckie's voice. The boy was still distant, obviously casting around virtually at random in the pine groves. Della stiffened.

"They're cute, Della-honey. I'll give 'em that." He giggled. "Terri and Tammi. God, didn't you and your husband have any more imagination than that?"

No, Della thought. We each had too much imagination. Tammi and Terri were simply the names we finally could agree on. The names of compromise.

"You know something?" Chuck raised his voice. "Now that I know where they live, I could drive over there in a while and say howdy. They wouldn't know a thing about what was going on, about what happened to their mom while she was out at the mall."

Oh God! thought Della.

"You want me to pass on any messages?"

"You little bastard!" She cried it out without thinking.

"Touchy, huh?" Chuckie slopped across the wet snow in her direction. "Come on out of the trees, Della-honey."

Della said nothing. She crouched behind a deadfall of brush and dead limbs. She was perfectly still.

Chuckie stood equally still, not more than twenty feet away. He stared directly at her hiding place, as though he could see through the night and brush. "Listen," he said. "This is getting real, you know, *boring*." He waited. "We could be out here all night, you know? All my buddies are gone now, and it's thanks to you, lady. Who the hell you think you are, Clint Eastwood?"

Della assumed that was a rhetorical question.

Chuckie hawked deep in his throat and spat on the ground. He rubbed the base of his throat gingerly with a free hand. "You hurt me, Della-honey. I think you busted my collarbone." He giggled. "But I don't hold grudges. In fact . . ." He paused contemplatively. "Listen now, I've got an idea. You know about droogs? You know, like in that movie?"

Clockwork Orange, she thought. Della didn't respond.

"Ending was stupid, but the start was pretty cool." Chuckie's personality seemed to have mutated into a manic stage. "Well, me droogs is all gone. I need a new gang, and you're real good, Della-honey. I want you should join me."

"Give me a break," said Della in the darkness.

"No, really," Chuckie said. "You're a born killer. I can tell. You and me, we'd be perfect. We'll blow this Popsicle stand and have some real fun. Whaddaya say?"

He's serious, she thought. There was a ring of complete honesty in his voice. She floundered for some answer. "I've got kids," she said.

"We'll take 'em along," said Chuckie. "I like kids, always took care of my brothers and sisters." He paused. "Listen, I'll bet you're on the outs with your old man."

Della said nothing. It would be like running away to be a pirate. Wouldn't it?

Chuckie hawked and spat again. "Yeah, I figured. When we pick up your kids, we can waste him. You like that? I can do it, or you can. Your choice."

You're crazy, she thought. "*I* want to," she found herself saying aloud.

"So come out and we'll talk about it."

"You'll kill me."

"Hey," he said, "I'll kill you if you *don't* come out. I got the light and the gun, remember? This way we can learn to trust each other right from the start. I won't kill you. I won't do nothing. Just talk."

"Okay." Why not? she thought. Sooner or later, he'll find his way in here and put the gun in my mouth and—Della stood up—but maybe, just maybe . . . Agony lanced through her knees.

Chuckie cocked his head, staring her way. "Leave the tools."

"I already did. The ones I didn't use."

"Yeah," said Chuckie. "The ones you used, you used real good." He lowered the beam of the flashlight. "Here you go. I don't want you stumbling and falling and maybe breaking your neck."

Della stepped around the deadfall and slowly walked toward him. His hands were at his sides. She couldn't see if he was holding the gun. She stopped when she was a few feet away.

"Hell of a night, huh?" said Chuckie. "It'll be really good to go inside where it's warm and get some coffee." He held the flashlight so that the beam speared into the sky between them.

Della could make out his thin, pain-pinched features. She imagined he could see hers. "I was only going out to the mall for a few things," she said.

Chuckie laughed. "Shit happens."

"What now?" Della said.

"Time for the horror show." His teeth showed ferally as his lips drew back in a smile. "Guess maybe I sort of fibbed." He brought up his hand, glinting of metal.

"That's what I thought," she said, feeling a cold and distant sense of loss. "Huey, there, going to help?" She nodded to a point past his shoulder.

"Huey?" Chuckie looked puzzled just for a second as he glanced to the side. "Huey's—"

Della leaped with all the spring left in her legs. Her fingers closed around his wrist and the hand with the gun. "Christ!" Chuckie screamed, as her shoulder crashed against the spongy place where his broken collarbone pushed out against the skin.

They tumbled on the December ground, Chuckie underneath, Della wrapping her legs around him as though pulling a lover tight. She burrowed her chin into the area of his collarbone and he screamed again. Kenneth had always joked about the sharpness of her chin.

The gun went off. The flash was blinding, the report hurt her ears. Wet snow plumped down from the overhanging pine branches, a large chunk plopping into Chuckie's wide-open mouth. He started to choke.

Then the pistol was in Della's hands. She pulled back from him, getting to her feet, backpedaling furiously to get out of his reach. She stared down at him along the blued-steel barrel. The pirate captain struggled to his knees.

"Back to the original deal," he said. "Okay?"

I wish, she almost said. Della pulled the trigger. Again. And again.

"Where the hell have you been?" said Kenneth as she closed the front door behind her. "You've been gone for close to three hours." He inspected her more closely. "Della, honey, are you all right?"

"Don't call me that," she said. "Please." She had hoped she would look better, more normal. Unruffled. Once Della had pulled the Subaru up to the drive beside the house, she had spent several minutes using spit and Kleenex trying to fix her mascara. Such makeup as she'd had along was in her handbag, and she had no idea where that was. Probably the police had it; three cruisers with lights flashing had passed her, going the other way, as she was driving north of Southeast Plaza.

"Your clothes." Kenneth gestured. He stood where he was.

Della looked down at herself. She'd tried to wash off the mud, using snow and a rag from the trunk. There was blood too, some of it Chuckie's, the rest doubtless from Vinh and Tomas.

"Honey, was there an accident?"

She had looked at the driver's side of the Subaru for a long minute after getting home. At least the car drove; it must just have been flooded before. But the insurance company wouldn't be happy. The entire side would need a new paint job.

"Sort of," she said.

"Are you hurt?"

To top it all off, she had felt the slow stickiness between her legs as she'd come up the walk. Terrific. She could hardly wait for the cramps to intensify.

"Hurt?" She shook her head. No. "How are the twins?"

"Oh, they're in bed. I checked a half hour ago. They're asleep."

"Good." Della heard sirens in the distance, getting louder, nearing the neighborhood. Probably the police had found her driver's license in Chuckie's pocket. She'd forgotten that.

"So," said Kenneth. It was obvious to Della that he didn't know at this point whether to be angry, solicitous, or funny. "What'd you bring me from the mall?"

Della's right hand was nestled in her jacket pocket. She felt the solid bulk, the cool grip of the pistol.

Outside, the volume of sirens increased.

She touched the trigger. She withdrew her hand from the pocket and aimed the pistol at Kenneth. He looked back at her strangely.

The sirens went past. Through the window, Della caught a glimpse of a speeding ambulance. The sound Dopplered down to a silence as distant as the dream that flashed through her head.

Della pulled the trigger and the *click* seemed to echo through the entire house.

Shocked, Kenneth stared at the barrel of the gun, then up at her eyes.

It was okay. She'd counted the shots. Just like in the movies.

"I think," Della said to her husband, "that we need to talk."

The Merry Widow

■

KATE WILHELM

*M*eg Summers was summoned to the district attorney's office late on a rainy November afternoon; the district attorney was present, and his chief assistant, Ricky Betz. Homicide Captain Al Cleves was slouched in a chair, scowling, and Detective Sergeant Don Ryerson sat as upright as a tree in another chair. They all looked very angry. Meg had met Folsum, the Texas lieutenant, earlier that day; he was standing at the window, a black shadow against the gray outdoors; even in silhouette he appeared angry. Cleves motioned toward a chair and she sat down warily, wondering why she was there at all. A detective for only four months, she was still in training.

"Okay, here's how it goes," Lieutenant Folsum said in a thick Texas accent. "Effie killed him." He made one-syllable words stretch out to two syllables; *"Kee-ild he-im.* And this time I intend to get her for it."

The district attorney was shaking his head. Folsum ignored him. He shifted a little; the rain on the windows behind him distorted the Portland city lights, creating a hallucinatory effect.

Meg sneaked a glance at her watch. Four-thirty, and Becky got out of preschool at five-fifteen. No way would Meg make it in time to pick her up. She had to call Clara, her backup, within the next fifteen minutes. Of course, the head of the school knew Meg's job sometimes kept her late, and they wouldn't turn Becky out, but they had made it clear that they didn't appreciate keeping one of the teachers late. Overtime, the head had said solemnly—which was meaningless, since Meg had to pay for any overtime.

"Effie was in Hawaii and met your local boy, Rollo Yates," the lieutenant was saying. "His mother had died recently and left him a bundle, and his father was in his seventies, in bad health, with an even bigger bundle. Another wedding, four weeks ago. Another death, yesterday. Rollo was victim number eight, gentlemen . . . and Ms. Summers."

Meg blinked. Obviously Folsum had filled in the others in some detail, but this was the first she had heard that Effie Yates was being accused of multiple murders. For a time no one spoke. Finally, the district attorney said, "Rollo Yates died in an accident. No way can we make it anything but an accident."

"They all died in accidents," the lieutenant said harshly. "Well, one had an aneurysm. Close enough."

Meg looked at her watch again, pretending she was simply moving to ease a cramped muscle.

"Two possibilities," Lieutenant Folsum said savagely. "One, she hires a woman to impersonate her, to be someplace else while *she* dispatches the new husband." He paused, then said, "Or she has a lover or accomplice who does the guy in for her." He moved away from the window and jerked a chair around to sit on it astraddle. Meg suspected he took his gun to bed with him.

"I don't care which scenario is right," Folsum said in a low, mean voice. "I want that little lady."

Captain Cleves was looking at his watch almost as often as she was, Meg realized. To her relief he stood up and said, "This looks like it's going to take a little time to plan. Let's have a break, meet back here in ten minutes."

Folsum scowled at him but made no objection. The district attorney and his assistant huddled; the captain reached for the telephone, then apparently changed his mind and walked to the outer office, where he sat at an empty desk to use a phone. Don Ryerson walked out with Meg. She headed for another desk, another phone. He stayed too close until she was actually seated, then continued on toward the men's room.

He never touched her, never made a pass, never uttered a word out of line. He never had to do anything overt; he broadcast his thoughts with every glance, every motion. In another time, another place, before the term "sexual harassment" had been invented, it would have been a different story, she understood, but here and now he was careful not to give her cause for a formal complaint. He was just always there, forty years old, six feet tall, a former football player running to fat now, with dissecting eyes and hands that came to life, opening, closing, while his eyes roamed over her. He gave her the creeps. Twice he had asked her to go out with him; now he simply looked.

She called Clara, who said no problem, she'd keep Becky until Meg showed up, give her some supper, bed her down if necessary.

Up here in the district attorney's office, the staff was closing down for the day. Not for the first time Meg felt envious of the secretaries and clerks who reported in at nine and left promptly at five. She saw Don Ryerson returning and hurried toward the ladies' room.

"She couldn't have planned this one much in advance," Folsum said when they had all gathered again. "No one knew Rollo's old man was that sick, and Effie and Rollo caught the first flight out when they got the word. So, we'll want all phone calls from that moment until Rollo got it. A list of all the passengers on that flight, and check them all out. Her movements minute by minute from the time she stepped off the plane. She got in touch with her accomplice somehow. I want to find out when, how, and who."

Captain Cleves was looking more and more unhappy as the list of what the lieutenant wanted stretched out. Finally he interrupted. "They arrived here within hours after the old man died. Two attorneys met them and took them to the hospital, and then to a hotel, and they went. Early yesterday morning the lawyers had them in meetings, making funeral arrangements, and in the afternoon Effie went to get her hair done, and later on Rollo went to the parking garage to get something from the car, a rental car. And the trunk lid fell on him. She didn't have time to set up anything."

"I never said she wasn't smart," Folsum drawled softly. His eyes glittered. "Ryerson and Summers come with me to talk to the little lady, and you get started on some of that other stuff. Right?"

Captain Cleves shrugged and nodded. Meg didn't understand how it had come about that the lieutenant from Texas was ordering her captain in Portland, but apparently Folsum was in charge. Even more apparently, he had had a run-in with Effie Yates in the past. Meg made a great effort not to reveal her dismay at being paired with Don Ryerson, who was looking at her again.

Effie Yates had a suite on the seventh floor of the plush Hanover House Hotel. She opened the door for them. She was a small woman in her midthirties, and surprisingly pretty, with dimples, blue eyes, blond hair done in a windblown style that suggested great care had gone into arranging it. Dressed in flowing green silk pants with a gold sash and a white silk blouse, she could have been a Barbie model. Her eyes widened when she saw Folsum. Then she dimpled and smiled. "For heaven's sake, it's the Lone Ranger himself! Well, come on in."

She put her hand on Folsum's arm, smiling broadly at him, and moved aside to let them all enter. "Folsum jerked away from her. "Sergeant Ryerson, Detective Summers," he said, motioning with his thumb toward them. "We'd like to ask you a few questions."

"Well, of course." Effie held out her hand to Meg to shake. Her hand was warm and firm. Then she shook hands with Don Ryerson, who looked bewildered, as if suspects weren't supposed to do this. She led the way to a sitting room with wide windows, beautiful furniture, and many vases of flowers.

Gesturing toward a couch and the chairs, she seated herself in a gold brocade-covered armchair. Folsum did not sit down. Don Ryerson started to, then, taking his cue from the lieutenant, continued to stand. Meg sat on the couch. Effie grinned at her.

"Okay," Effie said. "Shoot."

Folsum's expression made it clear that he would like to do just that. He said, "I have a tape recorder. Do you have any objection to our using it for this interview?"

She shrugged. "Nope. If your memory is as lousy as mine, that's the only way."

He set a tape recorder on a coffee table, finally sat down opposite her, and started. Don Ryerson sat in a straight chair, listening intently, his eyes now fixed on Effie Yates. Meg sat and watched and listened, but there was nothing to hear, she concluded quickly. Effie and Rollo had been entertaining friends when the call came about his father's death. Two friends had gone with Effie to help her pack a few things; the women had been the governor's sister and a visiting senator. Folsum's eyes were glittering again as Effie recounted her actions, minute by minute. It was obvious that there had not been an opportunity for her to plan anything or to get in touch with an accomplice.

Then Effie said, "Lieutenant, I told you all about it back in Dallas. Don't you remember?" She smiled at him, then at Meg. "I have such a peculiar gift, you see. For some reason I can always tell if someone is going to die within the next few months, and I know how it will happen. Not something I asked for. I mean, how on earth would anyone phrase such a request? I didn't believe it myself for a long time, but it's true. I always tell the guys about it. Rollo knew. Or he didn't know, I guess, because no one ever believes me. But I told him. And I told the lieutenant back in Dallas a few years ago."

Meg stared at her. Folsum cursed, not quite inaudibly, and Don Ryerson looked steely-eyed.

"Cut the crap, Effie!" Folsum said. He stood up. "We'll be checking out everything you said, everyone you saw and talked to, every phone call. Meanwhile, the body stays on ice. And you stay put."

Effie sighed mournfully. "In a city where I don't know a soul. No doubt my lawyer will be in touch with you tomorrow. I think we'll have a double funeral for Rollo and his father. That would be nice, wouldn't it?"

"Too bad you're so overwhelmed by shock and grief," Folsum muttered.

"Lieutenant, I hardly knew the man!"

Effie paused and looked at Meg appraisingly. Then she said, "Would you please stay and have dinner with me, Detective? I hate to eat alone in a hotel room, and it would look awfully funny if I went out and had a big meal, wouldn't it? But I am hungry. Besides, reporters are hanging around."

Swiftly Folsum said, "She'll stay. Come on, Ryerson, we have work to do."

Meg looked at her watch, then at Folsum, and she didn't say a word. It was fifteen minutes after seven. Becky would have to spend the night at Clara's house. And she would have to call to let Clara know.

"Well, good," Effie said. She got up and went to the door of an adjoining room and closed the door behind her.

"Okay," Folsum said to Meg, "This could be a break. It's why I picked you to come with us. I thought she might like to talk to a female, someone young. She's a real talker. Just let her go on, and remember every word she says, her expression, things she skips over. No point in trying to pump her; she's an old pro at this, but she might let something slip. Since you don't know anything, you can ask the kind of questions that anyone would. Get a cab when you're done, and as soon as you're home, write a full report before you forget anything. Got that?

After the two detectives left, Effie returned to the sitting room. She listened when Meg called Clara, and when she spoke to Becky. When Meg hung up, Effie said, "I'm sorry I asked you to stay. Do you want to go now, be with your daughter?"

"I can't. Orders," Meg said. "It's okay. It doesn't happen very often, and she loves her baby-sitter. It's okay." She realized her tone was not as upbeat as her words, but she couldn't help it.

"Well, since it's a done deed, let's see what the room service menu has to offer. I've found that if you want something not listed, they usually can find it for you. I hope you like wine. I love wine, a good Rhone white, or a Chardonnay. I happen to have both on and"—she went to a refrigerator and brought out two bottles—"you pick. I never touch the hard stuff, but a nice wine, that's different."

Meg shook her head. "I guess I'd better not. I think I'm still on duty."

"Nonsense. I'll pick and pour and put a glass at your elbow. By the time we eat and have coffee, you'll be sober again even if we both get a little bit tipsy first. She chatted as she opened the bottle and poured, chatted as she sipped her own wine and examined the menu, then handed it over to Meg. "At least taste the wine," she said. "If eating alone is bad, think how much worse drinking alone is."

Suddenly Meg laughed in spite of herself. Maybe Effie was a black widow who devoured one husband after another, but her friendliness was infectious. The wine was the best she had ever had. They ordered crab, and Meg listened in amusement as Effie added vegetables and salad, and steamed clams for starters, to be sent up immediately, and another bottle of the Rhone wine.

"There," Effie said in satisfaction. "See, I never would have done that alone. Tell me about your daughter."

To her surprise, Meg found herself talking about Becky, who was five, about Jack, who had walked out three years earlier, about her parents, who lived on the coast and ran a motel.

A waiter came, rolling a cart with the steamed clams and hot crusty bread, and more wine. As soon as he left again, Effie asked, "How on earth did you become a cop?" She took the lid off the bucket of clams and sniffed. "Oh, wow! Heaven! Dig in."

Going to the police academy together had been Jack's idea, Meg told her, digging in. The clams were as good as they smelled. Jack had flunked out and she had made it. At that point, Jack walked.

"It pays better than anything else I could do," Meg said. "The benefits are good—health insurance, sick leave, things like that. And I have a child to raise."

"Divorced or separated?" Effie asked. She dipped a piece of bread in the juice remaining in the bucket. "Try that," she said. "Good."

Meg tried it. Good. "Divorced," she said then.

"What I like to do is get up and move between courses," Effie said when the clams were gone, as well as all the juice. She went to the window. "Still raining." Then, facing out, she said softly, "I was crazy about Bobby, my first husband. I was twenty, he was twenty-three." At the table Meg stiffened, listening hard.

"I was still in college," Effie went on, "but he had graduated and had a job already. Then one night we were watching TV, sitting on the floor eating popcorn, laughing, and all at once it was just like a memory flashed into my head. You know how you remember things; a little bit at first, then more and more. It was like that. In my memory flash I saw him walking, saw something big and dark falling on him, saw him die.

"Then I remembered more. We were looking in a shop window on a street that I never had seen before. I had on a wedding ring. It was hot and sunny. I had on sandals and shorts, a tank top. It was June tenth. He started to walk on, but I looked in the shop window again and called him to come back. He laughed. We were so broke we couldn't buy a thing. We were putting it all on a credit card, his first credit card. We didn't have a clue about how we'd pay it off and we didn't really care. It was our honeymoon. Then the ice fell on his head."

There was a knock on the door, and this time two waiters appeared, one to bring food, one to clear away dirty dishes. No one spoke until they were gone. Effie came back to the table and began to remove covers, exclaiming over the dishes. She poured more wine for them both and sat down.

"Let's eat."

Meg reached across the table and touched Effie's hand. "I'm sorry about Bobby," she said.

"Honey, that was a long time ago. Sixteen years. It's all right." As if to prove that it was all right, she continued to talk between bites. She had been shaken by the flash of premature memory, she said, but Bobby had thought it was funny. Just to thwart fate, he had said, they'd go ahead and get married right them, in April. She could miss school for a few days; he could get a few days off work, and they would have a short honeymoon. They had gotten married in April, but a crisis had come up at work, and he had not been able to leave then. By June, when they took a trip to Mexico, she had forgotten the premonitory dream. Until it happened exactly as she had seen it.

She had been devastated, in severe shock, suicidal even, and then someone had brought a lawyer around, and he had explained to her the economics of a tragedy like that and seen to it that she was compensated. "He fell for me," she said with a slight grin. "He was twenty years older than I was, and he fell for me. I didn't encourage him; it just happened. He was so kind and gentle, and kept insisting that I was not to blame, that I hadn't done anything wrong, that all my guilt was misplaced. I was very grateful.

"And one day at lunch with him, I touched his hand and it happened again. A flash of memory. I told him I had seen him on a sinking boat that had run into a rock, and he laughed, exactly as Bobby had. He said he was safe because he didn't own a boat, never went near a boat, and didn't intend to go near one." She shrugged. "Two weeks after we got married a client took him out on his yacht, and it happened exactly as I had predicted. A submerged rock tore up the yacht, and it sank."

She had gone to a psychiatrist in New York, Effie continued. They started dating, and after some months she told him he would drop dead while a patient was talking. "He told me no one as healthy as he was could possibly just drop dead. But he did, two months later, four weeks after our wedding. I couldn't tell what killed him, of course. An aneurysm is pretty invisible. That's when the police got interested. They did an autopsy. I guess they thought I'd poisoned him. After that there's been an autopsy every time, no matter what the cause of death was. His patient was cured, by the way," she added. "He thought he had shocked his psychiatrist to death with his personal revelations, and he went on a power trip and was cured!"

She cracked crab legs and picked out the meat as she talked, now and then sighing over the succulent fare. Meg listened with mounting skepticism but did not interrupt. The crab was delicious.

"I traveled a little then, trying to think what was happening. I had to believe it was really happening by then, of course. Now and then I met someone and advised him to get a whole lot of insurance fast. No one ever did; they all thought I was wacko because I'd lost three husbands in three years. Then I found myself in Palm Beach. Talk about money! The first few times the guys had to work for it, but down there, they grow it on trees, or dig it out of family cellars or something. Anyway, there was a guy, single, a little older than me, rolling in dough. And he planned to leave it to some dippy aunt who already owned Fort Knox. I told him about my odd gift, of course. And he laughed. We got married and a shark ate him."

Effie dipped an asparagus spear in hollandaise and ate it thoughtfully. "By then I had a plan, though. I have a gift, and I have to share it with people. But how? Wouldn't an insurance company love to hire me! Anyway, I can't go around touching people and saying your okay, but you're dead. My range seems to be about four months. So I decided to become a distribution agent. I would collect bundles of dough, I decided, and give half to charity."

Finally Meg asked a question. "How did you meet Lieutenant Folsum?"

"Oh, that was in Dallas. Oil money. Guys all seem to carry guns down there, did you know that? Anyway, the oil man was at his broker's office and someone came in shooting and popped him. I had told him, too. I always tell them." She shrugged. "And the Lone Ranger made it his lifelong duty to bring me to justice." She laughed.

Meg pushed her plate back an inch, surfeited. "Don't you care at all?" she asked then. "I mean, to marry someone who dies so suddenly, doesn't it mean anything to you?"

Effie eyed the last piece of asparagus, shook her head, and picked up her wine. "I cared a lot the first time, and I cared the next two times, in a different way. After that?" She shrugged. "They were going to die, no matter what I did or didn't do. Others died, guys I didn't want any part of, and I knew they were going to. The ones I married had a lot of money, and I put it to good use. Half-and-half at first; now it's more like three-fourths to charities and the rest for me. That's better than any of them would have done with the dough. So I'm the highest-paid whore in the world. I can live with that."

Meg ducked her head, embarrassed, because that was exactly what she had been thinking. Or would have been thinking, she corrected herself, if she believed a word of this. Effie poured more wine, emptying the second bottle. They drank silently.

Then Meg asked, "Does it work with women too?"

"Sure. You're okay. I wouldn't have told you any of this if you hadn't been." Effie grinned reassuringly.

"Why did you tell me? It won't make a bit of difference if I believe you or not. Lieutenant Folsum is convinced you're a murderer. I couldn't change his mind."

For a moment Effie studied Meg. Then she said, "I don't want to use you, honey. I know what the Lone Ranger thinks. Forget him. The other one, though, what's his name?"

"Don Ryerson?"

"Yeah, the guy getting fat. I touched him and got my flash of memory. January sixth, a Saturday evening, six weeks from now. He's been sick in bed for three days with the mumps, and he's been married for three days. Too sick to do anything about it. He's alone watching television, and he gets really excited and jumps out of bed and goes to the window to yell at his bride, who has gone out to buy juice for him, and he falls out. Tough."

"Don Ryerson," Meg whispered. "I don't believe it."

"No one ever does," Effie said, smiling. "I'm not done yet. Listen.

The day of the wedding he shoots up a fever and takes to bed. The day before the wedding, he buys two lottery tickets and makes a big deal out of giving them to his bride-to-be for a wedding present. What excited him on Saturday was the announcement that one of the tickets had won big, real big, nine million big."

Meg put own her wineglass; her hand was shaking too hard to hold it. She was shaking all over. "That's crazy!" she cried. "If you know that, why don't you grab him?"

"Can't. Not in six weeks, not with the Lone Ranger breathing down my back, and fatso himself looking at me so steely-eyed. Besides, it would look bad to remarry that fast. But you could. I saw how he looked at you." She stood up. "I'll order some coffee now. And I have a box of chocolates that will make you think you're in heaven." She went to the phone, but before she lifted the receiver, she said, "Anyway, I said I have to share this gift. Remember?"

It was nearly midnight when Meg got back to her apartment, where she managed to write her report. She rewrote it three times; in the final version she did not mention what Effie had said about Don Ryerson. The next morning she gathered clean clothes for Becky and drove to Clara's house to collect her daughter and take her to preschool.

Lieutenant Folsum put her through a two-hour debriefing that left her exhausted and him bitterly unhappy. When he said she could go, she paused at the door to ask, "Is it true that she gives away millions?"

"True," he muttered. "Trying to ease her guilty conscience. Buy her way into heaven."

That week Meg read the entire file on Effie Yates. She read about the double funeral, and studied the pictures of the widow.

The lieutenant went back to Texas, and Effie returned to Hawaii; a few days later Meg received a postcard from her. "My address. Come visit. Next time, you buy the wine."

The following Monday when she reported to work Meg was assigned to partner with Don Ryerson, who was looking at her, his hands opening and closing. She stopped moving and asked, "Did you ever have mumps?"

He looked blank, then shook his head. "Hell of a question to ask."

She smiled at him.

Esther Goes on the Offensive

■

BEBE MOORE CAMPBELL

*T*he two women arrived at Charles's office right before noon. Charles rose from the chair behind his desk when they entered. "Have a seat," he said. Despite the redness in them, his eyes were alert, wary. Lord, please put the right words in my mouth, Esther thought as she sat down.

"Charles," Esther said, her voice sounding loud and almost strident in the silence of the office, "Mallory and I would like to discuss a matter of grave importance to us."

"I don't have a lot of time right now," he said, waving his hand as though he were telling them good-bye.

You better make time, fool. Esther's hands began to ball up into two tight fists. "This won't take long," she said. She took a deep breath, then stood up, opened her hands, and put them on the desk. She leaned across it so that her face was directly in Charles's. "Today you hinted that I mishandled this morning's robbery and that you were thinking about putting a negative evaluation of my performance in my personnel file. Then you told me that I smelled good and asked me if I smelled good all over. Am I remembering the sequence of events?"

"I don't know what the hell you're talking about." Charles's voice was calm, but his face had grown red and contorted. He looked ready to explode.

For a moment, even Esther felt like retreating. Don't be a punk, she told herself sternly. Punk. Punk. Punk.

Mallory eyed Esther, desperately wanting the black woman to back down. Esther took a deep breath and moved in closer to Charles. She could feel his breath on her face. "I think you do. Mallory certainly knows what I'm talking about. Isn't that right?"

Mallory managed to nod. "Yes," she said, her voice squeaky and thin.

Esther's voice got louder, stronger. "And so does Sandra Grossman. In the past several weeks we've all been the recipients of your threats and . . . sexual harassment." She wielded those last words like a weapon; Charles began to slump in his seat. "Neither Mallory, Sandra, nor I are interested in sleeping with you, Charles. We don't want to date you. Is that clear? You will be with us for another week, and during that week we don't want you staring at our breasts or our hips. We don't want you licking your lips at us. We don't want you calling us anything but our names. Do you understand me? Now, if my or Mallory's personnel records are changed, we'll go straight to Kirk and we'll be discussing some of your other offensive and highly suggestive remarks. Do I make myself clear?"

As Esther was speaking, Charles remained subdued; he acted like a defeated man. But as soon as she had finished, he sprang out of his chair like a wild dog on the attack, the gold pinkie ring and dangling bracelet sparkling as he waved his hand back and forth. "I never heard such a crock of shit in all my life," he said, snarling. "Who do you think you're talking to, some stupid kid? I never harassed either one of you." He stalked across the room until he stood directly in front of the two women. "You girls are looking for action, that's your problem," he said with a sneer. "You wish I would look at you. You've been coming on to me. Both of you. And when I do the write-ups, don't think I won't include that bit of information as well." He smiled, a triumphant grin full of malice. "Am I making myself clear?"

Esther stole a glance at Mallory and saw that her face was as pale as a piece of paper. Absolutely bloodless. Her own heart was pounding, frantic little thumps. She could feel rage coursing through her body. Her mouth was full of burning words. She knew she should take a deep breath and regain control, but she didn't want to calm down. She wanted to go off. Before Esther could stop herself, she put her left hand on her hip, craned her neck to the side, and pointed her right finger at Charles's face, almost touching his nose. "Fuck you, you bald-headed, polyester-suit-wearing, potbellied, drinking-on-the job, two-inch pudding-dick motherfucker. Let me make myself crystaldamnclear; I know some guys who'd take your litle pale, flat ass out for a hundred bucks. And I have a hundred bucks. Now," she said, getting right up in Charles's face, so close her eyes began to cross, "if you put a negative review in my personnel file, or any of our files, you'd better take a damn bodyguard with you when you go to work and when you go home at night. If you think I'm playing, try me."

She was panting when she finished, and her head felt light. Charles's shiny moon face was red; sweat was beading on his hairless pate. He opened his mouth to speak but could only make a faint gagging sound. Esther knotted her hand into a fist and slammed it into her other palm. Charles jumped back at least two feet. "It's been great talking with you," Esther said. "You just remember what I said. Do not try to fuck with us." She nodded toward Mallory, who, appearing nearly as frightened as their boss, looked at Charles and then at Esther. For a fraction of a second, it seemed as though she didn't know whose side she was on. But then she slowly stood up and followed Esther.

Neither woman said a word until they were inside Esther's office. Mallory cleared her throat and said in a high, whiny voice, full of wonder and just a little fear. "Do—you really know people like that?"

Esther tilted her head and watched Mallory as she fidgeted with her fingers. "Like what?"

"Like—like you told Charles about. Men who would hurt him."

Esther peered into Mallory's face and saw Barbie the Innocent. For a minute, she wanted to slap her more than she wanted to hit Charles. "What do you think, Mallory?"

The white woman shrugged her shoulders and shook her head. Had she said something wrong? "I don't know."

"Mallory," she said tersely, "it's straight out of *The Godfather*."

Mallory's head jerked a little, as though Esther had hit her. She stood there feeling stupid and a little ashamed, but at least she understood the anger in her friend's face. "I didn't mean . . . I just wish

I could be that angry and show it. But where did all that . . . all that come from?"

"Ghetto 101."

Mallory moved forward eagerly, her bright-gray eyes like headlight beams searching in the dark. "Do they have that at Cal State?"

Esther looked at Mallory's sincere face and burst out laughing. Mallory looked momentarily stricken, as if she'd been slapped, then the tiniest giggle escaped from her lips and she began to laugh too. Esther leaned against the wall with her head thrown back, her hunched shoulders shaking in a jerky rhythm. Each time they tried to stop laughing, the two women only had to look at each other to start up again.

"What do you think he's going to do?" Mallory asked between bursts of laughter. I have no idea.

"Suppose he still puts that stuff in our files?"

"Oh, yeah? He'll wake up with a horse's head in his bed. Shi-i-it." They fell against the glass partition, their bodies bent over and spasmodic, laughing so loudly, so wildly, that they didn't even notice the customers turning to stare at them.

this is a story

■

JANE YOLEN

this is a story,
but it is not my story:
There was first nothing,
and then more nothing,
and then an eternity of nothing.
Then out of that nothing
there came light,
and a word,
and man.
And afterward,
part of the light
and part of the word
and part of the man
and part of the nothing
split off and became woman.

This is a story
but it is not my story:
There was a god
who took his cock

and sprayed the nothing
and from those drops
came rams in the field,
and bulls, and boar,
and stallions and stag
and men.
And from those men
and rams
and bulls, boar, stallions, and stag
and their many cocks spraying
there also came women.

This is a story,
but it is not my story:
There was an egg
and out of that egg
there sprang men
with bows and spears
and stakes and clubs
And wherever they shot
their many arrows,
and threw their spears
and raked the earth
with their sharp stakes
and beat it with their clubs
there appeared women.

This is a story,
but it is not my story
which I carry in my secret place
where there is no light
and no word
and especially no men.

Over the Pass

■

SUSAN MARY MALONE

On a backroad byway between Idaho and Montana, through the Red Rocks Wildlife Refuge, I lost the feeling. My heart got out and took a hike and we were another day down the road before I realized it was gone.

From Missoula we had shot southward, past the goat-hunting grounds and into Idaho, then east to West Yellowstone. That one section of scenery, amid the postcard-laced miles, still gnawed at me. Over the most haunting of mountain passes, through years of flat valleys edged by rough and sculpted peaks, the path switchbacked forever.

Troy had taken a shortcut, traveling down an abandoned dirt road that reportedly joined the two states. Rand McNally and Co. lay sprawled on the pickup seat between us.

I loved to scan the atlas, loved to plot trips across country I would never see; to dream of journeys and adventures. Troy, on the other hand, never dreamed, rather drove on, often down these desolate, rutted roads that he swore led to somewhere but never did.

Most of the day, I hadn't a clue in which state we cruised. I was certain, however, that the crossing wouldn't be marked, not on an abandoned path such as this. But the mountains looked the same.

Funny, who'd have thought Idaho and Montana could be so similar? But there we had been, unable to discern the difference.

I had to keep telling him to slow down.

"Don't worry, Julie," Troy had said. "I'm good at this dirt driving."

I just sighed, too weary to explain. Too tired of explaining. I got so tired it was easy for those mountains to break my heart, slice a fissure straight down the middle of the muscle, as the river bisected the peaks.

The whole trip was a whirlwind. I had only wanted a weekend in the mountains, to try and get back to where we started from. The past months had drained any "give" from my heart, and now, well, now I just wanted to get back to Troy. To remember why I had fallen in love with him.

It had started well enough. The long drive from Missoula led right through goat country, where Troy would camp this winter in drifts of snow and stalk the elusive Angora. Or whatever. The goat.

This area was more closed-in than most of Montana. One mountain crowded into another with slivers of streams between them. We had camped early and built a fire, intending to fish, but never snapping our rods together. We hunted dry twigs, then branches, then started the fire and uncorked the first bottle of Chardonnay. Drinking the oaky nectar from a plastic cup and tearing chunks of bread and bites of cheese, I watched the flames spit and smelled the piney mountains. They smelled cold. At home, there was nothing like this, this cold.

Troy had talked through the evening of his business problems. This was not my intent, not on this trip, but well, that was how it went.

"Maybe we should move to California," he had said.

The words shaved softly across my skin.

"I sell so much work there anyway," he continued, "and my cousins could help. It's best to have family run your business."

I hadn't cringed when he said that, not as I usually did. I had quit defending myself for not helping, but until that instant, still cringed. Smiling and nodding instead, I watched as the final flicker of sunlight topped pine-forest edges, far, far above.

"My Aunt Betty could manage the business side, and you'd have all the time you need to work on your own stuff."

"I have all the time I want, Troy. What you do with your business won't affect me."

He had frowned, dark bushy eyebrows knitting together over the pools of shiny brown. But that hadn't spoiled the evening; there was too much wine for rancor. We drank and became jovial and discussed his brother's problems, which always brought us together. Them against us. Still, that wasn't what I wanted, this stolen weekend.

A sharp cold settled in with the darkness, and we fixed a bed in the back of the truck, snuggling into it and making love and all should have been perfect except that I couldn't sleep, staring through jagged spruce tops for most of the night.

The next morning, we had started this drive between Montana and Idaho, where we would spend the night on the Henry's Fork River with Troy's aunt and uncle. Tomorrow we planned to travel through the park and back to Troy's ranch in the flats of Montana. The Beartooths bordered that ranch, sparkling crystals on clear days, smoky, ghostly vestiges on foggy ones.

So close, so close. The mountains had called to me daily, only an hour away, but they may as well have been to Texas. Somehow, Troy couldn't find the time to go, not in all these months that I had been here. You are a fool, I told myself two days before. A fool. I then planned this trip and Troy had come along at the last minute, not believing I would go without him. When he saw that I would, he gathered his stuff and joined in.

"Please slow down," I repeated as we bounced over that dirt road. "I don't care what time we get to Island Park. I just want to look."

My wish was granted as we rounded a corner and came upon a pair of red-tailed hawks. The pair scarcely moved, intent on their lunch of carrion, then skirted to the half-inch shoulder. Unafraid. Man was not a predator here, just a passerby.

These birds of prey mated for life. What if you woke up one day and didn't like your hawkmate? You couldn't just defy the laws of nature, not as man did. You would be stuck.

Troy stopped to snap pictures and I grabbed a beer, settling back into the truck seat, staring straight through the windshield at lonely, isolated expanses of wild. This country would beat you, if you let it. No foothold would be strong enough to withstand the ravages of winter.

But summer had just finished and the valleys rolled for days. Long, wide stretches of land linked the snowed-over peaks. This was where the gods lived when they journeyed to Earth. That the winters here could cause a human heart to freeze in midbeat, I found consoling, though could not think why.

Yesterday we had passed Sandhill Cranes—on which there was now a hunting season. Troy said that the silvery cranes had turned into pests for the farmers. That the farmers might be the pests would have been too tiring to explain, so I hadn't tried.

Today, filled with wise hawk eyes, the predator-prey line smudged. One hawk soared skyward, and I felt a white flash in the deep muscle as my heart began to break. That first cut came with the sense of whatever called folks westward. I, too, would have followed the soughing of wind and wings. I followed it now.

Then Troy jumped back in and started talking and I forgot my heart and that was why, I figured later, I had missed its escape down the dirt road.

Somewhere we had crossed the Divide, over the Bitterroot Mountains. The pass blurred, blue-green and rocky in my memory. Had it not been marked either?

That night, we arrived at Troy's aunt's on the Henry's Fork and visited until late. By first light, I was on the porch, staring into glaring sunshine reflected from the water's surface. The river ran smooth and swift and soundless.

This was a famous tributary. The trout fishing here was heralded and oft-storied. Was *A River Runs Through It* fished here? No, Troy's aunt had explained, though smiling, pleased that I knew the story.

Only diehard fly fishermen had read it, and this aunt was of that variety. Or lovers of literature, I had wanted to say, but kept my mouth shut. I had learned both arts this summer—fly fishing *and* shutting my mouth.

Troy had taught me to cast, and I loved the feel immediately. Though no good at the art, knowing I never would be, I nevertheless held to it, at least in my mind. I might never actually cast another line, but would always think about it, talk about it, marvel at skilled anglers. It made me feel closer to Norman Maclean and his story, and caused the river to run through my heart.

I had fallen in love with Troy as he fished. In the beginning, when there was only attraction, we had gone to the gurgling Yellowstone.

After instructing me, he had taken up his own fly rod and soon, I stopped to watch. There is nothing more wondrous than the casting of a man with magic to his fishing. There seemed no four-count rhythm from ten to two o'clock, only rhythm, a flowing of line and tip all in one long, smooth action that graced the air like it skimmed the stream's gliding surface. No beginning, no end. Troy's arm rippled beneath his T-shirt, extending through the fiberglass and line to the water, in a dance with his lover, the river. He was beautiful.

I warmed now, sitting on that deck. A great blue heron coasted over the swift but glassy surface.

An urgency stabbed at me, though. As beautiful as the Henry's Fork was, this section lived in the flatlands. I had eked out the weekend to be in the mountains. Into the mountains I was pulled and wished to return. Perhaps that would steady and soothe the dull ache in my breast. Was this ache for something lost, or something longed for?

But we got going and off went Troy, reciting family troubles and work problems and my ears shut as the mountains grew larger in the windshield.

We entered the park.

Stopping at the gate, Troy asked, "Should we buy fishing licenses?"

"No."

"Oh, we might want them." He handed a wad of bills to the guard.

The charred remains of last summer's fires greeted me. Sunshine glistened and sparkled over the wet blackness. It was not, though, devastation that grinned back, but rather, new life. The charcoal ground sprouted carpets of emerald grass and fuchsia fire flowers. Yellow and blue cups interspersed, bringing images of a grade-school color wheel.

Four elk trotted beside the road, enormous animals, so much larger than the wildlife I had seen. Troy explained the significance of the biggest bull, in trophy terms, but my ears were still shut. When one sense was cordoned off, the others seemed to follow. I watched instead the shining light of fear in the bull's eyes as it veered up the hill.

The forest opened into great meadows and the park indeed looked replenished from the flames that had consumed it. Maclean had said that, having once fought for the fire service. Nature intended regular burns. It was the people who worried, attached to human structures, and worked themselves into a frenzy about fire. The land and forests and wildlife needed the clearing out for new growth. Troy pulled to the shoulder and stopped.

"You think I should try to sell the elk and grizzly through the California gallery, or wait'll they do me an entire show?"

Troy never missed a lick.

"I haven't a clue—you know that. I don't know selling or sculpting or what you should do with any of it."

"I just want your input," he said, pouting. "I just want you involved in my life."

"I know."

I wanted to say there was more to life than selling art, more than art, more than selling, more than the combination. I wanted to say this but couldn't, his brown eyes staring so unhappily at me.

"You always act like this," he said, "like you're sick of what I do."

I looked away. "It's just that that's all we ever talk about."

"No, it's not."

Two of the elk stopped on the ridgetop. Statue-still, frozen sculptures, more anachronistic than any of Troy's bronzes, they monitored the valley. Oh, what they must be able to see!

"So what do you want to talk about?" he said finally.

"The mountains."

"The mountains," he stated.

Did those elk ever lose their bearings? Ever wonder how the hell they got here? The big bull still stood, quiescent, silhouetted against the bluest sky in the universe.

"Okay, let's talk about the mountains," Troy said. "They say there's monster moose up there. Butch told me ever' so often, somebody kills a trophy bull and sneaks it out. The hardest part of the hunt is avoiding the bleeding-heart rangers." He shook his dark head. "Bastards."

"Bastards," I echoed.

Troy smiled at me. A breeze tickled my skin, bringing a biting chill. Summer was certainly finished.

He drove again and rambled more of his business. Oh, if he would just shut up, maybe my heart could quit this longing! I was in the middle of the mountains. Why the ache?

The park passing by did not halt my mind's return to that dirt road, to the wildlife refuge, the cold isolation, the keening of wind through the valleys.

I forced my concentration onto the fire's destruction. Singed bands weaved through untouched parts, as if a volcanic river had snaked through, carving away a section here, forming a crevice there, leaving the rest, as if to break up rootbound areas and open them to light. Finally all signs of fire vanished, as if the burning had been absorbed by the land. As if, as Maclean had said, eventually, all things merged into one, and a river . . .

"Go back!"

"What?" Troy slammed on the brakes and looked wild-eyed at me.

"Go back, I lost something. Go back." I was crying, a river of tears streaming down my cheeks.

"Where? Go back where? What did you leave?"

I shook my head, hard, unable to see the surrounding mountains, imagining only the pass, only the road, lost in the dirt byways of memory and knowing I would never find it again. That road lived on the wrong side of the great divide.

The wilderness receded before me. Had it ever been? Were the wilds just something I dreamt of? No. No, I had witnessed a wild place; *had* seen it.

The rest of my heart broke off, as does a branch after fire has eaten the tree substance out. It fled to find its other heart half, back down the rutted road. I let it slide away, let it slip through opened though grasping fingers. Let it go.

Cold Turkey

■

CAROLE NELSON DOUGLAS

"Hey, Big Blind Bertha, betcha can't get me!"
The boy jammed his hand in her chest, pushed,
and ran.

Bertha hardly noticed the jibe. She was one of those people born under the unlucky star stuck on the wand of a bad fairy, and she had figured it out at an early age.

Maybe the dead paternal aunt had been a lovely person, which was why her parents had perpetuated her name in their only daughter, but the aunt would have needed to be a lovely person with a name like that even seventy years ago.

Surely thirty-eight years ago the name was clearly on the comical list, but her parents had been losers like herself and ever ready to make what was bad worse.

Bertha.

She had fulfilled the prophecy of herself and became a chubby, pale child with poor eyesight who had to get spectacles at an early age so she could see for herself how hopeless she was.

She stuttered in school because the other kids laughed when she was called on. On the playground, they called her Big Bertha.

Only the boys, though. The girls didn't call her anything and they didn't ask her to play jump rope because her name was so ugly no one wanted to sing it out in one of the venerable rhymes. Not like Lin-da and Kar-en and Bam-bi. Besides, Bertha knew that she was clumsy and that her clothes were as ugly and laughable as she was (and always would be) and that her fat (and especially the fat where the boy had jammed his hand) would jiggle if she jumped.

She worked on the power of positive thinking as she rode the bus home after school, alone in the pandemonium of others at play. She repeated endlessly and silently, *invisible/disappear*. But she never was and she never did. Not enough.

She wasn't brilliant, but stubborn. All through school, she took home solid B's. Her parents seemed oblivious to her social flaws, but then they were fat, simple people too stolid to know how unworthy they were. Her brother was no better than herself, only older and a boy, and therefore mean in his frustration.

If the city streets and schoolyards were purgatory, the family's annual summer weeks on her uncle's farm were hell. All her cousins were older and boys, or seemed so, because the girls avoided her. The girls wanted to walk into town to slow-sip chocolate malts at the drug store soda fountain and then stroll the dusty, shaded streets in their new outfits so the older boys could watch them, and sometimes even say something nasty but nice.

Bertha was never asked to go with them, but she desperately wanted to, not because she had delusions of strolling around like a southern belle. She just wanted to get away from the nasty boys on the farm, who liked to dismember insects because it made her face pucker up and hot tears run into the creases and turn them raw.

The boy cousins had endlessly inventive fun on the farm. Usually it involved tormenting something. She tried to forget most of it as she grew older and didn't have to go there anymore.

"But *why* don't you want to go?" her parents would harp at her when she was old enough to stay home in the city alone. "Such good country air and so much fun, and all your cousins are there. Silly girl."

Her brother was off in the military by then, the only way he'd get educated beyond high school.

Bertha had held firm about the farm. She couldn't tell her parents why, but surely they knew. She remembered, when she didn't want to, pranks involving the animals, especially chickens and firecrackers.

Her mind winced at the details. She could conjure only scenes of laughter and of frantic birds running and clucking and bursting apart in panic and pain.

That's how they saw her, she thought, a stupid, clucking, running thing worth only laughing at.

Over the years, she had smothered the things too terrible to remember with food and then fat and then more food. She wasn't quite morbidly obese, but fat enough to sometimes almost disappear inside it. And sometimes too fat to disappear. She had been granted a quiet tenacity that got her through leaving home to go on her own, but she lost an early job or two with a craven phone call not to come back because her coworkers complained that she smelled.

She was meticulous about grooming and cleanliness, and she didn't smell, but she looked like she could. And her hair was the curly kind that seemed to have been subjected to a bad permanent, and everything she chose, from eyeglass frames to clothes, was somehow instantly out of date once it became hers.

So she plodded and still said *invisible/disappear* to herself on the bus, and sometimes lately she had even caught her lips moving, but maybe they would think she was praying. She put herself through nursing school because she thought it would be rewarding to take care of sick people and they might actually say thank you sometimes.

She hadn't counted on the laboratory dissections. That was awful, the frogs screaming as the needle pithed their brains, frog after frog, and the live specimens that sometimes mercifully didn't survive to lay before her dissecting team on the table. At least with all the formaldehyde no one could say for sure that she smelled.

She hated scalpel work, but her dissection partners were so clumsy that she took over. At least this way the animals would not be butchered. She had always been neat with her hands. After a while, she learned what the lab sessions were designed to teach her, to disassociate from the gore and fluids and smells, to do what she had to do professionally, and without fuss. To be a nurse.

She got so good at disassociation that when the hospital put her in the emergency room, she handled it with her usual slightly flustered competence. Haste and blood and moans had become white noise to her by then. *Invisible/disappear*. And the patients moved on so fast—either quick or dead, and that was that.

Disassociation worked off the job, too. On the rare times that scattering feathers and hysterical clucks fluttered into her mind, they vanished faster now. Even the wincing glimpse of a shadowed barn and the boys' voices low and laughing and mean and herself screaming the silent scream . . . fun on the farm.

She never ate chicken, or any fowl, or meat. She never ate eggs or milk or cheese. She liked what they called that. She was a vegan, she would tell people, and they looked at her like she had come from Mars, or even Venus.

I am a vegan. *Invisible/disappear.* Some day she just might.

But for now she was just Bertha the nurse, and she worked the night shift because all the most undesirable tasks always came to her. She volunteered to work holidays; she thought they might like her, then, and, besides, she lived alone in a semirural place crowded with the vagrant animals she had taken in. No one ever thought to invite her to a family holiday dinner, though she was always free or she wouldn't have been able to work those days. No one ever thought about Bertha. *Invisible/disappear* had finally worked.

And it was just as well. She hated holiday dinners and the roasted birds brought in headless, eviscerated, their vital organs extracted and chopped up and reinserted, then gobbled down by all the laughing, talking mouths. Assholes. She rarely even thought bad words, but that was one expression too deserved to pass by.

Bertha was working night shift the day before Thanksgiving. Funny that only Christmas and New Year's and Halloween had an "Eve" the day before, she often thought. She often thought of odd, insignificant facts other people never noticed. Just as they never noticed her.

Thanksgiving was hardly a busy holiday: a few accidental choking victims maybe, or the bloody but minor cuts from a carving knife. No one ever really lost a finger. Then the usual appendicitis and asthma cases. And once in a blue moon, a very blue moon, one of the truly freaky cases that descends on every emergency room eventually, that gets talked about forever after, and laughed about at cocktail parties in hushed corners where nasty boys still gather, only they call themselves doctors now, and they always know best and there are still certain crude things they let women hear only tiny, titillating, terrifying parts of, as if they were still in some barn plotting deviltry.

Dr. Cavanaugh the intern heard it first, by radio from the ambulance crew, and came out grinning in his greens. He was tall and thin and wore little round glasses like he'd been to an eastern med school, when he was really from Indiana.

"Got a live one coming in. Grease the latex gloves."

Everyone knows from *ER* on TV that a hospital emergency room is always busy, except during the rare dead time, and this was one of those down times.

"You aren't gonna believe this," Dr. Cavanaugh added. "A little early Thanksgiving turkey for one and all."

By then the ambulance was cruising silently into the parking zone by the intake entrance and Dr. Cavanaugh was first to greet it.

They could hear the guy squawking all the way in, calling on Jesus Christ like it was already Christmas.

They wheeled him in, accompanied by a similarly scruffy pal, one step up from wino, the blanket over his torso heaving with a life of its own.

"Jesus Christ! You gotta help me. Get me outta this!" His shouts hit the high notes of hysteria like a trumpet solo.

Bertha watched him pass, a man in his late twenties with long, dirty-blond hair, his unshaven lower face masked in wheatfield stubble, and blood on his grimy hands. His friend was no more appetizing, but who was a fat nurse to judge?

"Bertha," Dr. Cavanaugh called. "We need some big-time heft to hold this guy down."

The blanket reared up over the injured man's crotch; people with an obscene cast of mind might try to imagine what was going on under it.

Bertha thought she heard hoarse cries and saw pale, soft feathers swirling like snow in the summertime, amid a shower of fine, bloody raindrops.

She rushed alongside the gurney into an examining room. When the door hushed shut she could hear the ambulance attendants already answering questions from the jabbering staff. Then they all were laughing so hard no one could speak.

And she was inside, doing important things. Trying to calm the impatient patient and assisting Dr. Cavanaugh.

"Jesus Christ."

This time Dr. Cavanaugh echoed the words as he lifted the blanket off the writhing man.

A bird appeared, like a pretty little dove from under a magician's handkerchief, except a blanket was much bigger and so was the bird.

It flapped its clumsy wings and gargled piteously in the sudden light, bound to the patient's lower torso with torn, dirty sheeting, its beaked face a nightmare framed by obscene flaps of lumpy crimson skin. Turkeys were unattractive birds, like vultures, and considered stupid. But you never know, Bertha thought, still too surprised to grasp the situation.

The blood flowed from the man's pantless thighs and stomach, where the turkey's formidable, flailing talons had dug in. Horrible, deep rakes seven inches long. Urine and bowel smells mingled under the warm examining lights, man and turkey's.

"What a mess." Dr. Cavanaugh sounded disgusted. "How'd you get yourself into this, man?"

Bertha frowned, finally beginning to grasp what had happened. Mercifully, she felt the room miniaturize and pull away, like the barn shadows had done so long ago.

The turkey's wings sawed in hopeless racial memory of flight.

"My buddy and me, we got a chance to get this live turkey for Thanksgiving cheap, a couple days ago. So, we thought, let's get some double duty from the bird, right? Hey, we were drinking Dos Equis all day and didn't have nothin' better to do.

"Now I'm fuckin' stuck and gettin' clawed to hell and I'm stuck. Nobody can get this damn bird off me. Do it, Doc."

Dr. Cavanaugh rubbed his chin with a gloved hand. "Never had a case like this. Nurse!"

Bertha rushed to his side, her soft-soled shoes quiet as falling feathers on the vinyl tile floor.

"This guy needs a little tranquilizer. Phenergan should do it, whichever way it's easier to administer. You got someone can drive you home? Been drinking in the past couple hours?"

The guy nodded and shook his greasy head in turn. Dr. Cavanaugh withdrew to the door, Bertha accompanying him, and lowered his voice.

"We need him tranqed when we unwrap that winding sheet and do in the bird. Have to break its neck, I suppose. Or cut its throat with a scalpel. You didn't happen to do that on a farm, did you? I'll ask the others. Wonder what this thing weighs. What do you think? You're a woman. You cook these things."

She didn't, but she prided herself on knowing any information needed. "Ah . . . twenty-five pounds, maybe. It's a big one, bigger than a chicken."

"Not quite big enough," Dr. Cavanaugh added under his breath, his mouth quirking into a sneer. "Jeez. Maybe that guy will learn to be more choosy about where he stuffs it."

They could overhear staff titters outside in the hall. A rare moment of humor and idleness. Then all talk stopped as they heard a sudden flutter.

"Stat!" a man's voice ordered. "Stats" started echoing off the hard hospital walls like machine-gun fire. Stat-a-stat-a-stat.

"Sounds like all hands are needed." Dr. Cavanaugh opened the door. "Get him started on the tranq."

As the door whooshed open and closed, Bertha heard the words "apartment" and "fire." Seconds later the wails of arriving ambulances began.

"God, that bastard can't leave!" the man on the Gurney shouted. "I've got a situation here. Get this damn bird off me."

"This medication help. It's actually for nausea, but has a calming side effect. Just a moment, sir."

She had to call him "sir."

"It better not be no needle! I don't need nothin'. The turkey's the problem. Whatcha gonna do about that, huh?"

"I believe the doctor intends to . . . kill it." Bertha hesitated over the supplies, then picked the Phenergan in suppository form. "Just relax."

"God! What're you doing down there? Hey!"

"Just a small suppository, sir. Like a toothpick compared to what's in the turkey. This won't get stuck. It'll melt away."

And still the bird flapped and emitted its pathetic squawks.

Bertha suddenly saw the bird plucked and headless, protruding from the man's groin, its own life blood minging the red runes its claws had drawn on his flesh.

She saw the bird as white, plump, stupid and defenseless, like the babies they brought in, sometimes blue already, the pale flesh marked with the signs of nasty things done in shadowy corners, of mutilated orifices. Dead sometimes. And more often, unfortunately living to remember.

Or to disassociate.

She had disassociated from the bizarre scene before her. She was a nurse. She would do her duty. But the victim always paid, always suffered more, was always punished somehow, just for being there.

"Get this thing off me!" the man was screaming, barely audible above the rhythmic rise and fall of the sirens' warning chorus.

These whould be burned people. Pained people. Helpless people. Victims of circumstance. Not victims of deliberate abuse. Why did the perpetrators prove so hard to convict, and to punish? Why did they go on and on, to victimize again?

"Get this fucking bird off me, you stupid bitch!" the man screamed.

She really was in no position to object to his language, so she did exactly what he said.

"It was really simple," Bertha told the rape counselor from down the hall an hour later, a middle-aged lady with a plain face who looked as if she knew about invisible/disappear.

They had given her hot coffee and saltine crackers, but Bertha was a nurse and knew she wasn't really in shock.

"These boys like to think they're so mean, that it's so hard, like a bone. But that's a delusion of the circulatory system. It's all just blood and bluster. That's all. Not hard to cut, and once the blood leaked out, it shriveled and came out of the turkey like nothing. Like a narrow little thermometer. Poor bird. Don't let them kill her, please. She shouldn't be abused like that and then just die. I've a place in the country, I could take her home and I would never, ever eat her. Boys can be so mean, you know?"

The rape counselor's face looked odd, like she was disassociating, too. *Invisible/disappear.*

"I did the only thing I could," Bertha said. "I saved the victim. And they saved the leftover. They can sew it on again. And next time, he might think twice. Wouldn't you have done the same thing? Is it right to kill the victim? I'm not sorry. Wouldn't you have done the same thing?"

The woman never answered her, but Bertha was used to that.

Winter's Tale

■

CONNIE WILLIS

"Is the will here?" he said. "I need . . ."

"Thou hast no need of wills," I said, putting my hand upon his poor hot brow. "You have but a fever, husband. You should not have stayed so late last eve with Master Drayton."

"A fever?" he said. "Aye, it must be so. It was raining when I rode home, and now my head is like to split in twain."

"I have sent to John for medicine. It will be here soon."

"John?" he said, alarmed, half rising in the bed. "I had forgot Old John. I must needs bequeath the old man something. When he came to London—"

"I spoke of John Hall, thy son-in-law," I said. "He will bring you somewhat for thy fever."

"I must leave Old John something in my will, that he'll keep silence."

"Old John will not betray you," I said. He hath been silent, lo, these twelve winters, buried in Trinity Church, no danger to anyone. "Hush, thee, and rest awhile."

"I would leave him something of gaud and glitter. The gilt-and-silver bowl I sent thee from London. Do you remember it?"

"Yea, I remember it," I said.

* * *

The bowl had come at midday as I was making the second-best bed. I had already made the best bed for the guests, if any came with him, airing the hangings and putting on a new featherbed, and was going into my room to see to the second-best bed when my daughter Judith called up the stairs that a rider had come. I thought that it was he and left the bed unturned and forgot. Ere I remembered it, it was late afternoon, all the preparations made and we in our new clothes.

"I should have stuffed a new featherbed," I said, laying the coverlid upon the press. "This one is flattened out and full of dust."

"You will spoil your new gown, Mother," Judith said, standing well away. "What matters if the bed be turned? He'll notice not the beds, so glad he'll be to see his family."

"Will he be glad?" Susanna said. "He waited long enough for this homecoming, if it be that. What does he want, I wonder." She took the sheets and folded them. Elizabeth climbed onto the bed to fetch a pillow and brought it me, though it was twice her size.

"To see his daughters, perhaps, or his grandaughter, and make his peace with all of us," Judith said. She took the pillow from Elizabeth gingerly and brushed her skirts when she had laid it down. "It will be dark soon."

"Tis light enough for us to make a bed," I said, reaching my hands to lift it up. "Come, help me turn the featherbed, daughters." Susanna took one side, Judith the other, all unwillingly.

"I'll turn it," Elizabeth said, squeezing herself next to the wall at the foot, all eagerness to help and like to have her little fingers crushed.

"Wilt thou go out and see if they are coming, granddaughter?" I said. Elizabeth clambered over the bed, kirtle and long hair flying.

"Put on thy cloak, Bess," Susanna cried after her.

"Aye, Mother."

"This room was ever dark," Judith said. "I know not why you took it for your own, Mother. The window is high and small, and the narrow door shuts out the light. Father may be ill pleased at such a narrow bed."

It were well if he were, I thought. It were well if he found it dark and cramped and would sleep elsewhere. "Now," I said, and we three heaved the featherbed up and over the foot of the bedstead. Dust and feathers flew about, filling the room.

"Oh, look at my doublet," Judith said, brushing at the ruffles on her bosom. "Now we shall have to sweep again. Can you not get the serving boy to do this?"

"He is laying the fires," I said, pulling at the underside.

"Well, the cook then."

"She is cooking. Come, one more turn and we'll be done with it."

"Dost thou hear something?" she said, shaking out her skirts. She went out. "Have they come, Bess?" she called.

I waited, listening for the sound of horses' hooves, but I heard naught.

Susanna stood still at the side of the bed, holding the linen sheet. "What think thee of this visitation, Mother? Thou hast said naught of it since word arrived of his coming."

What could I answer her? That I feared this day as I had feared no other? The day the message had come, I'd taken it from Susanna's hand and tried to draw its meaning out, though she had read it out already and I had never learnt to read. "To my wife," it had read. "I will arrive in Stratford on the twelfth day of December." I had kept the message by me from that day to this, trying to see the meaning of it, but I could not cipher its meaning. To my wife, I will arrive in Stratford on the twelfth day of December. To my wife.

"I have had much to do," I said. I gave the featherbed a mighty pull and brought it flat across the bed. "New rushes to be laid within the hall, the baking to be done, the beds to make."

"He came not to his parents' funeral, nor Hamnet's, nor to my wedding. Why comes he now?"

I smoothed the featherbed, pressing the corners so that they lay neat and smooth.

"If the house be too full of guests, you can come to us at the croft, Mother," Susanna said. She folded out the sheet and held it to me. "Or if he . . . you ever have a home with us."

" 'Twas but a passing townsman," Judith said, coming back into the room. "Think you he will bring friends with him from London?"

"His message said he would arrive today," Susanna said, and bellied out the sheet, sweet with lavender, over the bed. "Naught else. Nor who should accompany him or why he comes or whether he will stay."

"Come, he will stay," Judith said, coming to fold the sheet against the side. "I hope his friends are young and handsome."

There was a creak upon the stairs. We stopped, stooped over the bed.

"Bess?" Susanna inquired.

"Nay, my little grandniece stands outside all uncovered," Joan said, and came, creaking, into the room. She wore a yellow ruff so high it seem'd to throttle her. It was the ruff that creak'd, or mayhap her leather farthingale. "I told her she will catch the sweating fever. I bade her put her on a heavier cloak, but she heeded me not."

"Hath it begun to snow, sister-in-law?" I said.

"Nay, but it looks to ere long." She sat upon the bed. "Are you not dressed, and my brother nearly here?" She spread her overskirts on either side that we might see her satin petticoat. "You look a common country wife."

"I am a common country wife," I said. "Good sister, we must make the bed."

She stood up, the ruff creaking as if it were a signboard on a tavern. "A cold welcome for your husband," she said, "the beds unmade, the children unattended, and you in rough, low broadcloth." She sat down on the coverlid on the press. "A winter's welcome."

I stuffed the pillows into their cases with something force. "Where is your husband, madam?" I said, and putting the pillows to the bed, boxed them a blow or two to make them plump.

"Home with the ague," she said, turning to look at Susanna, her ruff making a fearsome sound. "And where is yours?"

"Attending to a patient in Shottery," Susanna said, still sweetly. "He will be here anon."

"Why wear you that unbecoming blue, Susanna?" Joan said. "And Judith, your collar is so small it scarcely shows."

"At least 'tis silent," Judith said.

"He will not know you, Judith, so sharp-tongued have you become. You were a sweet babe when he left. He'll know not you either, Good Sister Anne, so pale and old you look. He'll not look so, I wot. But then, he's not as old as you."

"No, nor so busy," I said. I took the quilt from off the bed rail and laid it on the bed.

"I remember me when he was gone to London, Anne. You said you would not e'er see him again. What say you now?"

"He is not here, and dusk is fast upon us," Susanna said. "I say he will not come."

"I wonder what my brother will think of the impertinent daughters he hath raised," Joan said.

"He raised us not," Susanna said hotly, and on the same breath Judith cried out, "At least we do not trick ourselves out like—"

"Let us not quarrel," I said, putting myself between them and their aunt. "We all are tired and vexed with worry that it is so late. Good Sister Joan, I had forgot to tell you. A gift hath come from him this very day. A gilt-and-silver bowl. 'Tis on the table in the hall."

"Gilt?" Joan said.

"Aye, and silver. A broad bowl for the punch. I will with thee to see it."

"Let us go down, then," she said, rising from the chest with a great sound, like a gallows in a wind. I picked the coverlid up.

"They've come!" Elizabeth shouted. She burst into the room, the hood of her cloak flung back from her hair and her cheeks as red as apples. "Four of them! On horses!"

Joan pressed her hands to her bosom momently, then adjusted her ruff. "What does he look like, Bess?" she asked the little girl. "Doth he be very changed?"

Elizabeth gave her an impatient glance. "I never saw him ere this. I know not even which one he is."

"Four of them?" Judith said. "Be the others young?"

"I told thee," Elizabeth said, stamping her little foot. "I know not which is which." She tugged at her mother's sleeve. "Come!"

Susanna plucked a feather from my cap. "Mother . . . ?" she said.

I stood, the coverlid still held against me like a shield. "The bed's not yet made," I said.

"Marry, I'll not leave my brother ungreeted," Joan said. She gathered her skirts. "I'll go down alone."

"No!" I said. I lay the coverlid over the end of the bedstead. "We must all go together," I seized Elizabeth's hand and let her run me down the stairs ahead of them, that Joan might not reach the door before me.

"Now I remember me," he said. "I left the bowl to Judith. What was bequeath'd to Joan?"

"Thy clothes," I said smilingly. "You said 'twould keep her silent as she walked."

"Ay, she is possessed of strange and several noises of roaring, shrieking, howling, jingling chains. . . ." He took my hand. His own was dry and rough as his night smock, and hot as fire. "Silent. She must keep silent. I should have left her something more."

"The will bequeaths her twenty pounds a year and the house on Henley Street. You have no need of purchasing her silence. She knows naught."

"Aye, but what if she, seeing my cold corpse, should on a sudden realize?"

"What talk is this of corpses?" I said, pulling my hand vexatiously away. I pulled the sheet to cover him. "You had too merry a meeting with thy friends, and now a little fever. You'll soon be well again."

"I was sick when I came," he said. "How long ago it seems. Three years. I was sick, but you made me well again. I am so cold. Is't winter?"

I wished for John to come. " 'Tis April. It is the fever makes thee cold."

" 'Twas winter when I came, do you remember? A cold day."

"Aye, a cold day."

He had sat still on his horse. The others had dismounted, the oldest and broadest of them doubled, his hands to his knees, as though to catch his breath, the younger ones rubbing their hands against the cold. A white dog ran about their legs, foolishly barking. The young men had sharp beards and sharper faces, though their clothes bespoke them gentlemen. The one who was the master of the dog, if he could be called so, had on a collar twice wider than Joan's, the other a brown cap with russet feathers stolen from a barnyard cock.

"I should not have plucked the feather from your cap, Mother," Susanna whispered. "It is the fashion."

"Oh, look," Joan said, squeezing through the door. "He hath not changed a bit!"

"Which one is my grandfather?" Elizabeth said, her little hand clasped to mine.

They turned to look at us, the feathered one with a face canny as a fox's, the collared one with a gawking gaze. The bent man stood with a groan that made the dog run at him. His doublet was quilted and puffed as to make him look twice as broad as his own girth. "Come, come, Will," he said, turning to look at him still on his horse, "we've come to the wrong house. These ladies are too young and fair to be thy family."

Joan laughed, a screeching sound like the cackle of a hen.

"Is he the one on the horse?" Elizabeth said, squeezing my numbed hand and jumping up and down.

"You did not tell me that he was so well-favored, Mother," Judith said in my ear.

He handed down a metal chest behind him. The round man gave it to the feathered one and put a hand up to help him dismount. He came down off the horse oddly, grasping the quilted shoulder with one hand, the horse's neck with the other, and heaving himself over and down on his left leg. He stepped forward, stiff-gaited, watching us.

"See how he limps!" Joan cried.

I could not feel the wind, e'en though it bellied his short cloak and Elizabeth's hair. "Which one is my grandfather?" she said, fairly dancing in her impatience.

I would have made her answer, but I could not speak nor move. I only stood, quiet as a statue, and looked at him. He looked older even than I, the hair half gone on the crown of his head. I had not thought him to look so old. His face was seamed with lines that gave it a sadness of demeanor, as if he had endured many November's blasts. A winter's face, sad and tired but not unkind, and that I had not thought it to be either.

The round-bellied gentleman turned to us and smiled. "Come, ladies, well met," he said with a merry, booming voice that conquered the wind. "I was long upon the road from London and thought not to find such fair ladies at the end of it. My name is Michael Drayton. And these two gentlemen are Gadshill"—he pointed at the one with the ruff, then at the fox—"and Bardolph. Two actors they, and I a poet and lover of fair ladies." His voice and manner were merry, but he looked troubledly from Joan to me and back again. "Come, tell me your names and which of you his wife and which his daughters, that I speak not amiss."

"Come, Mother, speak and bid them welcome," Judith whispered, and nudged at my elbow, but still I could not speak nor move nor breathe.

He moved not either, though Master Drayton looked at him. I could not read his face. Was he dismayed, or vexed, or only weary?

"If you'll not greet him, I shall," Joan whispered, bending her head to me with a snapping sound. She stretched her arms toward them. "Welcome—"

I stepped down off the porch. "Husband, I bid thee welcome," I said, and kissed him on his lined cheek. "I could not speak at first, my husband, so struck was I to see thee after such an absence." I took his arm and turned to Master Drayton. "I bid thee welcome, too, and thee, and thee," I said, nodding to the young men. The ruffed one wore now a silly grin, though the one with the feathers looked foxy still. " 'Tis a poor country welcome we have to give, but we've warm fires and hot supper and soft beds."

"Aye, and pretty maids," Drayton said. He took my hand and kissed it in the French fashion. "I think that I will stay the winter long."

I smiled at him. "Come then, we'll out of the cold," I said.

"How looks he, Mother?" Susanna whispered to me as I passed. "Find you him very changed?"

"Aye, very changed," I said.

"I have bequeathed naught to Drayton," he said. "I should have done."

"There is no need," I said, laying a cool cloth on his brow. "He is thy friend."

"I would have left him some token of my friendship. And thee some token of my love. You know why I could not bequeath the property to you." He took hold of my hand with his own burning one. "If it were found out after my death, I would not have men say I bought your silence."

"I have my widow's portion, and Susanna and John will care for me," I said, loosing his hand to dip the cloth in the bowl again and wring it. "She is a good daughter."

"Aye, a good daughter, though she loved me not at first. Nor did thee."

"That is not true," I said.

"Come, Mistress Anne, when did you love me?" he said. I laid the cloth across his brow. He closed his eyes and sighed, and seemed to sleep.

"The very instant that I saw you," I said.

We made a slow progress into the house, he leaning on me as we stepp'd over the threshold and into the hall. "My leg grows stiff when I have ridden awhile," he said. "I need but to stand by the fire a little."

Joan crowded close behind, her farthingale filling the door so that the others could not follow till she was through. Master Drayton followed upon her skirts, telling Judith and Susanna in a loud and merry voice of what had passed upon the road from London. "As we came across the bridge, four rogues in buckram thrust at me." Drayton gestured bravely. Elizabeth stared at him, her eyes round.

The young men, Fox and Frill, entered the hall, bearing bags and the metal chest. They stopped inside the door to hear the tale that Drayton told. Frill dropped his sacks with a thump upon the floor. The Fox set the casket beside it.

"These four began to give me ground, but I followed me close."

"Husband," I said under cover of his windy voice, "thou must needs compliment thy sister Joan Hart on her new ruff. She is most proud of it." He gazed at me, and still I could not decipher his look. "Thy daughters, too, have new finery for this occasion. Susanna hath a blue—"

"Surely a man knows his own daughters," Joan said ere I could finish speaking, "though he hath not had a chance to greet them. Thy wife would keep thee all to herself."

"Good Sister Joan," he said. He bowed to her. "I would have greeted thee outside, but I knew thee not."

Joan said. "Thou did'st not know me?" Her voice was sharp, and I looked anxiously at her, but could see naught in her face but peevishness. The Fox turned to look, too.

"I knew you not for that you seem'd so young."

"Liar," the Fox said, turning back round to Drayton. "Those four were not knaves at all, but beggars. They asked for alms."

"Ah, but it makes a good tale," Drayton said.

"I knew you not. The years have been far kinder to you than to me, Sister," he said.

" 'Tis not true," Joan said, tossing her head. Her ruff groaned. "You look the same as on that day you left for London. Thy wife said on that day she'd not see her husband again. What say you now, Anne?" She smiled with spite at me.

"Thy gown is a most rare fashion, Sister," he said.

"Is't?" she said, spreading her skirts with her hands. "I thought it meet to dress in the fashion for your homecoming, brother." She gazed at my plain gown. "Though thy wife did not. Girls!" she called in a shrill voice that overmastered Drayton's. "Come meet thy father."

I had not had the opportunity to speak and say, "Susanna's gown hath a blue stomacher." They came forward, Bess holding to Judith's hand, and I saw with dismay that Judith's frontlet skirt was blue also.

"Husband," I said, but he had stepped forward already, limping a little. Joan folded her hands across her doublet, waiting to see what he would say.

Judith stepped forward, holding Elizabeth's hand. "I am thy daughter Judith, and this Susanna's little daughter Bess."

"And this must be Susanna," he said. She nodded sharply. He stooped to take Bess's hand. "Is thy true name Elizabeth?"

Bess looked up him. "Who are you?"

"Thy grandsire," Judith said, laughing. "Did you not know it yet?"

"She could not know her grandfather," Susanna said. "She was not born and I a child her age when you left us. Why have you come after all these years away, Father?"

"Susanna!" Joan said.

"I knew not how you looked, if you were fair," he answered quietly, "if you were well and happy. I came to see if there was aught that I could do for you."

"There's somewhat you can do for me, Will," Drayton said, clapping a hand to his shoulder. "Give me a cup of sack, man. I am half-froze and weary and was set upon by thieves. And hungry, too."

"I'll fetch it," Judith said, smiling at the Frill. " 'Tis in the kitchen, already warmed and mixed with sugar."

"I'll help thee," the Frill said.

The Fox said, "Madam, where shall I put these bags and boxes?"

"In the bedchambers," I said. "Husband, where would you have your chest?"

"Leave it," he said. "I'll bear it there myself."

Judith brought in the sack in a ewer with a cloth round it and poured it, steaming, into the bowl.

"I smell sweet savors," Drayton said, holding his cup out to her. "What's in it?"

"Cinnamon," Judith said, smiling the while at the Frill. "And sugar. And divers spices. Father, wilt thou drink a cup?"

He smiled sweetly at her. "I would put this in a safe place first." He raised the chest and turned to me. "Good wife, where would you have me sleep?"

"What's in the chest?" Elizabeth said.

"Infinite riches," Drayton said, and drained his cup.

I led the way up the stairs to my bedchamber, he following behind, dragging his leg a little under the weight of the chest.

"Where would you have me put it, Wife?" he asked when we came into the room. "In the corner?" He set the chest down and leant against the wall, his hand upon his leg. "I am too old for such burdens."

I stood against the door. He stood and looked at me, the lines in his unfamiliar face cut deep and sad.

"Where is my husband?" I said.

"Where is the will?" he said.

I had thought he slept and had stepped quietly to the door to see if John were come. "You must stop this talk of wills and assay to sleep," I said, folding the sheets under the featherbed that he might not cast them off. The featherbed made a rustling sound.

He started up, then lay back down again. "I thought I had heard Joan."

"Fear not," I said. "She'll not come. She is in mourning."

He looked as though he knew not what I spoke of. I said, "Her husband died these ten days since."

"Of the ague? Or overmuch noise?" he said, and smiled at me, and then his face grew sad, the lines deep-carved upon it. "She knew me not."

"Nay, and 'twere well she did not."

"Aye, well," he said. "When they first came to me, I thought not it would succeed. A one would say, I know him by his voice, or by his wit, or by his gait. But none said it. All believed, till at last so did I, and came to think I had a wife and daughters."

"And so thou hast," I said.

"Where is my husband?" I had asked, and he had not answered me at first, but let out his breath sighingly, as if he were relieved.

"I knew not that I had a wife and children till his father came to London to tell me that the boy had died," he said.

"What have you done with my husband?"

He sat down heavily upon the bed. "I cannot long stand on my bad leg," he said. "I killed him."

"When?"

"Near twenty years ago."

These twenty years since, he had lain in his grave. "How came you to kill him? Was it in a fight?"

"Nay, madam." He rubbed his leg. "He was murdered."

He answered me as plainly as I asked, more plainly, for my voice was so light and airy, I thought not it would carry the width of the room.

"How came he to be murdered?" I said.

"He had the misfortune to somewhat resemble me in countenance," he said.

I sat down on the coverlid-drap'd press. Dead. I had never thought him dead.

"I fell into some trouble with the queen," he said at last. "I had ... done her a service now and then. It made me overbold. Thinking myself safe from the fire, I spoke in jest of things that had got other men burnt, and was arrested. I fled to friends, asking their help to transport me to France. They told me to lie secretly in London at a certain house until they had arranged passage for me, but when they came, they said that it was all accomplished. The man was dead, and I was free to take his name for mine own."

His hand clutched the bedpost. "They had killed your husband, madam, at a little inn in Deptford and said I was the murdered man, not he. They testified that I had fought them over the reckoning of the bill, and they, in self-defense, had stabbed me. They told me this with pride, as of a job well done."

He stood, clasping the bedpost as it were a walking stick. "The queen's anger would have passed. The murder never. Your husband has had his revenge on me, madam. He took my life as sure as I took his."

I heard a sound from out the room. I waited, listening. I went, treading softly, into the gallery, but there was no one on the stairs, only the sound of laughter from below, and Drayton's voice. I came back in the room.

"How came my husband to that inn?" I asked.

"They lured him thence with promise of a part to play. He being an actor, they had seen him on the stage and marked his likeness to me. They passed a whole day with him ere they killed him, drawing him out with wine and questions, what were his habits, who his friends, that I might better play the masquerade. He did not tell them that he had a wife and children." He paced the narrow space between the bed and my skirts, and turned and paced again. "They even coaxed him to sign his name to a paper that I might copy it."

"And your deception succeeded?"

"Yes. The lodgings where I had stayed that fortnight since were his. I had already fool'd the owner of the house and all the neighbors without intention." There was another gust of laughter from below.

"What happened to your friends?"

"My friends," he said bitterly. "They were acquitted. Walsingham found me not overgrateful for his help and Poley's and has not seen me since. Skeres is in prison. Of Frizer, I know not. I heard that he was dead, but one cannot believe all that one hears."

"And none knew you?"

"No." He sat him down again. "I have been he this twenty years, and been not found out. Until now." He smiled a little. "What would you have me do, madam, now you have caught me out? Leave you in peace as I found you? I could away tomorrow, called to London, and not return. Or publicly confess my crime. What would you? I will do what you command."

"What's all this?" Drayton's voice bellowed from the stairs. "How now? The coverlet already off the bed? The host and his wife off to slumber so soon?" He lumbered into the room. "The dinner's not yet served, though you two feast your eyes upon each other." He laughed, and his very stomach shook with it, but when he turned his eyes to me, there was no laughter in them. "Good madam, I know we have dallied long upon the road, but tell me not 'tis time for bed so soon, supper missed, and all the trenchers cleared away. Tell me not that, or you shall break my heart."

He had stood up when Drayton came in, taking the weight of his body on his bad leg as if it were some lesson in pain, but he looked not at Drayton.

"For God's sake, come, man!" Drayton said, plucking at his arm. "I grow thinner by the minute!"

"Master Drayton, you are a most importunate guest," he said, looking at me.

"Whatever it is you speak of, sure it bears waiting till after supper."

"Yes," I said, "it hath already waited a long time."

"I am so cold," he said. I knelt beside the chest and took a quilt from out it. He raised himself to watch me. "What keep you in that chest now?"

I lay the quilt over him. "Sheets and pillowcoats and candles."

" 'Tis better so," he said. "Hast thou burned them all?"

"Aye, husband."

"I copied out his name so oft it was almost my own, but they are in my hand. If any come for them, you must say you burned them with the bedding when I died."

"I hear a sound upon the stairs," I said. I hastened to the door. "I am glad you've come, son-in-law," I said softly. "His fever is worse."

John set a lidded cup upon the press and put his hand upon my husband's brow. "Thou has a fever."

"I feel no fever," he said. He spoke through chattering teeth. "I am as two people lying side by side in the bed, both like to freeze. A little sack would warm me."

"I have somewhat for you better than sack." He slid his hand behind my husband's head to raise him to sitting. I put the pillows behind. "Drink you this."

"What is it?"

"A decoction of herbs. Flavored with cloves and syrup of violets. Come, father-in-law," John said kindly. " 'Twill help your fever."

He drank a swallow. "Vile potion!" he said. "Why did you not pour it in my ear and be done with it?" His hands shivered so that the liquid splashed onto the bedclothes, but he drank it down and gave the cup to John.

"Would you lie down again, husband?" I said, my hand to the pillows.

"Nay, leave them," he said. " 'Tis easier to breathe."

"Is there naught else I can do to help him?" I said, drawing John aside.

"See he hath warm coverings and clean bedding."

" 'Tis freshly changed, and the featherbed on the bed new. I made it with my own hands."

"The second-best bed," my husband said, and turned, and slept.

We went downstairs, Drayton between us like a father who has caught his children kissing in a corner, prattling of beds and supper so that we could not speak. "Come, man," Drayton said, "you've not had any sack from your own bowl."

The board was already laid. Judith was spreading the cloth, Joan bringing in the salts, little Elizabeth laying the spoons. Joan said, "You once again would steal my brother from me, Anne. You never were so affectionate in the old days."

I know not what I answered her, nor what I did, whether I served the fowl first or the sugar-meats, nor what I ate. All I could think of was that my husband was dead. I had not guessed that, through all the years when no word came and Old John cursed me for a shrew that had driven him away. I had not guessed it e'en when Old John nailed the coat of arms above the door of our new house.

I had thought mayhap my husband had suffered us to be stolen by a thief, as a careless man will let his pocket be picked, or that he'd lost us gaming, staking us all as he had staked my mother's plate, and the winner would come to claim us, house and all. But he had not. He had been murdered and laid in someone else's grave.

He sat at the head of the table, Drayton beside him. Drayton would not allow Elizabeth to be sent from table after she said her grace, but bade her sit on his broad knee. He talked and talked, following one story with another.

Joan sulked and preened by turns. Judith sat between Fox and Frill, feeding first one, then the other, her smiles and glances. "Remember you your father?" the Fox asked. "Had he a limp then?"

She answered him, all innocence, the way her father must have answered his assassins. He would have seen only what his desire showed him, 'twas ever his failing. And his father's, who could not see a stranger's face, so blinded was he by the colors of his coat of arms. His sister's failing, too, who could not e'en see over a starch'd ruff. All blind, and he the worst. He would not even have seen the knife blade coming.

When the meal was already done and the dishes carried away, Susanna's husband John came in, covered with snow, and was sat, and dishes warmed, and questions asked. "This is my grandsire," Elizabeth said.

"Well met, at last," John said, but I saw, watching from the kitchen, that he frowned. "I have been overlong at the birth of a cobbler's son, and overlong coming home."

Drayton called for a toast to the new babe, and then another. "We must toast Elizabeth's birth, for we were not present at her christening," he said. "Ah, and gave her not a christening gift." He bade Elizabeth look in his ear.

She stood on tiptoe, her eyes round. "There's naught in there but dirt," she said.

Drayton laughed merrily. "Thou has not looked well," he said, and pulled a satin ribbon from out his ear.

" 'Tis a trick," Elizabeth said solemnly, "is it not, grandsire?"

"Aye, a trick," he said. She climbed into his lap.

"He is not as I remembered him," Susanna said, watching him tie the ribbon in Bess's hair.

"Thou wert but four years old and Judith a babe when he left. Dost thou remember him?" I said.

"Only a little. I feared he would be like Aunt Joan, dressed in the fashion, playing the part of master of the house though he did not merit it."

"It is his house," I said, and thought of the name on the deed, the name that they had cajoled my husband into signing that he might copy it. "And all in it purchased with his money."

"Marry, it is his house, though he never saw it till now," she said. "I feared he would claim the house for his own, and us with it."

He fastened the ribbon clumsily, tying it round a lock of Bess's hair. "But he plays not that part," I said.

"No. Knowest thou what he said to me, Mother, when I brought him his sack? He said, 'Thy father was a fool to ever leave thee.' "

John Hall came and stood beside us, watching the tying of the ribbon. "Look how her ribbon comes loose," Susanna said. "I'll go and tie it."

She went to Bess and would have tied the ribbon, but she tossed her head naughtily.

"My grandsire will do't," she said, and backed against his knees.

"My hands are too clumsy for this business, daughter," he said. The lines had softened already in his face. He looked to her, and she, leaning o'er him, told him to loop the ribbon so and then to pull it through. Judith came and stood beside, smiling and advising.

"Notice you aught amiss about your husband?" John said.

"Amiss?" I said. I could not catch my breath. I had forgot that he had been to Cambridge, and to London, a learned man.

"I fear that he is ill," John said.

Bess ran to us. "Father!" she cried. "Look you at my new ribbon," and ran back again. "Grandsire, is't not pretty?" She fairly leaped into his arms and kissed him on the cheek.

"Sweet Bess, 'twas not my gift, but Drayton's."

"But you tied it."

"Is he very ill?" I said.

John looked kindly at me. "This country air will make him well again, and your kind ministrations. Shall we into the hall?"

"Nay," I said. "I must go up to make the bed."

I went out through the kitchen. The Fox and Frill stood by the stairs, whispering together. "You are mad," the Frill said. "Look how his family greets him, his daughters gathering round him. It was an idle rumor, and no more."

I hid inside the kitchen door that I might hear their conversation.

"His daughters were but babes when they last saw him," the Fox said.

"The sister says he has changed not at all."

"The sister is a fool. His wife greeted him not so eagerly. Saw you how she stood as a statue when first we came? 'Tis she should be the subject of our watch."

I came into the hall. They bowed to me. The Fox would have spoken, but Drayton came and said, "Good mistress, I had missed you in the hall."

"I'll follow you in a little. I would make up the second-best bed."

"No, I'll accompany thee," he said. "And you two see to the horses. They've not been fed."

The Fox and Frill put on their cloaks and went out into the snow. Drayton climbed the stairs after me, puffing and talking the while. I went into my room and lit the candles.

He looked about him. "A great reckoning in a little room," he said in a gentler voice than before. "I advised against his coming. I said it was not safe while any still lived who knew him, but he would see the daughters. Does the sister know?"

"Nay," I said. I laid the coverlid upon the bed and looked to put it so that it hung straight. I set the bolsters at the head of the bed. "Who is he?"

He sat upon the press, his hands on his stout knees. "There was a time I could have answered you," he said. "I knew him long ago."

"Before the murder?"

"Before the murders."

"They killed others?" I said. "Besides my husband?"

"Only one other," he said. His voice downstairs had been loud and bold, an actor's voice, but now it was so low I could scarce hear him, as though he spoke to himself. "You asked me who he is. I know not, though he was but a young man when first I knew him, a roguish young man, full of ambition and touched by genius, but reckless, over-proud, taking thought only for himself." He stopped and sat, rubbing his hands along his thighs. "Walsingham's henchmen killed more men than they knew that wicked day at Deptford. I saw him on the street afterward and knew him not, he was so changed. I would show you something," he said, and raised himself awkwardly. He went to the chest in the corner, opened it, and proferred me the papers that lay therein. "Read them," he said.

I gave them back to him. "I cannot read."

"Then all is lost," he said. "I thought to bargain with you for his life with these his plays."

"To buy me."

"I think you cannot be bought, but, aye, I would buy you any way I could to keep him safe. He hath been ill these two winters past. He has need of your refuge. The London air is bad for him, and there are rumors, from whence I know not."

"The young men you brought here have heard them."

"Aye, and wait their chance. I know that naught can replace your husband."

"No," I said, thinking of how he had stolen my honor and my mother's plate and run away to London.

"You cannot bring your husband back from the dead, if you tell all the world. You will but cause another murder. I'll not say one man's life is worth more than another's." He brandished the papers. "No, by God, I will say it! Your husband could not have written words like these. This man is worth a hundred men, and I'll not see him hanged."

He lay the papers back into the chest and closed the lid. "Let us go back to London, and keep silence."

Elizabeth ran into the room. "Come, granddame, come. We are to have a play."

"A play?" Drayton said. He lifted Elizabeth up into his arms. "Madam, he has no life save what you grant him," he said, and carried her down the stairs.

"The decoction will make him sleep," John Hall said.

He slept already, his face less lined in rest. "And quench the fever?"

He shook his head. "I know not if it will. I fear it is his heart that brings it on."

He put the cup into the pouch he carried. "I give you this," he said. He proffered me a sheaf of papers, closely writ.

"What is't?"

"My journal. Thy husband's illness is there, my treatments of it, and all my thoughts. I'd have thee burn it."

"Why?"

"We have been friends these three years. We'd drink a cup of ale, and sit, and talk. One day he chanced to speak of a play he'd writ, a sad play of a man who'd bartered his soul to the devil. He spoke of it as if he had forgot that I was with him: how it was writ and when, where acted. He marked not that I looked at him with wonder, and after a little, we went on to other things."

He closed the pouch. "The play he spoke of was Kit Marlowe's, who was killed in a brawl at Deptford these long years since." He took the papers back from me and thrust them in the candle's flame.

"Hast thou told Susanna?"

"I would not twice deprive her of a father." The pages flamed. He thrust them in the grate and watched them burn.

"His worry is all Susanna's inheritance," I said, "and Judith's. He bade me burn his plays."

"And Marlowe's?" he said, dividing the charring pages with his foot that they might the better burn. "Hast thou done it?"

A little piece of blackened paper flew up, the writing all burnt away. "Yes," I said.

"Judith said we are to have a play," Elizabeth said as we descended the stairs. She freed herself from Drayton's arms and ran into the hall.

"Judith?" I said, and looked to where she stood. The Fox was at her side, his feathered cap wet with snow. He leaned against the wall, seeming not even to listen. The Frill squatted by the hearth, stretching his hands to the fire.

"Oh, grandsire, prithee do!" Elizabeth said, half climbing into his lap. "I never saw a play."

"Yes, brother, a play," Joan said.

Drayton stepped between them. "We are too few for a company, Mistress Bess," he said, pulling at Elizabeth's ribbon to make her laugh, "and the hour too late."

"Only a little one, grandsire?" she begged.

"It is too late," he said, looking at me. "But you shall have your play."

The Fox stepped forward, too quick, taking the Frill by the sleeve and pulling him to his feet. "What shall we, Master Will?" he said, smiling with his sharp teeth. "A play within a play?"

"Aye," Drayton said loudly. "Let us do Bottom's troupe at Pyramus and Thisbe."

The Fox smiled wider. "Or the mousetrap?" All of them looked at him, Judith smiling, the Fox waiting to snap, Master Drayton with a face taken suddenly sober. But he looked not at them, nor at Bess, who had climbed into his lap. He looked at me.

"A sad tale's best for winter," he said. He turned to the Frill. "Do ye the letter scene from *Measure*. Begin ye, 'Let this Barnardine.' "

The Frill struck a pose, his hand raised in the air as if to strike. " 'Let this Barnardine be this morning executed and his head borne to Angelo,' " he said in a loud voice.

He stopped, his finger pointing toward the Fox, who did not answer.

Drayton said, " 'Tis an old play. They know it not. Come, let's have Bottom. I'll act the ass."

"If they know not the play, then I'll explain it," the Fox said. "The play is called *Measure for Measure*. It is the story of a young man who is in difficulty with the law and would be hanged, but another is killed in his place." He pointed at the Frill. "Play out the play."

" 'Let this Barnardine be this morning executed and his head borne to Angelo,' " the Frill said.

The Fox looked at Drayton. " 'Angelo hath seen them both, and will discover the favor.' "

The Frill smiled, and it was a smile less slack-jawed and more cruel than I had seen, a wolfen smile. " 'Oh, Death's a great disguiser,' " he said.

"An end to this!" I said.

Both of them looked at me, Fox and Frill, disturbed from their prey.

"The child is half-asleep," I said.

"I am not!" Bess said, rubbing at her eyes, which made the party laugh.

I stood her down from off his lap. "Thou mayest have plays tomorrow, and tomorrow, and the next day. Thy grandfather is home to stay."

Susanna hurried forward. "Good night, Father. I am well content that you are home." She fastened Bess's cloak about her neck.

"Will you a play for me tomorrow, grandsire?" Bess said.

He stroked her hair. "Aye, tomorrow."

Bess flung her arms about his neck. "Good night, grandsire."

John Hall picked up the child in his arms. She lay her head upon his shoulder. "I will take the actors with us," John said softly to me. "I trust them not in the house with Judith."

He turned to the Fox and Frill and said in a loud voice, "Gentlemen, you're to bed with us tonight. Will you come now? Aunt Joan, we will walk you home."

"Nay," Joan said haughtily, stretching her neck to look more proud. Her ruff moaned and creaked. "I would stay awhile, and them with me."

John opened the door, and they went out into the snow, Elizabeth already asleep.

"Marry, now they are gone, we'll have our play, brother."

"Nay," I said, kneeling to put my hands in his. "I am a wife long parted from her husband. I would to bed with him ere sunrise."

"You loved not your husband so well in the old days," Joan said, her hands upon her hips. "Brother, you will not let her rule you?"

"I shall do whatever she wills."

"I know a scene will do us perfectly," Drayton said. He spread his arms. " 'Our revels now are ended.' " He donned his wide cloak. "Come, Mistress Joan, I will accompany thee to thy home and these two to Hall's croft and thence to a tavern for a drop or two of sack ere I return."

Judith walked with them to the far end of the hall and opened the door. I knelt still with his hands in mine. "Why did you this?" he asked. "Hath Drayton purchased you with pity?"

"Nay," I said softly. "You cannot leave. Your daughters would be sad to have you go, and you have promised Elizabeth a play. You asked if there was aught that you could do for them. Be thou their father."

"I will and you will answer me one question. Tell me when you discovered me."

"I knew you ere you came."

His hands clasped mine.

"When Hamnet died, and Old John went to London to tell my husband," I said, "he came home with a coat of arms he said his son had got for him, but I believed him not. His son, my husband, would ne'er have raised his hand to help his father or to give his daughters a house to dwell in. I knew it was not he who did us such kindness, but another."

"All these long years I thought that none knew me, that all believed me dead. And so it was as I were dead, and buried in Deptford, and he the one who lived. But you knew me."

"Yes."

"And hated me not, though I had killed your husband."

"I knew not he was dead. I thought he'd lost us dicing, or sold us to a kinder master."

"Sold?" he said. "What manner of man would sell such treasure?"

" 'The iron tongue of midnight hath told twelve. Good night, good rest!' " Drayton called from the door. " 'Sweet suitors, to bed.' "

I rose from where I knelt, holding still to his hands. "Come, husband," I said. "The bed at last is made, in time for bed."

"The bed," he said, so weak I scarce could hear him.

"What is't, husband?"

"I have left you a remembrance in the will." He smiled at me. "I will not tell you of it now. 'Twill please thee to hear it when the will is read."

He had forgot that I sat by him when he made his will.

"John's foul decoction hath made me better," he said. "I am as one again, not split in two."

I laid my hand upon his brow. It was more hot than ever. I went to fetch another quilt from out the chest.

"Nay, come and sit with me and hold my hands," he said. "I have paid the sexton a French crown to write a curse upon my grave, that none will dig me up and say, 'That is not he.' "

"Prithee, speak not of dying," I said.

"I wrote not mine own will, but signed it only. They had him write out his name ere they killed him, that I might copy it."

"I know, husband. Soft, do not fret thyself with—"

"It matters not whose name is on the plays, so that my daughters' inheritance is safe. Hast thou burnst them all?"

"Yes," I said, but I have not. I have sewn them in the new featherbed. I will ensure it is not burnt with the bedding when he dies, and so will keep them safe, save the house itself burns down. I will do naught to endanger their inheritance nor the love they bear their father, but in after years the papers can be found and his true name set on them. The clew lies in the will.

"Wife, come sit by me and hold my hands," he says, though I hold them already. "I have left thee something in the will, a token of that night when first I came. I have bequeathed to thee the second-best bed."

A Woman Is Not a Potted Plant

■

ALICE WALKER

her roots bound
to the confines
of her house

a woman is not
a potted plant
her leaves trimmed
to the contours
of her sex

a woman is not
a potted plant
her branches
espaliered
against the fences
of her race
her country
her mother
her man
her trained blossom
turning

this way
& that
to follow
the sun
of whoever feeds
and waters
her

a woman
is wilderness
unbounded
holding the future
between each breath
walking the earth
only because
she is free
and not creepervine
or tree.

Nor even honeysuckle
or bee.

Is Anybody Listening?

■

DAWN RAFFEL

*S*he was under it all: knees raised and knobbed, the sheets a tent—stakeless, laundered—a house she had not built. "Not," she said, "mine"—this voice of hers a hum, little more, a seepage of breath; it sounded to her as if located nowhere, spleenless. Here is where it was: beneath a hand. There was hair on her face. A fan up somewhere shaved the air, its blades old wood. All curve, she was. She always had been—fetal, tight, and later rather ladylike and somewhat amiss. "Straighten yourself," her mother had said. "Chin up!" Words, ink. Things had been balanced on top of her head. *Britannica.* Step by step, A to Z, a headache of knowledge, of what she did not know. What a nomad she was, well thumbed—this house not hers, this fan refreshing nothing, useless, circling itself. She heard a flap of a sheet. A voice she heard, not hers, said, "You," said, "You?" She rolled, stilled, cheek against fabric. "Yes," she said in answer, and, answering again, said, "Do I what?"

Her hair was wet. She sat half-sunk and puckering. She heard the knock. A piece of soap, papery, a peeling, a little bit of nothing, really, floated. There was something quite abrasive in her hand. She was loosening skin. Sloughing was what it was properly called. Gray in the tub, this stuff of her, rubbed off. Her legs were pink. Or nearly. Or rather what they were was not so white. She lowered herself. The door—"Open up!"—was being worked. "Today," he said. "Open, I said." How not to hear it? She opened her mouth. Let in the slurry. Down on the bottom, she felt the ring of dirt.

"A silver, please," she said—made up and pinned, the hair in a particular elaborate twist—"less, please, half of that," she said. Her fork was to the crystal. A toast was under way—lucky twosome!—the chandelier aglow. It was all of it heirloom, all hand-cut. "Only a drop," she said, "for me."

Applause in the ballroom.

The bride, aswoon, was drunk.

She was not the bride.

"Must you?" he said.

She was pinching the flowers. She had been trained. Discretion was the better part. She'd learned their names, promptly forgotten. Arms crossed over a flattened chest: "It's close in here," she said. "Is it not? Do you think?"

The fountain in the cake had gone askew.

What were they, in fact? Severely exotic genus of flora? Purpled herbs? Bent grass?

She was at a doorway, a threshold—intemperate, the pain—hung over, and under a throw.

"Why can't you just stay put?" he said. "No faith," he said.

"Dear God," she said. A click of the jaw; she ground her teeth, averted—her glance, a long-lost blow. This last trait was handed down, it seemed to her. From where? It was not nice to look. Locked out one night, she had bloodied a window, scarring a girlish fist. "Under my roof . . . ," her father had said. The key ring, glasses: chronic, this misplacing jag. She did not look. A Gypsy might have read her distant past, all skin and fold. Her fortune: travel; tall, dark gent.

"Tell me am I right?" he said.

"You're right," she said. "I think." Although what was the question? Faithless in what? She was smoothing a wrinkle. Easy this, synthetic that, perfect for washing; cooling herself with a wooden sun. Still, it was humid, wasn't it?

He was chin into hands.

There was some kind of rule, some test. Was it fibers per inch? These were quality issues.

She had a woman's sense of things.

Lovely, she'd said, regarding whatever. Rounds of bread, the roe atop; pumps to the floor squares, crossing her legs. A napkin with which she had tidied herself. The kiss was in her palm. Blotted. There were no two prints alike. She had been born this way, like this, for this, pledging allegiance, singing, or rather mouthing, like a scout: Heigh-ho, nobody home, meat nor milk nor money have I none, still I will be . . . what? Buffed to a finish, holding her body like a glass of sand; she would not eat that cake—"Very lovely," she'd said, a shade below whispering, running out again. So here had come attendants, here came the inadmissible aunt, convex and verbal, inviting a not-nice look. The voice no flute—the voice is like an instrument for cutting, apportioning a serving to itself. Oh, aunt! Oh, florid relation!

She, herself, not loose with words, had trusted in posture, relying on the value of a face. Intuiter: She'd kept the house. She'd minded his appearances. Sidelong, she saw him, rubbing himself.

"Headache?" she said. "Eyeache? Toothache? Ingrown nail?"

They'd been hospital corners, primly tucked.

"Some wedding," he said.

"Help me," she said. Let it be said that she was a woman who used herself, what gifts she had received—nose to the cream pot, pinky in the air, as if seeking or maybe calling for judgment, hand to the disinfected phone.

He had given her perfume, bath salts, mints.

When he was gone she would stand on chairs—mother of necessity. The ladderbacks as if in a salute to grand ancestral dead, not hers, and no, not his, retrieved from some false past. The rugs were Oriental.

"Help me, please," she said again, inventing, as ever, a need.

She stood at the sink.

She splashed herself.

When he was gone, she would cripple a bureau. Wall-to-wall, knots per blinding, knotty foot; inscrutable frictions, always, it seemed. She was always dragging something: Her life in her head, her finger in a drawer, a little toe on the varnish—impossible to get to where she would.

She was that short.

"I believe it starts with *s*," she said, still in the bathroom. "Statice or something. A lavender bud."

He sat on the tub lip.

"Iris?" he said.

"Not iris," she said.

He had often told her this: How often had he told her this: How was he to know? The things she asked! Was it cream? Taupe? Puce? Was it poly-whatever?

What was it that she smelled?

Whatever had she said?

What was she thinking?

"Reach me a towel, please," she said.

Was he to read her mind? Receded, as if in an emotional crease. Days, years. The hair in the face, no pride. Or was it shameless?

He gave her what she asked for.

She patted herself. She was still in the bed, why not? It was the place she had begun—a rosy, absorbent, a purely subcutaneous creature. Flesh, bone, labor—she had made this tent. Encamped herself, again, again, tent after tent, as if devoted to the enterprise: ghost town.

It was the body reformed.

He was questioning her.

There was all of her knowing at the tip of her tongue. Her breath, let out, dispersed.

She had listened to the whirring.

She was her witness.

It was she who, after all, had answered yes.

Incident On and Off a Mountain Road

■

JOE R. LANSDALE

Whether Ellen came to the moonlit mountain curve, her thoughts, which had been adrift with her problems, grounded, and she was suddenly aware that she was driving much too fast. The sign said CURVE: 30 MPH, and she was doing fifty.

She knew too that slamming on the brakes was the wrong move, so she optioned to keep her speed and fight the curve and make it, and she thought she could.

The moonlight was strong, so visibility was high, and she knew her Chevy was in good shape, easy to handle, and she was a good driver.

But as she negotiated the curve a blue Buick seemed to grow out of the ground in front of her. It was parked on the shoulder of the road, at the peak of the curve, its nose sticking out a foot too far, its rear end against the moon-wet, silver railing that separated the curve from a mountainous plunge.

Had she been going an appropriate speed, missing the Buick wouldn't have been a problem, but at her speed she was swinging too far right, directly in line with it, and was forced, after all, to use her brakes. When she did, the back wheels slid and the brakes groaned and the front of the Chevy hit the Buick and there was a sound like an explosion and then for a dizzy instant she felt as if she were in the tumblers of a dryer.

Through the windshield came: Moonlight. Blackness. Moonlight.

One high bounce and a tight roll and the Chevy came to rest upright with the engine dead, the right side flush against the railing. Another inch of jump or greater impact against the rail, and the Chevy would have gone over.

Ellen felt a sharp pain in her leg and reached down to discover that during the tumble she had banged it against something, probably the gearshift, and had ripped her stocking and her flesh. Blood was trickling into her shoe. Probing her leg cautiously with the tips of her fingers, she determined the wound wasn't bad and that all other body parts were operative.

She unfastened her seat belt, and as a matter of habit, located her purse and slipped its strap over her shoulder. She got out of the Chevy feeling wobbly, eased around front of it and saw the hood and bumper and roof were crumpled. A wisp of radiator steam hissed from beneath the wadded hood, rose into the moonlight, and dissolved.

She turned her attentions to the Buick. Its tail end was now turned to her, and as she edged alongside it, she saw the front left side had been badly damaged. Fearful of what she might see, she glanced inside.

The moonlight shone through the rear windshield bright as a spotlight and revealed no one, but the backseat was slick with something dark and wet and there was plenty of it. A foul scent seeped out of a partially rolled-down back window. It was a hot, coppery smell that gnawed at her nostrils and ached her stomach.

God, someone had been hurt. Maybe thrown free of the car, or perhaps they had gotten out and crawled off. But when? She and the Chevy had been airborne for only a moment, and she had gotten out of the vehicle instants after it ceased to roll. Surely she would have seen someone get out of the Buick, and if they had been thrown free by the collision, wouldn't at least one of the Buick's doors be open? If it had whipped back and closed, it seemed unlikely that it would be locked, and all the doors of the Buick were locked, and all the glass was intact, and only on her side was it rolled down, and only a crack. Enough for the smell of the blood to escape, not enough for a person to slip through unless they were thin and flexible as a feather.

On the other side of the Buick, on the ground, between the back door and the railing, there were drag marks and a thick swath of blood, and another swath on the top of the railing; it glowed there in the moonlight as if it were molasses laced with radioactivity.

Ellen moved cautiously to the railing and peered over.

No one lay mangled and bleeding and oozing their guts. The ground was not as precarious there as she expected it. It was pebbly and sloped out gradually and there was a trail going down it. The trail twisted slightly and as it deepened the foliage grew denser on either side of it. Finally it curlicued its way into the dark thicket of a forest below, and from the forest, hot on the wind, came the strong turpentine tang of pines and something less fresh and not as easily identifiable.

Now she saw someone moving down there, floating up from the forest like an apparition; a white face split by silver—braces perhaps. She could tell from the way this someone moved that it was a man. She watched as he climbed the trail and came within examination range. He seemed to be surveying her as carefully as she was surveying him.

Could this be the driver of the Buick?

As he came nearer Ellen discovered she could not identify the expression he wore. It was neither joy nor anger nor fear nor exhaustion nor pain. It was somehow all and none of these.

When he was ten feet away, still looking up, that same odd expression on his face, she could hear him breathing. He was breathing with exertion, but not to the extent she thought him tired or injured. It was the sound of someone who had been about busy work.

She yelled down, "Are you injured?"

He turned his head quizzically, like a dog trying to make sense of a command, and it occurred to Ellen that he might be knocked about in the head enough to be disoriented.

"I'm the one who ran into your car," she said. "Are you all right?"

His expression changed then, and it was most certainly identifiable this time. He was surprised and angry. He came up the trail quickly, took hold of the top railing, his fingers going into the blood there, and vaulted over and onto the gravel.

Ellen stepped back out of his way and watched him from a distance.

The guy made her nervous. Even close up, he looked like some kind of spook.

He eyed her briefly, glanced at the Chevy, turned to look at the Buick.

"It was my fault," Ellen said.

He didn't reply, but returned his attention to her and continued to cock his head in that curious dog sort of way.

Ellen noticed that one of his shirt sleeves was stained with blood, and that there was blood on the knees of his pants, but he didn't act as if he were hurt in any way. He reached into his pants pocket and pulled out something and made a move with his wrist. Out flicked a lock-blade knife. The thin edge of it sucked up the moonlight and spat it out in a silver spray that fanned wide when he held it before him and jiggled it like a man working a stubborn key into a lock. He advanced toward her, and as he came, his lips split and pulled back at the corners, exposing, not braces, but metal-capped teeth that matched the sparkle of his blade.

It occurred to her that she could bolt for the Chevy, but in the same mental flash of lightning, it occurred to her she wouldn't make it.

Ellen threw herself over the railing, and as she leaped, she saw out of the corner of her eye, the knife slashing the place she had occupied, catching moonbeams and throwing them away. Then the blade was out of her view and she hit on her stomach and skidded onto the narrow trail, slid downward, feet first. The gravel and roots tore at the front of her dress and ripped through her nylons and gouged her flesh. She cried out in pain and her sliding gained speed. Lifting her chin, she saw that the man was climbing over the railing and coming after her at a stumbling run, the knife held before him like a wand.

Her sliding stopped, and she pushed off with her hands to make it start again, not knowing if this was the thing to do or not, since the trail inclined sharply on her right side, and should she skid only slightly in that direction, she could hurtle off into blackness. But somehow she kept slithering along the trail and even spun around a corner and stopped with her head facing downward, her purse practically in her teeth.

She got up then, without looking back, and began to run into the woods, the purse beating at her side. She moved as far away from the trail as she could, fighting limbs that conspired to hit her across the face or hold her, vines and bushes that tried to tie her feet or trip her.

Behind her, she could hear the man coming after her, breathing heavily now, not really winded, but hurrying. For the first time in months, she was grateful for Bruce and his survivalist insanity. His passion to be in shape and for her to be in shape with him was paying off. All that jogging had given her the lungs of an ox and strengthened her legs and ankles. A line from one of Bruce's survivalist books came to her: *Do the unexpected.*

She found a trail among the pines, and followed it, then abruptly broke from it and went back into the thicket. It was harder going, but she assumed her pursuer would expect her to follow a trail.

The pines became so thick she got down on her hands and knees and began to crawl. It was easier to get through that way. After a moment, she stopped scuttling and eased her back against one of the pines and sat and listened. She felt reasonably well hidden, as the boughs of the pines grew low and drooped to the ground. She took several deep breaths, holding each for a long moment. Gradually, she began breathing normally. Above her, from the direction of the trail, she could hear the man running, coming nearer. She held her breath.

The running paused a couple of times, and she could imagine the man, his strange, pale face turning from side to side, as he tried to determine what had happened to her. The sound of running started again and the man moved on down the trail.

Ellen considered easing out and starting back up the trail, making her way to her car and driving off. Damaged as it was, she felt it would still run, but she was reluctant to leave her hiding place and step into the moonlight. Still, it seemed a better plan than waiting. If she didn't do something, the man could always go back topside himself and wait for her. The woods, covering acres and acres of land below and beyond, would take her days to get through, and without food and water and knowledge of the geography, she might never make it, could end up going in circles for days.

Bruce and his survivalist credos came back to her. She remembered something he had said to one of his self-defense classes, a bunch of rednecks hoping and praying for a commie takeover so they could show their stuff. He had told them: "Utilize what's at hand. Size up what you have with you and how it can be put to use."

All right, she thought. All right, Brucey, you sonofabitch. I'll see what's at hand.

One thing she knew she had for sure was a little flashlight. It wasn't much, but it would serve for her to check out the contents of her purse. She located it easily, and without withdrawing it from her purse, turned it on and held the open purse close to her face to see what was inside. Before she actually found it, she thought of her nail file kit. Besides the little bottle of nail polish remover, there was an emery board and two metal files. The files were the ticket. They might serve as weapons; they weren't much, but they were something.

She also carried a very small pair of nail scissors, independent of the kit, the points of the scissors being less than a quarter inch. That wouldn't be worth much, but she took note of it and mentally catalogued it.

She found the nail kit, turned off the flash and removed one of the files, and returned the rest of the kit to her purse. She held the file tightly, made a little jabbing motion with it. It seemed so light and thin and insignificant.

She had been absently carrying her purse on one shoulder, and now to make sure she didn't lose it, she placed the strap over her neck and slid her arm through.

Clenching the nail file, she moved on hands and knees beneath the pine boughs and poked her head out into the clearing of the trail. She glanced down it first, and there, not ten yards from her, looking up the trail, holding his knife by his side, was the man. The moonlight lay cold on his face and the shadows of the wind-blown boughs fell across him and wavered. It seemed as if she were leaning over a pool and staring down into the water and seeing him at the bottom of it, or perhaps his reflection on the face of the pool.

She realized instantly that he had gone down the trail a ways, became suspicious of her ability to disappear so quickly, and had turned to judge where she might have gone. And, as if in answer to the question, she had poked her head into view.

They remained frozen for a moment, then the man took a step up the trail, and just as he began to run, Ellen went backward into the pines on her hands and knees.

She had gone less than ten feet when she ran up against a thick limb that lay close to the ground and was preventing her passage. She got down on her belly and squirmed beneath it, and as she was pulling her head under, she saw Moon Face crawling into the thicket, making good time; time made better, when he lunged suddenly and covered half the space between them, the knife missing her by fractions.

Ellen jerked back and felt her feet falling away from her. She let go of the file and grabbed out for the limb and it bent way back and down with her weight. It lowered her enough for her feet to touch ground. Relieved, she realized she had fallen into a wash made by erosion, not off the edge of the mountain.

Above her, gathered in shadows and stray strands of moonlight that showed through the pine boughs, was the man. His metal-tipped teeth caught a moonbeam and twinkled. He placed a hand on the limb she held, as if to lower himself, and she let go of it.

The limb whispered away from her and hit him full in the face and knocked him back.

Ellen didn't bother to scrutinize the damage. Turning, she saw that the wash ended in a slope and that the slope was thick with trees growing out like great, feathered spears thrown into the side of the mountain.

She started down, letting the slant carry her, grasping limbs and tree trunks to slow her descent and keep her balance. She could hear the man climbing down and pursuing her, but she didn't bother to turn and look. Below she could see the incline was becoming steeper, and if she continued, it would be almost straight up and down with nothing but the trees for support, and to move from one to the other, she would have to drop, chimpanzeelike, from limb to limb. Not a pleasant thought.

Her only consolation was that the trees to her right, veering back up the mountain, were thick as cancer cells. She took off in that direction, going wide, and began plodding upwards again, trying to regain the concealment of the forest.

She chanced a look behind her before entering the pines, and saw that the man, whom she had come to think of as Moon Face, was some distance away.

Weaving through a mass of trees, she integrated herself into the forest, and as she went the limbs began to grow closer to the ground and the trees became so thick they twisted together like pipe cleaners. She got down on her hands and knees and crawled between limbs and around tree trunks and tried to lose herself among them.

To follow her, Moon Face had to do the same thing, and at first she heard him behind her, but after a while, there were only the sounds she was making.

She paused and listened.

Nothing.

Glancing the way she had come, she saw the intertwining limbs she had crawled under mixed with penetrating moonbeams, heard the short bursts of her breath and the beating of her heart, but detected no evidence of Moon Face. She decided the head start she had, all the weaving she had done, the cover of the pines, had confused him, at least temporarily.

It occurred to her that if she had stopped to listen, he might have done the same, and she wondered if he could hear the pounding of her heart. She took a deep breath and held it and let it out slowly through her nose, did it again. She was breathing more normally now, and her heart, though still hammering furiously, felt as if it were back inside her chest where it belonged.

Easing her back against a tree trunk, she sat and listened, watching for that strange face, fearing it might abruptly burst through the limbs and brush, grinning its horrible teeth, or worse, that he might come up behind her, reach around the tree trunk with his knife, and finish her in a bloody instant.

She checked and saw that she still had her purse. She opened it and got hold of the file kit by feel and removed the last file, determined to make better use of it than the first. She had no qualms about using it, knew she would, but what good would it do? The man was obviously stronger than she, and crazy as the pattern in a scratch quilt.

Once again, she thought of Bruce. What would he have done in this situation? He would certainly have been the man for the job. He would have relished it. Would probably have challenged old Moon Face to a one-on-one at the edge of the mountain, and even with a nail file, would have been confident that he could take him.

Ellen thought about how much she hated Bruce, and even now, shed of him, that hatred burned bright. How had she gotten mixed up with that dumb, macho bastard in the first place? He had seemed enticing at first. So powerful. Confident. Capable. The survivalist stuff had always seemed a little nutty, but at first no more nutty than an obsession with golf or a strong belief in astrology. Perhaps had she known how serious he was about it, she wouldn't have been attracted to him in the first place.

No. It wouldn't have mattered. She had been captivated by him, by his looks and build and power. She had nothing but her own libido and stupidity to blame. And worse yet, when things turned sour, she had stayed and let them sour even more. There had been good moments, but they were quickly eclipsed by Bruce's determination to be ready for the Big Day, as he referred to it. He knew it was coming, if he was somewhat vague on who was bringing it. But someone would start a war of some sort, a nuclear war, a war in the streets, and only the rugged individualist, well-armed and well-trained and strong of body and will, would survive beyond the initial attack. Those survivors would then carry out guerrilla warfare, hit-and-run operations, and eventually win back the country from . . . whomever. And if not win it back, at least have some kind of life free of dictatorship.

It was silly. It was every little boy's fantasy. Living by your wits with gun and knife. And owning a woman. She had been the woman. At first Bruce had been kind enough, treated her with respect. He was obviously on the male chauvinist side, but originally it had seemed harmless enough, kind of Old World charming. But when he moved them to the mountains, that charm had turned to domination, and the small crack in his mental state widened until it was a deep, dark gulf.

She was there to keep house and to warm his bed, and any opinions she had contrary to his own were stupid. He read survivalist books constantly and quoted passages to her and suggested she look the books over, be ready to stand tall against the oncoming aggressors.

By the time he had gone completely over the edge, living like a mountain man, ordering her about, his eyes roving from side to side, suspicious of her every move, expecting to hear on his shortwave at any moment World War III had started, or that race riots were overrunning the United States, or that a shiny probe packed with extraterrestrial invaders brandishing ray guns had landed on the White House lawn, she was trapped in his cabin in the mountains with him holding the keys to her Chevy and his jeep.

For a time she feared he would become paranoid enough to imagine she was one of the "bad guys" and put a .357 round through her chest. But now she was free of him, escaped from all that . . . only to be threatened by another man—a moon-faced, silver-toothed monster with a knife.

She returned once again to the question, what would Bruce do, outside of challenging Moon Face in hand-to-hand combat? Sneaking past him would be the best bet, making it back to the Chevy. To do that Bruce would have used guerrilla techniques. "Take advantage of what's at hand," he always said.

Well, she had looked to see what was at hand, and that turned out to be a couple of fingernail files, one of them lost up the mountain.

Then maybe she wasn't thinking about this in the right way. She might not be able to out fight Moon Face, but perhaps she could outthink him. She had outthought Bruce, and he had considered himself a master of strategy and preparation.

She tried to put herself in Moon Face's head. What was he thinking? For the moment he saw her as his prey, a frightened animal on the run. He might be more cautious because of that trick with the limb, but he'd most likely chalk that one up to accident—which it was for the most part. . . . But what if the prey turned on him?

There was a sudden cracking sound, and Ellen crawled a few feet in the direction of the noise, gently moved aside a limb. Some distance away, discerned faintly through a tangle of limbs, she saw light and detected movement, and knew it was Moon Face. The cracking sound must have been him stepping on a limb.

He was standing with his head bent, looking at the ground, flashing a little pocket flashlight, obviously examining the drag path she had made with her hands and knees when she entered into the pine thicket.

She watched as his shape and the light bobbed and twisted through the limbs and tree trunks, coming nearer. She wanted to run, but didn't know where to.

"All right," she thought. "All right. Take it easy. Think."

She made a quick decision. Removed the scissors from her purse, took off her shoes and slipped off her panty hose, and put her shoes on again.

She quickly snipped three long strips of nylon from her damaged panty hose and knotted them together, using the sailor knots Bruce had taught her. She cut more thin strips from the hose—all the while listening for Moon Face's approach—and used all but one of them to fasten her fingernail file, point out, securely to the tapered end of one of the small, flexible pine limbs, then she tied one end of the long nylon strip she had made around the limb just below the file, and crawled backward, pulling the limb with her, bending it deep. When she had it back as far as she could manage, she took a death grip on the nylon strip, and using it to keep the limb's position taut, crawled around the trunk of a small pine, curved the nylon strip about it, and made a loop knot at the base of a sapling that crossed her knee-drag trail. She used her last strip of nylon to fasten to the loop of the knot, and carefully stretched the remaining length across the trail and tied it to another sapling. If it worked correctly, when he came crawling through the thicket, following her, his hands or knees would hit the strip, pull the loop free, and the limb would fly forward, the file stabbing him, in an eye if she were lucky.

Pausing to look through the boughs again, she saw that Moon Face was on his hands and knees, moving through the thick foliage toward her. Only moments were left.

She shoved pine needles over the strip and moved away on her belly, sliding under the cocked sapling, no longer concerned that she might make noise, in fact hoping noise would bring Moon Face quickly.

Following the upward slope of the hill, she crawled until the trees became thin again and she could stand. She cut two long strips of nylon from her hose with the scissors, and stretched them between two trees about ankle high.

That one would make him mad if it caught him, but the next one would be the corker.

She went up the path, used the rest of the nylon to tie between two sapling, then grabbed hold of a thin, short limb and yanked at it until it cracked, worked it free so there was a point made from the break. She snapped that over her knee to form a point at the opposite end. She made a quick mental measurement, jammed one end of the stick into the soft ground, leaving a point facing up.

At that moment came evidence her first snare worked—a loud swishing sound as the limb popped forward and cry of pain. This was followed by a howl as Moon Face crawled out of the thicket and onto the trail. He stood slowly, one hand to his face. He glared up at her, removed his hand. The file had struck him in the cheek; it was covered with blood. Moon Face pointed his blood-covered hand at her and let out an accusing shriek so horrible she retreated rapidly up the trail. Behind her, she could hear Moon Face running.

The trail curved upward and turned abruptly. She followed the curve a ways, looked back as Moon Face tripped over her first strip and hit the ground, came up madder, charged even more violently up the path. But the second strip got him and he fell forward, throwing his hands out. The spike in the trail hit him low in the throat.

She stood transfixed at the top of the trail as he did a push-up and came to one knee and put a hand to his throat. Even from a distance, and with only the moonlight to show it to her, she could see that the wound was dreadful.

Good.

Moon Face looked up, stabbed her with a look, started to rise. Ellen turned and ran. As she made the turns in the trail the going improved and she theorized that she was rushing up the trail she had originally come down.

This hopeful notion was dispelled when the pines thinned and the trail dropped, then leveled off, then tapered into nothing. Before she could slow up, she discovered she was on a sort of peninsula that jutted out from the mountain and resembled an irregularly shaped diving board from which you could leap off into night-black eternity.

In place of the pines on the sides of the trail were numerous scarecrows on poles, and out on the very tip of the peninsula, somewhat dispelling the diving-board image, was a shack made of sticks and mud and brambles.

After pausing to suck in some deep breaths, Ellen discovered on closer examination that it wasn't scarecrows bordering her path after all. It was people.

Dead people. She could smell them.

There were at least a dozen on either side, placed upright on poles, their feet touching the ground, their knees slightly bent. They were all fully clothed, and in various states of deterioration. Holes had been poked through the backs of their heads to correspond with the hollow sockets of their eyes, and the moonlight came through the holes and shined through the sockets, and Ellen noted with a warm sort of horror that one wore a white sundress and pink, plastic shoes, and through its head she could see stars. On the corpse's finger was a wedding ring, and the finger had grown thin and withered and the ring was trapped there by knuckle bone alone.

The man next to her was fresher. He too was eyeless and holes had been drilled through the back of his skull, but he still wore glasses and was fleshly. There was a pen and pencil set in his coat pocket. He wore only one shoe.

There was a skeleton in overalls, a wilting cigar stuck between his teeth. A fresh UPS man with his cap at a jaunty angle, the moon through his head, and a clipboard tied to his hand with string. His legs had been positioned in such a way it seemed as if he were walking. A housewife with a crumpled, nearly disintegrated grocery bag under her arm, the contents having long fallen through the worn, wet bottom to heap at her feet in a mass of colorless boxes and broken glass. A withered corpse in a ballerina's tutu and slippers, rotting grapefruits tied to her chest with cord to simulate breasts, her legs arranged in such a way she seemed in mid-dance, up on her toes, about to leap or whirl.

The real horror was the children. One pathetic little boy's corpse, still full of flesh and with only his drilled eyes to show death, had been arranged in such a way that a teddy bear drooped from the crook of his elbow. A toy metal tractor and a plastic truck were at his feet.

There was a little girl wearing a red, rubber clown nose and a propeller beenie. A green plastic purse hung from her shoulder by a strap and a doll's legs had been taped to her palm with black electrician's tape. The doll hung upside down, holes drilled through its plastic head so that it matched its owner.

Things began to click. Ellen understood what Moon Face had been doing down here in the first place. He hadn't been in the Buick when she struck it. He was disposing of a body. He was a murderer who brought his victims here and set them up on either side of the pathway, parodying the way they were in life, cutting out their eyes and punching through the backs of their heads to let the world in.

Ellen realized numbly that time was slipping away, and Moon Face was coming, and she had to find the trail up to her car. But when she turned to run, she froze.

Thirty feet away, where the trail met the last of the pines, squatting dead center in it, arms on his knees, one hand loosely holding the knife, was Moon Face. He looked calm, almost happy, in spite of the fact a large swath of dried blood was on his cheek and the wound in his throat was making a faint whistling sound as air escaped it.

He appeared to be gloating, savoring the moment when he would set his knife to work on her eyes, the gray matter behind them, the bone of her skull.

A vision of her corpse propped up next to the child with the teddy bear, or perhaps the skeletal ballerina, came to mind; she could see herself hanging there, the light of the moon falling through her empty head, melting into the path.

Then she felt anger. It boiled inside her. She determined she was not going to allow Moon Face his prize easily. He'd earn it.

Another line from Bruce's books came to her.

Consider your alternatives.

She did, in a flash. And they were grim. She could try charging past Moon Face, or pretend to, then dart into the pines. But it seemed unlikely she could make the trees before he overtook her. She could try going over the side of the trail and climbing down, but it was much too steep there, and she'd fall immediately. She could make for the shack and try and find something she could fight with. The last idea struck her as the correct one, the one Bruce would have pursued. What was his quote? "If you can't effect an escape, fall back and fight with what's available to you."

She hurried to the hut, glancing behind her from time to time to check on Moon Face. He hadn't moved. He was observing her calmly, as if he had all the time in the world.

When she was about to go through the doorless entryway, she looked back at him one last time. He was in the same spot, watching, the knife held limply against his leg. She knew he thought he had her right where he wanted her, and that's exactly what she wanted him to think. A surprise attack was the only chance she had. She just hoped she could find something to surprise him with.

She hastened inside and let out an involuntary rasp of breath.

The place stank, and for good reason. In the center of the little hut was a folding card table and some chairs, and seated in one of the chairs was a woman, the flesh rotting and dripping off her skull like candle wax, her eyes empty and holes in the back of her head. Her arm was resting on the table and her hand was clamped around an open bottle of whiskey. Beside her, also without eyes, suspended in a standing position by wires connected to the roof, was a man. He was a fresh kill. Big, dressed in khaki pants and shirt and work shoes. In one hand a doubled belt was taped, and wires were attached in such a way that his arm was drawn back as if ready to strike. Wires were secured to his lips and pulled tight behind his head so that he was smiling in a ghoulish way. Foil gum wrappers were fixed to his teeth, and the moonlight gleaming through the opening at the top of the hut fell on them and made them resemble Moon Face's metal-tipped choppers.

Ellen felt queasy, but fought the sensation down. She had more to worry about than corpses. She had to prevent herself from becoming one.

She gave the place a quick pan. To her left was a rust-framed rollaway bed with a thin, dirty mattress, and against the far wall was a baby crib, and next to that a camper stove with a small frying pan on it.

She glanced quickly out the door of the hut and saw that Moon Face had moved onto the stretch of trail bordered by the bodies. He was walking very slowly, looking up now and then as if to appreciate the stars.

Her heart pumped another beat.

She moved about the hut, looking for a weapon.

The frying pan.

She grabbed it, and as she did, she saw what was in the crib. What belonged there. A baby. But dead. A few months old. Its skin thin as plastic and stretched tight over pathetic little rib bones. Eyes gone, holes through its head. Burned match stubs between blackened toes. It wore a diaper and the stink of feces wafted from it and into her nostrils. A rattle lay at the foot of the crib.

A horrible realization rushed through her. The baby had been alive when taken by this madman, and it had died here, starved and tortured. She gripped the frying pan with such intensity her hand cramped.

Her foot touched something.

She looked down. Large bones were heaped there—discarded Mommies and Daddies, for it now occurred to her that was who the corpses represented.

Something gleamed among the bones. A gold cigarette lighter.

Through the doorway of the hut she saw Moon Face was halfway down the trail. He had paused to nonchalantly adjust the UPS man's clipboard. The geek had made his own community here, his own family, people he could deal with—dead people—and it was obvious he intended for her to be part of his creation.

Ellen considered attacking straight-on with the frying pan when Moon Face came through the doorway, but so far he had proven strong enough to take a file in the cheek and a stick in the throat, and despite the severity of the latter wound, he had kept on coming. Chances were he was strong enough to handle her and her frying pan.

A backup plan was necessary. Another one of Bruce's pronouncements. She recalled a college friend, Carol, who used to use her bikini panties to launch projectiles at a teddy bear propped on a chair. This graduated to an apple on the bear's head. Eventually, Ellen and her dorm sisters got into the act. Fresh panties with tight elastic and marbles for ammunition were ever ready in a box by the door, the bear and an apple were in constant position. In time, Ellen became the best shot of all. But that was ten years ago. Expertise was long gone, even the occasional shot now and then was no longer taken. . . . Still . . .

Ellen replaced the frying pan on the stove, hiked up her dress, and pulled her bikini panties down and stepped out of them and picked up the lighter.

She put the lighter in the crotch of the panties and stuck her fingers into the leg loops to form a fork and took hold of the lighter through the panties and pulled it back, assured herself the elastic was strong enough to launch the projectile.

All right. That was a start.

She removed her purse, so Moon Face couldn't grab it and snare her, and tossed it aside. She grabbed the whiskey bottle from the corpse's hand and turned and smashed the bottom of it against the cookstove. Whiskey and glass flew. The result was a jagged weapon she could lunge with. She placed the broken bottle on the stove next to the frying pan.

Outside, Moon Face was strolling toward the hut, like a shy teenager about to call on his date.

There were only moments left. She glanced around the room, hoping insanely at the last second she would find some escape route, but there was none.

Sweat dripped from her forehead and ran into her eye and she blinked it out and half-drew back the panty sling with its golden projectile. She knew her makeshift weapon wasn't powerful enough to do much damage, but it might give her a moment of distraction, a chance to attack him with the bottle. If she went at him straight on with it, she felt certain he would disarm her and make short work of her, but if she could get him off guard . . .

She lowered her arms, kept her makeshift slingshot in front of her, ready to be cocked and shot.

Moon Face came through the door, ducking as he did, a sour sweat smell entering with him. His neck wound whistled at her like a teapot about to boil. She saw then that he was bigger than she first thought. Tall and broad-shouldered and strong.

He looked at her and there was that peculiar expression again. The moonlight from the hole in the roof hit his eyes and teeth, and it was as if that light was his source of energy. He filled his chest with air and seemed to stand a full two inches taller. He looked at the woman's corpse in the chair, the man's corpse supported on wires, glanced at the playpen.

He smiled at Ellen, squeaked more than spoke, "Bubba's home, Sissie."

I'm not Sissie yet, thought Ellen. Not yet.

Moon Face started to move around the card table and Ellen let out a bloodcurdling scream that caused him to bob his head high like a rabbit surprised by headlights. Ellen jerked up the panties and pulled them back and let loose the lighter. It shot out of the panties and fell to the center of the card table with a clunk.

Moon Face looked down at it.

Ellen was temporarily gripped with paralysis, then she stepped forward and kicked the card table as hard as she could. It went into Moon Face, hitting him waist high, starling but not hurting him.

Now! thought Ellen, grabbing her weapons. Now!

She rushed him, the broken bottle in one hand, the frying pan in the other. She slashed out with the bottle and it struck him in the center of the face and he let out a scream and the glass fractured and a splash of blood burst from him and in that same instant Ellen saw that his nose was cut half in two and she felt a tremendous throb in her hand. The bottle had broken in her palm and cut her.

She ignored the pain and as Moon Face bellowed and lashed out with the knife cutting the front of her dress but not her flesh, she brought the frying pan around and caught him on the elbow and the knife went soaring across the room and behind the rollaway bed.

Moon Face froze, glanced in the direction the knife had taken. He seemed empty and confused without it.

Ellen swung the pan again. Moon Face caught her wrist and jerked her around and she lost the pan and was sent hurtling toward the bed, where she collapsed on the mattress. The bed slid down and smashed through the thin wall of sticks and a foot of the bed stuck out into blackness and the great drop below. The bed tottered slightly, and Ellen rolled off of it, directly into the legs of Moon Face. As his knees bent, and he reached for her, she rolled backward and went under the bed and her hand came to rest on the knife. She grabbed it, rolled back toward Moon Face's feet, reached out quickly and brought the knife down on one of his shoes and drove it in as hard as she could.

A bellow from Moon Face. His foot leaped back and it took the knife with it. Moon Face screamed, "Sissie! You're hurting me!"

Moon Face reached down and pulled the knife out, and Ellen saw his foot come forward, and then he was grabbing the bed and effortlessly jerking it off of her and back, smashing it into the crib, causing the child to topple out of it and roll across the floor, the rattle clattering behind it. He grabbed Ellen by the back of her dress and jerked her up and spun her around to face him, clutched her throat in one hand, and held the knife close to her face with the other, as if for inspection; the blade caught the moonlight and winked.

Beyond the knife, she saw his face, pathetic and pained and white. His breath, sharp as the knife, practically wilted her. His neck wound whistled softly. The remnants of his nose dangled wet and red against his upper lip and cheek and his teeth grinned a moonlit, metal goodbye.

It was all over, and she knew it, but then Bruce's words came back to her in a rush. "When it looks as if you're defeated, and there's nothing left, try anything."

She twisted and jabbed out at his eyes with her fingers and caught him solid enough that he thrust her away and stumbled backward. But only for an instant. He bolted forward, and Ellen stooped and grabbed the dead child by the ankle and struck Moon Face with it as if it were a club. Once in the face, once in the midsection. The rotting child burst into a spray of desiccated flesh and innards and she hurled the leg at Moon Face and then she was circling around the rollaway bed, trying to make the door. Moon Face, at the other end of the bed, saw this, and when she moved for the door, he lunged in that direction, causing her to jump back to the end of the bed. Smiling, he returned to his end, waited for her next attempt.

She lurched for the door again, and Moon Face deep-stepped that way, and when she jerked back, Moon Face jerked back too, but this time Ellen bent and grabbed the end of the bed and hurled herself against it. The bed hit Moon Face in the knees, and as he fell, the bed rolled over him and he let go of the knife and tried to put out his hands to stop the bed's momentum. The impetus of the rollaway carried him across the short length of the dirt floor and his head hit the far wall and the sticks cracked and hurtled out into blackness, and Moon Face followed and the bed followed him, then caught on the edge of the drop and the wheels buried up in the dirt and hung there.

Ellen had shoved so hard she fell face down, and when she looked up, she saw the bed was dangling, shaking, the mattress slipping loose, about to glide off into nothingness.

Moon Face's hands flicked into sight, clawing at the sides of the bed's frame. Ellen gasped. He was going to make it up. The bed's wheels were going to hold.

She pulled a knee under her, cocking herself, then sprang forward, thrusting both palms savagely against the bed. The wheels popped free and the rollaway shot out into the dark emptiness.

Ellen scooted forward on her knees and looked over the edge. There was blackness, a glimpse of the mattress falling free, and a pale object, like a whitewashed planet with a great vein of silver in it, jetting through the cold expanse of space. Then the mattress and the face were gone and there was just the darkness and a distant sound like a water balloon exploding.

Ellen sat back and took a breather. When she felt strong again and felt certain her heart wouldn't tear through her chest, she stood up and looked around the room. She thought a long time about what she saw.

She found her purse and panties, went out of the hut and up the trail, and after a few wrong turns, she found the proper trail that wound its way up the mountain side to where her car was parked. When she climbed over the railing, she was exhausted.

Everything was as it was. She wondered if anyone had seen the cars, if anyone had stopped, then decided it didn't matter. There was no one here now, and that's what was important.

She took the keys from her purse and tried the engine. It turned over. That was a relief.

She killed the engine, got out and went around and opened the trunk of the Chevy, and looked down at Bruce's body. His face looked like one big bruise, his lips were as large as sausages. It made her happy to look at him.

A new energy came to her. She got him under the arms and pulled him out and managed him over to the rail and grabbed his legs and flipped him over the railing and onto the trail. She got one of his hands and started pulling him down the path, letting the momentum help her. She felt good. She felt strong. First Bruce had tried to dominate her, had threatened her, had thought she was weak because she was a woman, and one night, after slapping her, after raping her, while he slept a drunken sleep, she had pulled the blankets up tight around him and looped rope over and under the bed and used the knots he had taught her, and secured him.

Then she took a stick of stove wood and had beat him until she was so weak she fell to her knees. She hadn't meant to kill him, just punish him for slapping her around, but when she got started she couldn't stop until she was too worn out to go on, and when she was finished, she discovered he was dead.

That didn't disturb her much. The thing then was to get rid of the body somewhere, drive on back to the city, and say he had abandoned her and not come back. It was weak, but all she had. Until now.

After several stops for breath, a chance to lie on her back and look up at the stars, Ellen managed Bruce to the hut and got her arms under his and got him seated in one of the empty chairs. She straightened things up as best as she could. She put the larger pieces of the baby back in the crib. She picked Moon Face's knife up off the floor and looked at it and looked at Bruce, his eyes wide open, the moonlight from the roof striking them, showing them to be dull as scratched glass.

Bending over his face, she went to work on his eyes. When she finished with them, she pushed his head forward and used the blade like a drill. She worked until the holes satisfied her. Now if the police found the Buick up there and came down the trail to investigate, and found the trail leading here, saw what was in the shack, Bruce would fit in with the rest of Moon Face's victims. The police would probably conclude Moon Face, sleeping here with his "family," had put his bed too close to the cliff and it had broken through the thin wall and he had tumbled to his death.

She liked it.

She held Bruce's chin, lifted it, examined her work.

"You can be Uncle Brucey," she said, and gave Bruce a pat on the shoulder. "Thanks for all your advice and help, Uncle Brucey. It's what got me through." She gave him another pat.

She found a shirt—possibly Moon Face's, possibly a victim's—on the opposite side of the shack, next to a little box of Harlequin Romances, and she used it to wipe the knife, pan, all she had touched, clean of her prints, then she went out of there, back up to her car.

Wolfer

■

GENE WOLFE

She dropped the bar, she shot the bolt, she fed the fire anew,
For she heard a whimper under the sill and a great gray paw came
through.

Janet listened with attention and an eerie foreboding while the lecturer spoke forcefully and knowledgeably, talking about things he
clearly knew well and had known for a long time.

"With only trifling exceptions, our surnames originated as notations
on tax rolls. There were a great many Johns and Williams and so on,
just as there are now. Some means had to be found to distinguish
among them. Let us suppose that a certain man named John, living
in England, had been born in Ireland. The tax collector would record
his name, John . . ."

A haunting wail overpowered the calm and reasonable words—a
sound no one but she could hear. Later, when she was walking through
the snow to the bus stop, the howl would be louder and more insistent;
but it was frightening even now.

"And so a notation appeared after John's name, Ireland or perhaps
Irish. Check the telephone directory in any big city and you will find
those names, borne by John's descendants to this day. Franz and Fran-

cis are familiar names of this type, both indicating that the bearer was originally French. Not long ago I read, with a certain amusement, about historians searching the archives of Liège, a city in Belgium, for mention of Jacques de Liège, the inventor of the jackknife. Anyone who knew anything about the history of surnames could have told them that the very last place to look for Monsieur de Liège was in Liège itself." The lecturer paused, smiling as he glanced from face to face.

Kyoto howls like that sometimes, Janet thought. Kyoto was one of the Scotties she was caring for while Rachael and Andy were in Europe; but she knew Kyoto did not really sound like that, and that the howl was in her mind, not in the freezing February night outside the lecture hall. What would the dogs say when she told them about it?

"Physical peculiarities presented another fertile source of surnames. Thus we have John Short, John Stout, John Small, and even John Talman. John White had white or at least light-colored hair. John Black had a dark complexion in an area in which fair complexions were the rule.

"Trades were the exception at a time when most people farmed the land. John Hooper made barrels, while John Fletcher made arrows. I need not explain names like Smith and Taylor, I hope. Thus we know that Oliver Goldsmith's ancestor made jewelry, and that Geoffrey Chaucer's made shoes."

Janet fidgeted, and tried to still the wild wailing in her mind. What a fool she had been to come!

"And now I'd like to learn your own surnames, each of which I will endeavor to explain as well as I can. I must warn you that those drawn from Slavic languages—Polish and Russian, for example—are liable to stump me."

He studied the audience and pointed. "How about you, sir? Are you willing to stand and tell us your name?"

A middle-aged man rose, straightening his heavy overcoat. "I don't mind, but you will. I'm George Dembinski."

The lecturer smiled again. "I said that some Slavic names might stump me, not that all of them would. Your ancestor lived in an oak wood, sir. If he had lived in England instead of Poland, your name would be Oakely, or something of the sort.

"Which brings us back to place names. In addition to such names as French and England, derived from nations, we find many names like Mr. Dembinski's. John Ford's house was near the point at which you could wade the river, for example. Somewhat less obviously, John Clough lived in a clearing in the forest."

He scanned his audience again. "Are you willing to stand up so I can explain your surname, madam?"

The gray-haired woman he had indicated stood, proving to be taller than Janet expected. "You'll be talking about Bishop John," she told him. "My name is Margaret Bishop."

"Ah. That's an interesting class, names taken from an employer's position. Your ancestor—or your husband's—was not the bishop but the bishop's servant, probably an upper servant. The author Stephen King furnishes a good example of this type of name. His ancestor was John Who-serves-the-king."

Another search. "What about you, sir?"

A man younger than Janet, in jeans and a leather jacket. "Bill Noble."

"Another name of the same type. I came across a very clear example recently. The gentleman's name was James M'Lady. Your ancestor, sir, was John Who-serves-the-noble-family, just as his was John Who-serves-my-lady. Most of you are probably familiar with the very interesting name of a chain of bookstores—Barnes & Noble. John Barnes may have been John Who-cares-for-barns or John Who-lives-near-barns. But the name Barnes is most often derived from the old Scottish word *bairn,* meaning a child and especially a younger son in a noble Scottish family. Mr. Barnes and his junior partner Mr. Noble show how frequently these old relationships are continued or resumed when their thousand-year-old origins are utterly forgotten. Forgotten, I should say, except by me.

"What about you, madam?"

Here it was.

"Will you give us your name?"

Janet stood, conscious that her knees were trembling and perfectly certain that the lecturer knew it. "Of course I will. That was why I came. I'm . . . you said that—that Ms. Bishop's ancestor . . . or her husband's. So I ought to tell you I'm not married anymore, and it's my maiden name. I'm Janet Woolf." She paused, floundering mentally. "You know. Like Virginia Woolf? With two *o*'s. Does that matter?"

The lecturer shook his head. "All such names are merely variants of *Wolf.* I take it you're not Jewish?"

"No, I'm a—no."

"If you were, your name would indicate membership in the tribe of Benjamin. Since you're not, you're presumably descended from someone called Wolf or Vulf . . ."

Janet wanted to protest but did not.

"Someone who exhibited the courage and ferocity thought characteristic of wolves."

Too softly she murmured, "I don't think so."

"I might note that though the various forms of *wolf* are unusual as first names, they remain in use. The Irish patriot Wolfe Tone is an example, as is Jack London's fictional captain, Wolf Larson. You're shaking your head."

"I don't believe any of that." Janet took a deep breath. "I think my name—" Louder! "Belongs to the same group as that other woman's. That it's really a servant name and maybe even a friend name, because back then a servant wasn't just somebody who cooked and cleaned, he was somebody who went out and fought for you when that was what you needed. I think that we were John and Joan and Jane Who-serve-the-wolves, once."

The lecturer started to say something, but she raised her voice again, overriding him shrilly. "I can't prove it, but I feel it. You'll make fun of me, I know, but half the time I was listening I was laughing at you. You're so sure you know everything that went on back when people like us were savages with bows and spears. Where everybody lived. What everybody did."

The audience was buzzing; she had to shout to make herself heard. "But I know what I feel in my heart! And I don't believe you know nearly as much as you think you do!"

She dropped back into her seat, her face burning. Somewhere high overhead, the lecturer was saying something—something presumably crushing. She did not hear it.

As she left the lecture hall, a tall, gaunt, gray-haired woman edged closer to her. Mentally Janet snapped her fingers. Margaret Bishop.

"Wolves! Take the crosstown bus."

Abruptly, Margaret Bishop strode ahead and vanished into the crowd.

She's crazy, Janet thought; but there had been something so urgent and compelling in that whisper that she went to the bus stop, all the while worrying frantically about her little Geo in the parking lot. There were two men at the bus stop; both looked tired, and neither so much as glanced at her. No, she thought, Margaret Bishop's perfectly sane—I'm the one who's crazy.

When the almost-empty bus arrived, Margaret Bishop was sitting by herself in the last seat. A slight motion of her head and something welcoming in her eyes indicated that Janet was to sit beside her.

Janet did. "I guess I went to the wrong stop. I thought that was the closest."

"It is." Margaret Bishop spoke under her breath. "You're a godsend, Janet. Is it all right if I call you Janet? You're gold and diamonds and rubies to me. Do you have some kind of big car, a van, or a minivan? Anything at all like that? Don't look at me when you answer."

Responding to the last, Janet said, "Yes. All right."

"I knew you would!" There was heady exultation in Margaret Bishop's whisper. "You listen, you follow instructions, and you don't ask questions. You're perfectly wonderful!"

I've often tried to be, Janet thought. Maybe this time I'm succeeding.

"We need somebody to transport three young wolves. You'll do it. I know you will."

"Wolves?" She nodded. "I'll certainly try."

"We're trying to reestablish wolves throughout the United States. Maybe you've heard about us?"

"I've read something, I think."

"They call us wolfers, and there are a lot more of us than they think. Ranchers who doom thousands of cattle every year," the whisper grew bitter, "and rent thousands of acres of public land for pennies, are afraid that somewhere, sometime, a wolf may kill a calf. But wolves are a vital part of this country's ecology."

"I know," Janet whispered back. "I've read a great deal about them."

The bus lurched to a stop; a tired-looking man got off and an even tireder-looking one got on, stamping snow from his overshoes. "That's not one of them," Margaret Bishop whispered, "or I don't think so. They're behind us in a car."

Janet forgot about not asking questions. "Who are they?"

"Feds. Probably Fish and Game, but it might be the FBI or even the ATF."

"That's scary."

"Of course it is, and there are dozens of those secret police agencies, though nobody's got the guts to call them the Secret Police. Are you particularly frightened of the ATF? You shouldn't be, because they're really all the same. Someone who shows you a U.S. marshal's badge today may show somebody else credentials from the CIA tomorrow." A slight smile tugged at Margaret Bishop's thin lips. "Their names aren't like Woolf and Bishop, you see, Janet. Theirs mean nothing."

"Young wolves, you said. You want me to take them somewhere."

"Yes, three. Two females and a male." Margaret Bishop opened her purse and rummaged through it. "To a certain park in Michigan. There's a new place in Texas, too, but I'm going to send you to Michigan. I assume you work."

Janet nodded—almost imperceptibly, she hoped.

"Can you take a few days off work?"

"I already am. I won't have to go back until a week from Monday. I—do you mind if I tell you something personal? I don't want to burden you with my problems. I really don't."

"I'd *love* for you to tell me something personal, Janet. I'm eager to get to know you."

"It was because I was getting so depressed, because of the divorce. I divorced Steve, you see. He didn't want it, but—"

"You just didn't get along." Margaret Bishop sounded sympathetic.

"He was always bossing me, always crowding me. I'd say, 'Stop! Stop! You're killing me and you're killing the last bit of the love we used to have.' "

"Yes."

"And he'd say, 'Why can't you be sensible, Janet?' And then when I failed, it was all my fault and he started talking about the good times we'd had. That was what he said, the good times. Only they hadn't been good times for me, and I could never make Steve understand that."

Margaret Bishop's hand found hers.

"The day he moved out, I threw a frying pan at Wasabe—at dear little Wasabe! She's the best little dog anybody ever saw, but I threw a great big cast-iron skillet at her. I could've killed her."

"You had been hurt, and wanted to hurt someone else."

"Yes, exactly. So I explained to my boss and he let me take my two weeks of vacation. I'd been planning to fly to Florida, but I couldn't because of the dogs, so I thought I'd just stay here at home and go to museums and, you know, cultural things, and get some extra sleep and snap out of it. Only I didn't. And because of taking my old name back I kept thinking about wolves, real wolves and werewolves and all the rest of it, and getting bluer and bluer, until you came along. But now I'm not depressed at all. When you get off this bus I'll get off, too—"

"No you won't," Margaret Bishop told her. "We can't let them see us together. Stay on for another two stops."

"All right, I'll stay on for another two stops, and then I'll get off and take another bus back to the campus and get my Geo. That's not the big car I told you about. It's just little. The big one's a Ford Expedition."

"Perfect!"

"And I can start tomorrow. I will, if that's all right."

For the first time, Margaret Bishop turned and looked at her. "If you're caught, caught with the wolves, you'll be fined. You could even be sent to prison. I doubt that it will happen, but it could. Do you understand?"

"Yes. I'll try very hard not to be caught. Kyoto and Wasabe and I will, because I'll have to take them with me. And we won't be."

"Let us pray," Margaret Bishop had said, and had handed her this piece of paper. At the top was the name and address of the man in Minnesota who had the wolves—and, supposedly at least, cages for them. At the bottom was the name and address of the Michigan man who knew all the back roads around the new park and would sneak the wolves in, one at a time and at night.

Home at last, Janet was showing the paper to Kyoto, the wheaten

Scottie, who sniffed and inspected it, and cocked her head wisely. "This is very important information," Janet told Kyoto. "You're not to tear it up! Not under any circumstances. Understand?"

I don't do that, Kyoto said quite plainly. It's Wasabe who tears things up, and she mostly tears up house plants burying her toy.

"Let me rephrase that. You are not to tear this up unless we're raided by the Feds. That's what Margaret Bishop calls them, Feds. If we're raided by Feds, I want you to bark as loud as you can, and eat it."

Eat what? Wasabe inquired, interested. (Wasabe was the black Scottie.)

"This is a very valuable paper." Janet showed it to Wasabe, who sniffed it even more thoroughly than Kyoto had.

"It doesn't have phone numbers because their phones might be tapped. The Feds might even be putting a tap on *our* phone right now, so if either of you makes a call, don't speak English. Speak Dog."

We will, Kyoto and Wasabe declared in unison.

"Tomorrow I'm going to have to see Steve. It will be ugly, I know it will, but I've got to do it. After that, we'll go to Minnesota and get three wolves, fierce big animals that eat little puppy dogs for lunch. Understand? You two have Japanese names so you ought to be polite, but I can't really say I've noticed it so far. You'd darned well better be polite to the wolves, though, and keep your distance, too. And so had I."

Don't worry, Janet, Kyoto said. I'll protect you.

They had said "Hi. How are you?" and not listened to the answers, and Steve had invited Janet in. Now she sat on the edge of a chair big enough to hold a man bigger even than Steve, and clutched her purse in both hands. "When we separated I swore I would never ask you for help."

Steve nodded, his hard, handsome face guarded.

"Now I am. I have to borrow your truck. It shouldn't be for more than two days, and you'll have my Geo to drive to work." She hesitated. "It could be three, I hope not, but it could be. Not any longer than that."

"It's not a truck. It's a sport utility vehicle."

This was encouraging—he had not said no. "I'm sorry. I really am. Your sport utility vehicle. I simply have to have it. I'll take good care of it, and I'll owe you a big, big favor if you let me borrow it. I know that. Will you, Steve? Please?"

A guarded nod. "What do you want it for?"

"Thank you! Oh, Steve, thank you very, very much." It would be too dangerous to kiss him, she decided, although she wanted to. "Do you remember Rachael's dogs?"

"With the funny names? Sure."

"Well, I stuck my neck out. I shouldn't have, but I did. I promised to take some other dogs for another woman, a new friend. And they're big, really big dogs—"

He chuckled.

"I said I'd take them to Michigan for her." Janet's voice fell. "Three of them."

"If they piss on my upholstery, Janet—"

"They won't! They'll be in a cage in back. You've seen big dog cages like that. Everybody has. They'll never get near your upholstery, I promise, and if they—you know—relieve themselves, I'll clean it up."

"You'd better."

"I will, Steve. Really, I will." She paused to swallow; there was the money for Florida, money that she would never use now. "In fact, before I bring it back to you I'll take it to that detailing place. They charge a lot, I know—"

"It'll be two hundred if it's a dime," Steve declared.

"But I will. It'll be just like a new car—I mean sport utility vehi-cle—when you see it again."

She gave him the keys to her Geo, and he gave her his, which she put in her purse.

"Steve . . . ?"

He cocked an eyebrow. "You need another favor?"

"No. But—but I'd like one. I said I'd be careful with your car? I'll be twice as careful with this. I want you to lend me a gun."

"What?"

"I know I never liked them. I know I always complained about your having them. But these are really big dogs, and they're not nice dogs like Kyoto and Wasabe. Do you know what I mean? And there are three of them, and I'll have to—to let them out to exercise them, I guess. So will you? Not one of your hunting rifles, the little one, the pistol."

"The Smith & Wesson?"

She swallowed again. "I guess so. I don't think I'll need it. I certainly hope I don't. . . ."

To her surprise he nodded sympathetically.

The Smith & Wesson was in the pocket of Janet's parka as she drove up to the Minnesota farmhouse. The house was dark, the barnyard brilliantly illuminated by a light on a high pole. She switched off her headlights before the Expedition rolled to a stop, jumped out, and ran up the steps onto the dark front porch, joyfully accompanied by Wasabe and Kyoto.

There was no response to her knock. She listened for a time, found the bell and rang it, looked back at the dark front yard and the darker road, watched the silent ghost that was her breath floating in the frigid air, and knocked a second time. Nothing.

Wasabe was sticking close, an almost invisible furry presence around her feet; Kyoto had decided the wolves were probably in the rusty hulk of an old truck on the other side of the driveway, and was investigating. A third knock, as loud as she could make it.

Nothing.

Janet whistled Kyoto to her and went back to the Expedition, sat in it for ten minutes or so watching the front door, and restarted the engine. "Nobody." She scratched Kyoto's ears and switched the headlights back on.

"A farm's not like a house," she told Kyoto. "You can't just go off and leave it. Who's going to feed the chickens?"

It seemed a compelling argument, but as is the case with most compelling arguments, nobody listened. Slowly she backed up and out onto the road again. "Well, I'm not going back to say I tried once but there was nobody home. No way!"

Not us! Kyoto declared. As usual, Wasabe seconded her: Not us. Right, Janet?

"No, indeed. I'm going back to—what was the name of that little town?"

Thief River Falls, Kyoto declared. Wasabe laid a paw on Janet's arm. Viking.

"Whatever." She put the Expedition in drive and glanced at the instruments. "There's bound to be someplace to stay there. A motel or a bed and breakfast or something. Tomorrow we'll come back—"

She hit the brakes as a big man in a red cap and a big red checkered coat appeared in her headlights. The Expedition skidded a little on the icy asphalt and came to a stop.

The man in the checkered coat came to her window and the Smith & Wesson into her hand without her consciously wanting either one of them. There seemed to be little to do with the latter except point it at the face of the former, so she did and said, "I darned near killed you. What do you want?"

"A ride." He held up one big hand as though its leathery palm would stop a bullet. "You are looking for me? Granstrom is my name."

"You weren't at your house." Janet hesitated. "Are you afraid they're watching it?"

"Put that away." Granstrom took a deep breath. "I get in the car, all right?"

"This?" She glanced at the Smith & Wesson and put it back into the pocket of her parka. "Yes. Get in. You'll have to chase the dogs into the back."

He did, settling himself into the deep bucket seat. "Nice car. You come to get my wolfs, ya?"

"Wolves. Yes, I did."

"All right."

She waited for him to say more; when he did not, she asked, "Should we go back to your house?"

He shook his head and pointed. "Go slow."

"Right." She let the big Expedition drift ahead.

"There." He pointed again.

"You want to go through all that snow?"

"Ya."

Her headlights showed an opening in a sagging fence of rusty wire. Cautiously the Expedition edged forward, crossing what might or might not have been cattle bars.

"I say turn off those light, you do that?"

"Ya," Janet said, and did. Dark pines and white snow, lost in inky darkness when the moon vanished behind snow-laden clouds.

"Go slow."

It was impossible to go much slower, but she tried. No doubt there was a dirt road under the snow; presumably the Expedition was on it, more or less. "Are the Feds watching your house?" she asked him.

He scratched his head without removing his cap, knocking it to one side. "I don't think so."

"But you went outside in this cold to wait for me half a mile down the road."

"Ya. A certain fellow, he said you would be coming."

"A friend of yours."

"Oh, ya."

"And of Margaret Bishop's."

He turned to look at her. "Ya, her, too."

"You let me go past you so you could look me over, and maybe so you could see if anybody came out of the bushes to grab me when I stopped at your place."

This time he did not speak.

"But you don't think your place is watched?"

"Here stop."

He got out, walked away at an angle until he was only just visible in the moonlight, then motioned for her to follow. She did, and in a minute and a half was enveloped in the deeper night of pines. A faint light motioned her forward. From outside the Expedition there came a throaty yelping cry that was not in her mind. The faint light shone down upon crisp, undisturbed snow: She was to stop. She put the transmission in park and got out, followed by the Scotties.

"They are here," Granstrom said. "My wolfs." He did not shine his flashlight on them, but their eyes glowed. Shadows in the shadows, they passed back and forth, moaning and whining, clinking faintly like icicles rattling down from the highest branches of a big tree. She felt Wasabe tremble as she pressed against her calf. Kyoto was broadside to the wolves, tail erect as an obelisk, fur on end making her look larger than Janet had ever seen her.

"That is a brave little dog you got." Granstrom had followed the direction of her eyes.

"Yes. She's not really mine, but she is."

"Don't let her get too close to my wolfs."

"I don't think we have to worry about that." Janet paused, looking around. "Don't you have cages for them?"

"A big pile of brush." Granstrom's light shot over the wolves' heads to illuminate it. "They go in there, ya? Get out of the wind, sleep all together. I got them on chains."

"You have to have a cage for them!"

He indicated the Expedition with a nod. "I chain them for you in back so they don't get at you."

For a moment they stared at each other. "Open the back," he said.

She did and he did. One wolf snapped at him, and he slapped its muzzle. When all three were inside the Expedition and the rear hatch was shut again, he motioned for her to get in.

"Aren't you coming? I could give you a ride back to where you live."

"No." When he saw that she expected some further answer he added, "I stay to clean up."

"In the dark?"

He did not reply.

She got back into the Expedition, followed reluctantly by Kyoto. Granstrom picked up Wasabe and handed her to Janet. "Thank you," she said. "Sure you don't want a ride home?"

He shook his head. "You go slow, ya? Till you get to the county road, you go slow."

"I will," she promised.

She had covered perhaps one tenth of a mile when she saw him running behind her and stopped, and rolled down her window as she had before.

"My—wolfs." He was out of breath and panting. "Where do—you bring them?"

"I don't know if—"

"Where?"

Margaret Bishop had said nothing to indicate she should not tell him. "To a Larry Ventris in Michigan. There's a big park close to where he lives. He'll smuggle them into it and let them go."

"Good—good." Granstrom's hands, clutching the top of the Expedition's door, relaxed a trifle. "That is good. A good man." She had assumed unconsciously that Granstrom never smiled, but he smiled now. "Up Suicide Road he will take them. This he tells once. Suicide Road or else Harrison Road."

"You know him."

"Ya."

She waited for him to release the door so that she could roll up her window again, but he did not. At last she said, "If you don't want a lift . . . ?"

"The mother wolf, she is dead." He spoke slowly. "A trap or a hunter. Someone shoots, or else poisons. I don't know. Three days I watch their den, and the little wolfs, they are weaker each day."

Janet found herself nodding. "I understand."

"Littler than your dogs they are. I keep them in the house till they get big. Larry Ventris, he is a good man."

She nodded. "I feel sure he is."

"You." He did not point to her, but made a small gesture to indicate her; in the back of the Expedition one of the wolves whimpered. "You are a good woman. Such a good woman most men don't ever see."

She thanked him, sounding—to herself—exceedingly inadequate.

"I was going to tell your their names," Granstrom said, "but they are wild wolfs again now. Wild wolfs in the woods, they got no names."

Once they stopped beside the road, and she slept for two hours before the cold and Kyoto woke her. Once, too, she stopped for gasoline (careful to pay cash), bought five hamburgers and coffee at the gas station, and a mile down the road stopped again to eat a hamburger herself, share another between the Scotties, and feed the remaining three to the wolves, throwing the pieces at first, then letting them eat—each growling to keep the others away—from her fingers as Granstrom must have.

No one answered her repeated knocks at the Ventrises', and at last a neighbor came to tell her that neither Ventris nor his wife were at home. Her voice dropped. "I think he was arrested. He always seemed like such a nice, nice man, but I think that they've arrested him."

Janet said, "That was why they arrested him, I suppose." But she did not say it loudly, and said it only to Wasabe and Kyoto after she was back in the Expedition with the doors closed and locked.

She looked into the rearview mirror, and one of the wolves, meeting her eyes there, spoke in Wolf: Aren't we ever going to be free?

"You will," Janet told it. "I swear you will. You'll be free today. Kyoto, do you remember where in that park—Suicide Road. That was one. Who could forget Suicide Road?"

Nobody, Kyoto declared; to which Wasabe added, We only need one.

In another gas station, this one quite near the park, a mechanic who looked as weary as she felt gave her directions to Suicide Road. "It's a pretty place, ma'am. Lot of people go snowmobiling there." He himself looked out at the snow with longing. "This's probably the last big fall this winter. Should be real pretty out there."

"It sounds awful, but it's where my boyfriend said he was going to go, so I've got to find it." She had forgotten already who was dying—the father or the mother; it probably did not matter, she decided.

"Well, you just take Ninety-four and stay with it, then turn off where you see the red barns, like I said. I don't believe there's a sign, though."

"Will I be in much danger of going off the edge? Suicide Road sounds so scary." One of the wolves was starting to howl. Janet wondered whether the mechanic heard it.

He grinned, weary still. "Not 'less you jump. It goes up to Suicide Cliff. That's why they call it that."

"How far?" she asked Kyoto. "That's the question. We're about a mile into this park already."

A little farther, Kyoto advised. So they won't run out right away and get shot.

She nodded, too tired to be sleepy. Kyoto was right as always. Go in deep, let out the wolves. . . .

For the first time it occurred to her that she, unaided by Larry Ventris, Granstrom, Margaret Bishop, or anyone else, was going to have to unchain the wolves and release them. "You wolves," she spoke to them over her shoulder, "had darned well better remember that I'm your friend and I've got a gun."

One howled, then another; Wasabe began to yip in sympathy.

"Shut up!" She tapped the horn, and they did. "What I'm going to do is drive way deep in this park. Have you noticed that we haven't seen any other cars?"

Kyoto had, and said so.

"I'm going to enjoy this winter scenery, which really is spectacular. Then I'm going to stop and let you wolves out. Let me do it, and you're free. Bite me while I'm trying to unchain you, and you're going to have a fight on your hands. Understand?"

A wolf met her eyes in the mirror but said nothing.

"You think you're big, tough wolves, but you're not even half grown up yet. It'll be three against three if we fight. Speaking for myself and the dogs, we don't want to. It's entirely up to you."

A second wolf appeared in the mirror, saying in Wolf, Let us out here.

"Okay," Janet told it. "That sign said there was a scenic overlook up ahead. We can pull off right up there."

She did and got out, followed by both Scotties. "We'll go on through the park," she told them. "Did I say that?"

Wasabe nodded. I think so, Janet.

"Then we'll find someplace that will take dogs and I'll have a bath and sleep till next Wednesday." She unlocked the hatch of Steve's Expedition and held out her hand to the most docile-looking wolf. "That is the hand of friendship. Remember the hamburgers?"

The wolf said nothing, but allowed her to unsnap the chain around its neck. She took three quick steps backward as Kyoto barked a warning.

Almost fearfully the wolf stood for a moment on the rear of the Expedition, looking at her and the dogs, the rocks, the snow, and the trees. It lifted its head, sniffed the wind, and jumped down, loped across the little snow-covered parking lot and across Suicide Road to what appeared to be a sheer cliff, so steep that the snow had found only scattered points in which to lodge. Passing behind a roadside bush, it never reappeared.

Janet discovered that she had been holding her breath, and she let it out with a whoosh. "That was the greatest moment of my life," she told the emptiness beyond the railing.

Wasabe, sniffing at the wolf's trail, looked up with snow on her nose. Mine, too, Janet.

She had almost gotten up the courage to release the second wolf when the park ranger's car pulled in. He marched grimly toward her, a good foot taller than she in his Smokey Bear hat. "Miss—" he began. His eyes opened very wide when he saw the Smith & Wesson.

"Were you about to say that I'm under arrest?"

He shook his head, the motion almost imperceptible.

"That's good," Janet told him. "Because if you do I'm going to shoot you and roll your body over that drop." For a moment it seemed to her that she might actually do it.

"You're bringing in wolves." There was an odd, undecided quality to his voice.

She pointed to the back of the Expedition. "There they are."

"Letting them go in the park."

"I *was*. But that was before you came." Something in her voice made Wasabe bark at him and Kyoto growl. "Now you are. If you want to keep breathing, you get over there and unchain them."

He looked at the two remaining wolves, and back at her. "You don't need that gun, miss."

"I'm glad to hear it. Get busy."

"In a minute."

She raised the gun. "The trigger was pretty stiff when I got it, but I had a gunsmith smooth it out." It was something Steve had said. On her own she added, "I don't have strong hands, but I can pull this trigger now, and it's a lot easier to pull after the first time. It's called double action."

"I know what it's called," the park ranger said.

"Sure you do. And you know that if you can keep me talking somebody will come by. Get over there and unchain them."

He took a hesitant step toward the wolves.

"I'm going to count to ten." She tried to make her voice hard, and at least succeeded in frightening herself. "Is that understood? I don't want to, but on the count of ten I shoot. One. Two. Three . . ."

Like playing hide-and-seek, she thought.

"Four. Five. Six. I am not joking. Do it!"

He edged nearer the wolves, but one lunged at him, snarling.

"Never mind, I'll do it."

She was no longer tired. It's getting out of the truck and into the fresh air, she thought, or it's getting to stretch my legs, and whatever it is, it's wonderful.

She gestured with the Smith & Wesson. "Get over closer to your car, but don't get in."

"I am not going to rush you," he said. He sounded sincere.

"That's good. If you're not going to rush me I'm not going to shoot you, and that's the way we both like it."

"I was going to warn you, that's all. Tell you to come in at night, because if somebody else saw you I'd have to—"

She made an angry gesture, and he backed away. She said, "I'm going to put this in my pocket. See?"

He nodded.

"If you can get to me before I can get it out again, you win. But you'd better be careful not to slip in the snow." The wolf that had snarled at him snapped at her; she cuffed its muzzle and unhooked its chain. "Now get out of here," she told it. "We're tired of feeding you. Go kill a gopher or something."

When she looked around at the ranger, his hands were no longer raised. "There," she told him, "that's another one. You arrested a friend of mine yesterday, but you still haven't stopped us." *Us* was Margaret Bishop, Granstrom, Larry Ventris, and how many others? It really wasn't a question of how many others, she decided; it was a question of how many wolves.

The ranger had spoken, but she had been too occupied with her thoughts to hear him. As she unchained the third wolf she said, "Come again?"

"I said I was sorry about your friend. It wasn't me."

The third wolf jumped from the back of the Expedition and for perhaps fifteen seconds stood nose-to-nose with Kyoto and Wasabe. I'm going to live in these woods and have cubs, the third wolf said in Wolf, because that's what I want to do.

It's up to you, Kyoto declared in Dog. We want to stay with Janet.

Wasabe added, Until Rachael and Andy get back.

Kyoto glanced up at Janet, saying, How long? And the third wolf trotted away as if she meant to trot straight down Suicide Road, but went someplace else before she reached it.

Good-bye, Kyoto called; and Wasabe, Janet, and the ranger joined her. Good-bye! "Good-bye!" "Good-bye!"

"Do you know what I worry about?" Janet asked him.

"Sure. You're afraid one might bite a kid."

She nodded. "I'm afraid one may kill a child. How did you know?"

"Because I worry, too. I worry about every kid who comes into this park, but we have bears and wildcats. Do you know how many kids have been bitten by bears and wildcats put together since I've been here? I've been here six years."

She shook her head.

"Not a one. They've got wolves in Canada, just about everywhere except in the cities, and they've got wolves in Minnesota that came down from Canada. Do you think the TV news in Minneapolis and Toronto is yelling every day about kids torn to pieces by wolves?"

When she did not reply, his voice softened. "Can I tell you something? Wolves aren't half as dangerous as deer. Deer aren't nearly as smart, and the males get very aggressive in the fall. We've got more than a thousand deer in this park."

She pointed toward his car. "You've got a radio in there?"

He nodded. "I'm not going to use it, though."

"But if I put a bullet in it, you'll have to explain what happened."

He nodded again.

"All right." With her hand on the gun in her pocket, she shut the Expedition's hatch. "I'll take my chances."

"Thanks . . ." he said.

"What is it?"

He pointed to her left hand. "You're not married."

"No."

He tried to smile. It was not something he did well. "My name's Jerry, miss. Jerry Baumgarten."

She got back into the Expedition and whistled for the dogs. "This is the wild, wild woods," she told him. A glance took in rocks and pines and snow that she knew she would never forget. "In the wild woods, we Woolfs have no names."

As the Expedition pulled away, she watched its side mirror to see whether he ran for his car and its radio. He did not.

Suicide Road struck another road, a Michigan state highway, and she turned onto it, singing under her breath, a happy little song about a winter wonderland. There were curves and more curves, hills and valleys, pines, white birch and snow-covered bushes.

Then suddenly and incredibly an impossibly tall man in snowy white, with outstretched arms and the finest smile she had ever seen. She slammed on the brakes so hard that the Expedition nearly skidded off into the ditch.

In the blinking of an eye, the man in white was gone. Where he had stood, three snowmobiles flashed across the road.

Janet turned off the ignition, told the dogs to stay inside, and got out. There were no footprints where the man in white had stood, only the tracks of the racing snowmobiles that, if she had not seen him and braked . . .

It did not bear thinking about. She looked up and down the empty road, and listened to the sound of their racing engines until they faded to bright winter sunshine and clear blue sky. Slowly and stiffly she knelt in the snow, clasped her hands, and closed her eyes. *Thank you. Thank you very, very much. It was a pleasure, Lord, a pleasure and an honor to look after your dogs, even if it was only for a day. I'll be happy to do it again anytime.*

Back in the Expedition, traveling the state highway at a cautious twenty-five miles an hour, she waited for some word of thanks and approval from Him. There was none; instead, a vast questioning, as though God (too big to be seen) were waiting expectantly for something more from her.

What was it Margaret Bishop had said? Michigan, and another park someplace? Janet cast her mind back to the dark, crawling, jolting bus. A certain park in Michigan, and a new place . . .

"Saddle up, you li'l Scottie gals." She risked a small nudge of the accelerator. "Round up them wolves 'n' head 'em on out. We're a-goin' to Texas."

"Yip-yip-yippee!" the wheaten Scottie replied, speaking even more plainly than usual.

Ever loyal, Wasabe seconded her. "Yippee-ki-yi, Kyoto!"

> *She loosed the bar, she slid the bolt,*
> *she opened the door anon, And a*
> *grey bitch-wolf came out of the dark*
> *and fawned on the Only Son!*
> —Kipling

Oral

■

RICHARD CHRISTIAN MATHESON

"What do you want me to do?"

"Seashells. Have you ever touched one?"

"Yes."

"In a detailed way?"

"What do you mean?"

"Describe it to me."

"The shell I touched was on a beach in Florida. It was a nautilus with a pearly spiral. Rough and sharp on the . . . skin of it."

"Analogy of touch. Good. Go on."

"It was heavy."

"How heavy?"

"A pound. Maybe a pound and a quarter."

"Tell me about the inside."

"There were . . . slender twists. Corkscrews. Glassy surfaces like . . ."

". . . yes?"

". . . feeling the interior of an ancient bottle."

"Did you put your hands into it?"

". . . three fingers. I reached them in and they moved as if sliding on curved glass and they felt like they were gliding into a glove, they fit so perfectly. The walls were cool, and there were grains of sand that scraped my fingertips."

"Did your fingers get wet?"

"The interior was a little moist. I forgot that."

"Try to remember everything."

"I will. It felt . . . petrified. Is that the word?"

"Yes. Like rock. Hard and cold. Dead."

"But still alive. Able to sustain temperature and color. The contours were like a body. The textures seemed to be . . . feeling me."

A pleased stare.

"I made you feel something when I described the shell?"

"Yes."

"Like it was real?"

"Yes."

"Were you excited?"

"Yes."

"You could buy a shell."

"I don't come near what others have touched."

"People have touched everything. It's life."

"No. The opposite. Fingerprints signal oncoming death. Germs cling to surfaces. Waiting to cause illness, suffering. Disinfection is impossible."

Silence.

"But you miss touching things. You must."

Silence.

"Is that why I'm here?"

"Let's go on." Points. "The pencil."

"It's wooden. Painted to feel smooth. No heavier than a sugar cube. The name of the hotel is etched into the side like . . . inverted braille."

"What about the curves? How does the rubber feel on the eraser? Sticky? Firm? Angular? And the tip?"

"Well . . ."

"Frayed? Shredded? Or softly worn? Rounded? There's a difference." Impatient. "How about the sharpness of the point? Somewhat blunted and oval-ended or almost pinpoint? And the lead. Soft? Chalky? Hard like bone? Cracked on one side? Does it bend between fingertips?" Almost angry. "You didn't describe the metal collar that anchors the eraser. Is it serrated? Grooved? Does it have a curved rise? Several rings? A sharp edge at the seam where it anchors the eraser? Could it draw blood if you ran skin over it? Is the pencil tubular, or seven-sided, as is common design? Are the painted letters and numbers on the side more smooth than the painted section?"

"It's very . . ."

"Generalities. You have no feel for it."

"I'm sorry."

"I felt *nothing*."

Eyes downward. "Do you want me to go? You don't have to pay me anything."

A moment. A sigh. Gesturing. "The drinking glass."

She delicately picks it up.

"It's light, almost no weight at all. Cylindrical, warm from the hotel room heater. So smooth it seems to have no surface. So hard it has a brittle strength. A kind of tension like it could explode unexpectedly from the compacted frustration of the molecules."

"Interesting. Keep going."

"The edge where you touch it to your lips is rounded."

"Touch it to your lips."

"It rests on my mouth. Presses down my bottom lip. The upper edge of the glass touches my nose. It fits into my hand. Separates my thumb and index finger by two inches. It feels good to hold it. The weight and shape are comforting."

"Pour water into it. A little at a time."

"All right." Pouring. "It's getting heavier, I can feel the weight in my wrist. My fingers have to grip more tightly."

"Can you feel the coolness of the water through the glass?"

"Yes."

"Describe it to me."

"It feels the way it feels when you take your glove off on an early winter day. The first seconds your skin can notice the cold."

"Vague. Give me another example."

". . . the sensation of adding cold water to a hot bath and feeling chilly tendrils, struggling through the warm liquid to find you."

"Better."

"Can you remember that?"

"Yes."

"The water is climbing higher in the glass. A quarter inch at a time, splashing softly against the glass, spraying my hand with tiny, heatless droplets . . . can you feel it?"

"Yes."

". . . as it fills the glass, I feel the rising coolness, inside the glass, climb my palm. . . ."

". . . yes."

". . . there's a dew forming on the outside of the glass. I can feel it with the sponge of my fingertips."

"Keep going."

"I feel the droplets from this moist film seep between my fingers. And I feel the weight of the glass shift, as the water tips from side to side."

"Drink it."

She leans the glass back, against full mouth, swallows; a voluptuous drain. Looks at him.

"I can feel it going down inside me like . . ."

He breathes harder. Tightens; bends. Releases.

"Do you want me to describe it?"

"Later. I need to rest now."

Silence.

"We'll start again in a few minutes."

"All right."

"Think about the lamps. The phone. The faucet handles. I want to hear about them." His voice shrinks; a whisper. "Before I forget."

He closes eyes. Leans back on the motel bed.

She watches him from her chair. Wants to gently touch him. To reassure, stroke his sad face. Calm his heart. She wonders what happened to him. What hurt had crept oddly inward; shaken his world.

As he rests with eyes shut, she moves to him and slowly reaches. Then, as her warm palm nearly touches his cheek, she looks at her hand.

All at once, she sees the small, healing cut on one knuckle that provides an unlocked door to the viral body within. The fingerprints that provide soft alleys and canyons for the poisons of mankind; infinite hiding places for illness, invisible beginnings of pain and plague. The immeasurable death affixed to the underside of her nails, barnacled in the deep creases of her palm.

She quietly withdraws her hand. Sits back down in her chair, waiting for him.

Straw Dogs

■

TAEKO TOMIOKA

*E*ikichi was in the habit of saying "To make it short." I had no idea what he was making short, but he certainly liked the expression.

My favorite question was, "What would you do if we had a baby?" I always asked this question after I'd had sex with a young man, and I always looked forward to hearing their responses. This time Eikichi didn't say "to make it short"; he was silent.

"Well, what would you do? Shall I mail it to you through UPS?" I said, smiling. Eikichi looked relieved. But he still couldn't come up with any response to my teasing. I didn't pursue the question. It was only the initial reaction I found interesting.

More than once Eikichi had said that his name reminded people of an old man's name. He said it was his granddad who had named him. Not "grandfather" nor "grandpa" but "granddad"; that's what he called him. Seventysome years old now, he was a farmer in the countryside.

Ever since he'd entered the room I'd thought of nothing except what I could do to get Eikichi to have sex with me. No, actually, it wasn't only since he'd entered the room, rather I'd been thinking of nothing but seducing him ever since the first time I saw him. This was not just the case with Eikichi. I've always wondered whether a relationship can be established simply by the entry of part of a stranger's body into mine.

Eikichi hadn't said a word since he'd taken off his clothes. Our sex ended quickly. He didn't look embarrassed. He didn't attempt to explain. After he dressed he talked for a while about his dormitory and the people he worked with, frequently using the expression "to make it short." He also talked about a cheap nightclub he went to once with a guy from work.

"To make it short, I'll say that the girls are better off. The popular ones at that club are only twenty-one or so, the same age as I am, and they earn ten times what I make. They can make that much money simply because they're women." He became more adamant about the topic as he went on.

Listening to him, I said to myself: He'll tell his roommate at the dorm about this, our single encounter in our physical "relationship." He'll make it into a funny story. "To make it short, those ladies, those middle-aged women, aren't actually bad at all," he might say. Eikichi hadn't held my hand, and he didn't try to kiss me. When I sat on the bed, he went ahead and took off his clothes as if he were about to take a bath.

I've always been amazed by how easily and quickly that part of the male body can enter the female body. It seems almost comical the way it so smoothly slides inside me, and momentarily appears to achieve physical unity. Although this unity happens quickly and with amazing ease, most people expect connection to continue on through the dramatic stages of conflict, cooperation, ecstasy, and so on. I did not expect any of those dramatic experiences with Eikichi or, for that matter, with any other young men.

Still, each time I find that I'm impressed, even moved, by the fact that this part of a total stranger's body can come inside me so easily. Eikichi, for instance, was a complete stranger until yesterday. Today he is not only here with me, but for a while his body is inside me. I can't help marveling at the fact that a man who'd been walking outside on the boulevard in his suit came into a room and became naked. It was strange to see a naked man standing in front of me wearing only a wristwatch. Once I saw a naked body wearing only socks, which I found amusing. Another time I was struck by the sight of part of a man's penis showing under the hem of a white cotton undershirt. For some reason Eikichi didn't take off his wristwatch when he removed his clothes, and he didn't use that commonplace technique of sliding it off against my skin. I liked him because of this. When he was done, he stood up like a person who'd just finished moving his bowels and he put on his clothes, returning to his original self.

I didn't know why Eikichi had responded to my invitation and why he'd come without asking questions—I didn't care to find out. I only looked forward to the moment when a stranger, more specifically a young man I'd taken a fancy to, would enter my body, slipping inside me. I had no interest in finding out whether he did so because he was curious, or because he wanted to achieve ejaculation, or because he was attracted to me. As a rule I do not see the same man twice. What I couldn't help expecting was that a young man like Eikichi would be left with a certain vile feeling, an awful aftertaste, when the act was over. A woman who was no longer young, a total stranger, had made a pass at him and he had gone to bed with her without the involvement of either money or love. Secretly I expected to see this create a small, inexplicable dark space in his mind. Eikichi didn't satisfy this expectation. But his lack of response gave me a kind of sadistic pleasure.

"Sure, I've been to one of those places before, but the cafés with private booths were something else. With those setups you can't call it a café anymore. When I used to go to them you could sometimes see a woman's leg sticking out from the bottom of a thin curtain, you know. To make it short, people went there because they didn't have money to go to a hotel, don't you think so?"

Eikichi was chatting away as if he were talking to his buddy. According to him, these cafés had booths lined up in a row, like train compartments, each with two small chairs and a table only big enough to hold two teacups. They were divided by a thin board. When a man and a woman sit next to each other in these booths, there's no space for them to move about. In these booths young couples kissed and caressed each other, even had intercourse, Eikichi told me. No matter what people said, the space was too small for intercourse, so sometimes the table was kicked over and cups fell and broke. At other times you might hear a male voice trying to suppress a cry of excitement and see a woman's leg flying out through the curtain.

"Guys who have money wouldn't go to such a tacky place. To make it short, it's us who came out of the sticks with ninth-grade educations who would go there. If you're one of those who has his own room and parents who pay the rent, you wouldn't go to such a place. But if you live in a dorm you've got no choice. It's the same with girls most of the time. They agree to come along because they're interested in sex, right? But in the end most of them don't like it there. After letting you touch them a lot they say they won't do it in a place like that. In those days all I thought of was doing it. Thinking about it now, I was miserable, you know. All you'd see was a woman's leg sticking out from under a dirty curtain. You'd hear the noises from the next booth, you'd hear the guy asking to be let in. It's really cramped there, one square meter, that's all. Guys who can take women wherever they want in a car would never understand the feeling. To make it short, it reminds you of the night train carrying groups of kids into the city to work." Eikichi finished talking. Then he drank his tea, apparently without enjoying it, and prepared to go. When he returned to his dormitory, he would tell his roommates about his sexual encounter. As he was leaving, a gold metal button fell off his black sport coat. He picked it up carefully and put it in his pocket.

Yōji Tomoda left the university without graduating from the drama department when he was accepted by a theater group as a student actor. Soon he was given the lead in a play, a small studio production.

I saw Yōji for the first time on the day of the group's initial script reading. The moment I saw him I began fantasizing about having sex with him. He wasn't particularly good-looking but his features were large, well suited to a stage actor. He wore a black sweater and jeans, and carried his script in a dirty canvas bag.

"I saw a large mole on Yō's chest," said the middle-aged actress who played opposite him, smiling.

Yōji Tomoda was called Yō by the people in his theater group, who were all older than he was. When the producer said something to him, he simply said "yes." He wasn't talkative; between rehearsals he rarely spoke unless he had to.

I'd decided to wait until closing night. In the meantime I tried not to speak to him.

"Yōji isn't bad, what do you think?" the producer said to me.

"He's your type," said the actress. I felt that they were both trying to encourage me. It sounded as though the producer was asking my opinion of Yōji as a young man rather than as an actor.

"Yō, come and sit next to this lady," the actresses would say, pointing at me whenever we sat down to eat between rehearsals. Since no one in the group was his age, Yōji was isolated most of the time.

However, once he started acting, Yōji's voice was loud and powerful. He wasn't intimidated by the two middle-aged, experienced actresses. This attitude didn't seem to stem from naïveté; rather he seemed to be challenging someone, though not specifically the actress who played across from him. He was possessed by a free-floating, inexplicable anger.

"Yō's something else. During the second scene when he pushes me against the wall, trying to embrace me, you know, he kept stroking my back with his left hand. He knew no one could see it," said one of the actresses, the shorter one. They all laughed a little.

"Maybe there's a stage direction in his script," said the other actress. She seemed to have something in mind. They all laughed again. Yōji, who'd heard them as he came in carrying tea for everyone, didn't laugh.

"Do men serve tea here?" I asked.

"Yō is a student actor, not yet a member, that's why," said one of the actresses.

Rehearsals are usually boring for those who aren't involved in the play, but I went to the studio frequently in order to see Yōji. During my visits I didn't speak to him at all.

The two actresses are about the same age as I am, and I've known the tall one for many years. She is a large woman, but she has a voice and manner of speech too dainty for her role. However, when I heard her speak to Yōji her voice sounded cruel. I empathized with Yōji and felt his humiliation.

The closing night party wasn't very big. After all, it had only been a studio performance with three players. We went to a bar nearby and had some beer and snacks. Still, there ended up being about twenty of us altogether, including stagehands, friends of the players, and a few other members of the group. Yōji, who had served tea during rehearsals, refrained from serving drinks at the bar. He sat alone in the corner with his beer.

"I know you were looking at Yō all the time, I was watching you from onstage. It's disgusting," said the tall actress. She repeated this many times.

"I think Tomoda played well," said the producer, calling Yōji by his surname, with a hint of formality in his voice.

"Yō, come here now. The main actor can't be sitting in a corner," someone said, inviting him to join the producer and the actresses. He came, glass in hand, and sat diagonally across from me. After a while the stagehands and the producer left. Only a few of us remained in the bar.

"Please excuse me now. I have a rehearsal tomorrow," said Yōji to the actresses.

"You're in the next one, too?"

"Yes. A soldier," said Yōji. Soldiers simply walk across the stage when they aren't standing, so this meant he was returning to his original status of student actor.

The actresses and their friends started talking about Yōji, making it difficult for him to leave. Again they brought up the fact that I had been looking at him onstage.

"Mr. Tomoda, why don't we go somewhere else to drink?" I said, keeping my eyes on him as I stood up.

The others were amazed at my brazenness and watched us leave without a word.

Outside the bar there was a narrow street with cars lined up on one side. It was a place where taxis often waited for fares. When I realized I'd been grabbing Yōji's upper arm, I let it go and held his hand instead.

"We were able to get rid of those middle-aged women, weren't we?" I said. This was the first time I'd spoken since we'd left the bar.

"Let's go get a drink somewhere," said Yōji in a tone quite different from that I'd heard at rehearsals; he sounded like a young man talking to a friend.

He soon went back, however, to being reticent, even gloomy. It was rather cold out, but instead of a coat he wore a thin black sweater and pale blue jeans. He had on white high-top shoes, and carried his dirty canvas shoulder bag. He could pass as a student, but perhaps not as an actor. While we walked I kept telling myself that I had to make love to this man, as if I were on an important mission. I heard the loud voices of the actresses and the others talking all at once inside my head. You guys don't have to fuss and talk so loud, I answered them silently, with peculiar confidence. I won't fail to carry this out.

Yōji didn't attempt to pull his hand away from mine, and he didn't say anything. Earlier he had said that he wanted to drink more, but now he kept walking. He looked as glum as a student who'd just failed his entrance exams.

"Was it nice after that?" the tall actress would ask a few days afterward.

"I'm not interested in kiddy menus," I would say, to put a stop to her curiosity.

But now I started to feel depressed with Yōji next to me. When I realized that walking with his hand firmly in mine meant that we already had a physical relationship, I felt as if my sweaty hand were a part of my sex organs. I released his hand.

"Do you want to play pachinko?" Yōji asked when we came to a big pinball game parlor. Loud music blasted from inside. I told him I disliked pachinko. However, I couldn't think of a bar I could take Yōji to, and I disliked being with people who drank anyway. What I wanted was to find some place, like a shady spot under a tree, where we could sniff each other's bodies as animals do. Cafés with private booths like the one Eikichi described might exist for such purposes, but I couldn't imagine going to one of them, it wasn't my style. Now I didn't know what to do with my fussiness.

I kept walking, holding Yōji's arm. I sensed in him the humiliation and anger of a youth who, though first mentioning more drinking, had ended up inviting me to play pachinko. I felt like pouncing on his shame as if it were some helpless prey. Yōji wasn't glum just because a woman had made a pass at him, or because he was broke, or, for that matter, because he lacked the smooth words to turn the situation around. There was something else. I wanted to pull out the guts of his dark mood and devour them with my teeth. This desire was combined with my strange sense that my mission was to make love to him. I wondered if Yōji was humiliated because he sensed that he was being insulted by a woman. Perhaps his embarrassment was made all the more real because there hadn't been any sex between us. I continued to walk with Yōji, holding on to his arm. I must not do anything until he makes a move, I said to myself.

Before sex with Eikichi, I had fed him steak. Blood scattered from the steak as it cooked in the frying pan. When the blood mixed with fat, it turned transparent as water and ran out from the meat. This is like feeding and fattening an animal before slaughter, I'd thought as I watched Eikichi enjoying the food I offered. Now I wanted this gloomy Yōji to do something entirely different, but I was too anxious to wait until his shame and anger were neatly wrapped up, like tempura in batter, fried, and ready to eat.

We came across a takoyaki snack wagon. I bought a plateful and ate some as I walked. Yōji walked a few steps ahead of me, and when I offered him the takoyaki, he pretended not to hear. I thought if I had been a friend or a sweetheart his own age, he would eat. Or, perhaps if he didn't want to eat while walking, he would have said something like, "Don't do that; it's unsightly."

"But it's really good. People tease me for liking them so much, but these are my favorite snack. I can't resist the smell," I told Yōji in a loud voice. He walked ahead of me, looking even more despondent. However, he didn't leave me.

"Wait, don't walk so fast. My right leg's stiff. I have neuralgia, and when I get chilled, it gets worse," I said to Yōji. Then I grabbed his arm, dragging my leg. The neuralgia bit was only partly true. It was a ploy I used frequently to jar young men with the fact that they were going to have sex with an older woman.

I saw a telephone booth and went inside to check the yellow pages. Watching Yōji standing outside the booth, I dialed the numbers of several hotels, none of which had vacancies. I was finally able to make reservations at the last hotel, the farthest out and the most expensive. I stopped a taxi and told the driver to take us there. When we got to the hotel, I paid for the room. Then I tapped Yōji on the shoulder with the plastic tag that the room key was fastened to, and made him follow me. He'd been standing in front of the elevator like an animal that had been drenched in rain. Don't make an issue of your shame or anger now; you came with me because you wanted to, I said silently while we were in the elevator. I looked at him as if he were already my lover. There is really nothing two strangers, a male and female, can do but have sex.

Yōji didn't undress as if he were about to take a bath, like Eikichi had done. He remained silent except when he pulled open the curtain and said how beautiful the lighted streets were. When I turned around, there was this man in brand-new, white underpants instead of a black sweater and soiled jeans. For a fleeting moment the whiteness of his underpants told me something about his life. Then he slid under the white sheet without taking them off and lay there with his head sticking out.

"I've never been in an expensive hotel like this," he said distantly.

While I'd been walking with Yōji, I'd spotted places beneath trees where an animal straying from its herd could take refuge and rest. I thought such a place would make this young man feel more comfortable and natural. We were not like those rutting young lovers who went to cafés with private booths and let their legs stick out from the curtains. What we actually did, however, was the same. It was obvious that Yōji disliked this "expensive hotel," but I was ready to attack his gloom. Never mind his mood, I said to myself, trying to suppress a cruelty inside me.

His young, slender torso covered mine, and before I knew it, that part of him slipped into me. Somehow, from that moment on, I began to feel how superb Yōji's body was. It wasn't because of his sexual experience; it was something more subtle, as if his body actively sought physical contact with other bodies. This was a quality I'm sure he was born with. I remembered how this tongue-tied, gloomy youth had talked onstage in such a strong, sure voice. I felt at this moment that he was still onstage. His whole body seemed to reach every corner of mine. And yet I didn't think he was acting. There was an innate expressiveness to his body. He wasn't experienced with women and he didn't try to conceal it, nor did he take his partner for granted. His body told all of this eloquently. I was moved by this.

"You've done something naughty to Yō," said the tall actress to me sometime later.

"I didn't do anything naughty. I did something good," I replied.

Women my age are interested in the details of sex. They are eager to hear about the stage setting and dialogue that surrounded the act, and the techniques the male partner used to induce physical delight. I wasn't interested in giving out any details, and the actress's curiosity remained unsatisfied.

"A good thing? Was it very good?" she kept asking.

"Yes, it was good, so good that I contemplated a double suicide."

"How frightful! But I'm relieved. I thought you had some problem in that area. People tell me you're seducing young men right and left."

"Thanks for your concern but I think I'm normal. I believe in getting what I need, no more. I don't expect more than I need. But what I did with Mr. Tomoda was beyond my needs, you see."

"Then you're fickle."

"If you call it fickle, life itself is fickle."

"You're disgusting, as always."

Yōji spoke little and responded with his body to what I, a stranger, sought from him, and I understood intuitively what type of person he was. He approached me as an equal. His body was not affected by my age or my social status. I sensed some hostility, but he didn't seem to be conscious of it. His withdrawn mood continued, and it excited me. By the bed I saw a pair of neatly placed white shoes. Yōji Tomoda told me he was twenty-two years old.

I was surprised that he was still next to me when I woke up around six the next morning. Without opening his eyes he thrust his knee between my legs, and instantly his body was united with mine. In a moment of confusion, I thought we were lovers. He used his body as if he knew me well, and I couldn't help noticing his tendency toward a kind of commonplace male sincerity. I was slightly disappointed. I also felt peaceful, and lay there awhile.

I left the hotel alone. Stepping outside, I was assaulted by the bright light of morning and the sight of people on their way to work. The sight hit me like hard rain on concrete. In spite of such an assault, I did not let myself fall to the ground.

Shunsuke seemed to enjoy talking to me, but he gave no hint that he had sexual interest in women. His body didn't give off the semen smell characteristic of most young men. His thin chest, skinny loins, and childish face made him look like a high school student. But he said he was twenty-four years old. He was the nephew of a friend, and he'd been sent to my house by his uncle. When I met him, as usual I thought only of sex. I wouldn't have been interested if he had been one of those young men who seem to have semen stuck to their skin.

"You wear interesting clothes," I said, running my hand down the back of his jacket to the jeans that tightly covered his waist and loins. His jacket had a down lining, the kind that people wear for outdoor sports. It was bright red.

"You're warm from the waist up, but you must be cold down here. Tight jeans don't have any space for air, you know. Down is warm because it allows for a lot of air," I said.

"I heard ostrich down is hard to come by nowadays so they use guinea hens. But I think this is ostrich," Shunsuke said, smiling.

"When I'm on the train and a boy like you wearing tight jeans comes and stands in front of me, I always stare at him, you know. I wonder how that thing in there is doing in those tight jeans."

Shunsuke laughed in a childish way.

"Would you mind having a date with me next Sunday?" I said. I held his hand as he laughed innocently.

"Sure, it's okay." He looked at me expectantly.

"Then kiss me to show you've promised."

Shunsuke clumsily held my head between his hands, and I touched his chest. I felt the thumping of his heart; it made me think of ejaculation, not the pulsing of blood.

"Don't tell your uncle," I said, making him my accomplice.

The following Sunday, when I spotted him standing by the ticket booth, I was disappointed. Although I didn't expect him to come in a three-piece suit, I'd hoped to see him dressed in something other than such ordinary clothes. There was nothing about his dress or manner to indicate he was taking an overnight trip with a woman. He wore his usual jeans, an ordinary shirt and jacket, and carried a leather shoulder bag, which he seemed to have with him all the time. He was tall and skinny, and looked like a teenager. But he'd arranged for train tickets, a hotel reservation, and an itinerary without a hitch. And before he boarded the train he bought all the necessities: a newspaper, a magazine, cigarettes, canned beer, some peanuts, chocolates, and Kleenex.

At the hotel, which was the oldest and best known in the area,

Shunsuke inquired about departure times for the cable car and the pleasure boat. When we got to our room he immediately turned on the shower to check the water pressure. "This building was built in the old days," he commented.

"The boat leaves at four. We can make it if we go now," he said after a while.

"Let's do it tomorrow," I said, moving close to him.

The room was bright with strong sunlight leaking through the shutter of the western window. I was interested in nothing but sex with this man who looked like a high school student. I wanted to find out if sex would make some kind of connection between us.

Shunsuke started to take off his clothes and asked if I wanted him to undress. Then he placed his jeans, shirt, and underwear neatly on the back of a chair; even his socks were paired together. My clothes were scattered here and there on the floor.

"What would you do if we had a baby?"

"I'd put it on my back and go to school with a milk bottle," he said.

Through sex I try to discover something metaphysical about my and my partner's body. This is why I allow my body to be completely exposed, like a bag being turned inside out, with my sex organ as the opening. I'm curious to know if there are such things as spirituality and maliciousness hidden in the corners of this bag, waiting to be revealed when the bag is turned inside out by a stranger's sex organ. Shunsuke lifted one of my legs, and I wondered what he saw in there. "Is this good?" he asked, and I said, "More." "Look more carefully," was what I meant to say. The fluid coming out of my body would instantly dry up if my body were turned inside out.

The naked body of a man stepped across the stripes of sunlight made by the blinds. There was no trace of the darkness I'd felt moments ago as I clung to this thin, naked body; it had disappeared the way mist blows away. I felt comfortable, as if I'd just had a bath. Touching the shoulders of strangers always alarms me when I walk in crowded places; my body tenses. People's gazes often make me feel so uncomfortable that I look away. And yet I held the naked body of this man, a stranger, simply because I felt like it. This woman, who is reluctant even to shake hands with people when such a formality is required, connected her body to a stranger's without hesitation. This is a mystery, I thought, while absently gazing at Shunsuke's naked back in the stripes of sunlight. He had none of the heavy sullenness that I'd seen in Yōji.

"I find it erotic to do this at this time of the day, don't you?" said Shunsuke.

"What? Erotic? Why?"

The word "erotic" repulsed me; it stuck in my throat. And I'd lost interest in him now that sex was over.

A man's small buttock was in front of my eyes, looking like an alien thing. Now it was on the other side of a plastic shower curtain, with hot water splashing over it. I sat on the toilet seat. The wet face of a stranger peered from the plastic curtain. Shocked to find a woman on the toilet, he disappeared back inside.

"It's all right, you can come out. Haven't you ever seen a woman peeing before? You can see it now," I said to him. The stranger rushed out of the bathroom, all wet, trying not to see the woman. Inside the toilet bowl I noticed some opaque fluid floating. The semen of this man-boy. Suddenly, I felt like laughing—the whole thing seemed comical. There must be men who have wives at age twenty-four, some even have children. Shunsuke came here with me like a boy being invited to a picnic. He showed he knew how to deal with a woman in bed. He wasn't even timid when he caressed me. Afterward, he took a shower, enjoying it like a child would after a play in the pool.

"We should have our dinner somewhere else. I heard there are some well-known restaurants here that serve freshwater fish," said the man-boy in tight jeans cheerfully.

I opened the blinds and I saw a lake in the distance. I felt like staying in the room, alone.

"Doesn't this view of the lake make you want to try double suicide?" I said. I wanted to provoke him. Sightseeing wasn't what I had in mind at all. Shunsuke looked at me, bewildered. His slender torso and long, skinny legs were now in his clothes; his white-socked feet inside his high-top shoes. When he talked, his canine teeth showed a bit. I thought a lover might find this charming.

"Don't you feel like going somewhere now, just disappearing?"

"Shall we? Let's go somewhere far away," he said. He called me by name for the first time. Then he looked down with an intensity in his face, provoked by my words. I felt that my interest in him would last another day.

                              *   *   *

"Does your mother wear glasses?" I asked Shunsuke later as I took my glasses out to read the menu. This was one of my usual schemes, like my neuralgia bit, although I actually did need glasses.

"I think she uses them when she reads."

"I can't read anything without my glasses, even if I go like this," I said, holding the menu away from me.

"Have you had that problem since you were a child?"

"Don't be silly. These are bifocals."

Shunsuke just looked at me, not knowing what to say.

"There's nothing strange about wearing these after forty, you know."

"But you don't look so—"

"Appearance and reality are two different things," I said, staring at Shunsuke's face through my glasses.

"I don't believe you're forty," he said in an angry voice.

"But I am."

"Still, I do want to go somewhere far and disappear," I added after a while.

"You don't mean abroad, do you? I know I can manage anywhere in Japan, but I've never been abroad. But let's go anyway, somewhere far."

"We're not going for a picnic."

"You want to live somewhere far away, don't you? I can work and support us."

"You can?"

"Since I decided to come here with you, I've been thinking of marrying you. It's true."

"You're still in school."

"I've finished college. I'm in graduate school because I don't want to work. I'll quit school if you marry me."

It was hard to believe he was in graduate school, but I didn't think he would lie. Just as I'd been eager to have sex with him, I now felt a certain excitement in cornering him.

"You are still a dependent, so you have no idea how much money one needs to live on, even for a month. I detest living in poverty," I said.

"A dependent?"

I held Shunsuke's hand under the table while I kept my eyes on a young waiter in a white jacket and black tie. The way he was standing indicated he was a temporary. He didn't deal with the diners like the other waiters did. As I continued staring at him, his white jacket and trousers disappeared, and he became a naked man, looking down at his feet. I wanted to say something to him. I was already imagining having sex with him.

Shunsuke's gloom, which until now had been hidden deep inside him, started to surface. Just a short while ago his body had been on top of mine. He had looked like a gymnast on the horse, his legs and arms stretching and bending; in the end he had collapsed with a low cry. Now he was in front of me, dressed in his clothes, eating and talking about work. The time Shunsuke spent naked in bed with this woman was now forever sealed; it floated in the air, untouched, while real time passed. No one else could see how Shunsuke had changed in this passage of time. A male peacock spreads his feathers to show off before a female prior to copulation; the human male gives gifts to a woman whom he is going to marry. Someone once told me these are parallel courtship rituals. It is only humans who attempt to seal away what has come out of their sexual intercourse. The semen that came out of Shunsuke, so boyish and not very sexual, was left floating in the toilet bowl; it got there after passing through a woman's body. Shunsuke entered a woman's body without spreading his feathers. Now he had removed himself from all smell of sex and had talked about supporting this woman. I enjoyed this contradiction. In Shunsuke, whose outward appearance was asexual, I had nonetheless detected, like an animal with a keen nose, the smells of maleness and sex—and these smells compelled me to seduce him.

"You don't have to worry," he was saying. It was as if his voice came from a far distance. I was imagining that I was an animal quietly eating the food brought to me in my cave by a young man called Shunsuke. At that moment I had a feeling that people might call happiness, a sensation I hadn't experienced before. It hovered in the air momentarily, then disappeared.

"In this faraway place what would I do all day while you work?" I asked. I intended to let myself fall into the chasm of happiness, dragging Shunsuke along. I wanted to indulge myself for a while.

"You've lived forty years already. You can take it easy, sleep."

"I'll probably date another young man."

"You won't make me give up. I'm going to marry you. I don't give up easily once I make up my mind."

We bantered like this for a while before returning home. My anger had increased so much by then that I was ready to kick Shunsuke and be rid of him.

The relationship established through sex with Shunsuke made it clear to me that I could hope to live as an animal. I believed that the happiness I would gain then would surpass even the rapture of sexual climax, when we momentarily forget everything else. Men who boast of their skill in giving women sexual pleasure have never interested me because of this belief. To live as an animal would mean to give up both physical relationships and words. For this reason Shunsuke's sexuality would have to be destroyed, just as straw dogs are burned after the festivities.

I dialed the number printed on the matchbook I'd picked up at the hotel. I wanted to speak with that tall, temporary waiter. I had managed to obtain his name from another waiter. "That tall waiter is Mr. Yamamoto, isn't he," I asked. I got the response I wanted: "No. That's Unno." As I dialed, I remembered my excitement at hearing his name.

Rin'ichi Unno probably came out of curiosity.

"You remember me having a dinner with a young man, don't you?" I said to him.

"People often approach me like that," he responded.

"You're approached by customers often, then?"

"I'd say so. But I usually say no. If the manager finds out, he'll fire me," said Rin'ichi.

"Even temporary employees?"

"I'm not a temporary. I have another month of provisional status, though. I dropped out of high school so that's why I have to work hard."

"Well, I appreciate that you've come then. I wanted to see you, you know."

"What do you want by seeing me?"

"I want to go to bed with you."

"You say things very bluntly," said Rin'ichi, averting his eyes from me and looking down.

Rin'ichi glanced at his wristwatch, then he lit a cigarette. His fingers were unusually long. I imagined that those fingers were going to touch my body. He ground out his half-smoked cigarette in the ashtray, took out another, and tapped it on the table. I watched the movements of his bony, slender fingers. He wore a blue jacket, and perhaps because of it, his face looked a bit pale.

"When I approach a girl, I don't say things as directly as you do," he said, forcing a smile.

"Do you do it as they do in the old-fashioned love stories then?"

"Girls like that, you know."

I felt my desire to have sex (which is not the same as sexual desire) quickly fading as I listened to this young man sitting across the table.

"Why did you pick me?" he asked as he stretched his long legs under the table.

Why did I pick this man: a waiter who looked like a kid working as a temporary? He wore exactly the same uniform as the rest of the waiters. My eyes had spotted him among several other men who looked the same. Why indeed had my eyes settled on this particular man, Rin'ichi Unno? But they had, and that seemed enough. Yet Rin'ichi asked me to explain. Does he want me to say that he looked particularly handsome among all those in uniform, or that he made a good impression on me? Does he want us to go through those same lines: "Why do you like me?" "Because I do."

That my eyes went to Eikichi, Yōji, Shunsuke, and then Rin'ichi seemed to be the same as when some people are always noticing strange-looking plants with large flowers, while others are absorbed by looking at dilapidated houses, or the faces of old people. It wasn't that my eyes simply fell on these young men. Rather I'd say that they had seemed larger than life to me, as if I were looking at them through a magnifying glass. Eikichi came along when I'd told him I'd treat him to a steak; he hadn't asked why. When he'd finished eating his steak, he took off his clothes as if he were about to take a bath. I didn't have to say that I wanted to go to bed with him.

"I think women shouldn't say those things so openly," said Rin'ichi. "Of course women have sexual desire, too," he added.

"Sexual desire?" I said in a low voice, which came out of me in spite of myself, like vomit.

"Yes. I said women have sexual desire."

"That's obvious. But I don't, you can bet on it."

"But you said you wanted to go to bed with me."

"Wanting to go to bed and feeling sexual desire are two different things."

"How old are you really? Young women don't say things like that. Men have pride, if you really want to know," said Rin'ichi, smiling at me.

"I feel a lot of sexual desire now, but I don't feel like going to bed with you." I smiled as I stood up.

Outside, the street was full of people sightseeing. There were small children everywhere. Because it's a holiday, I thought. I walked, trying to avoid them, thinking they looked like worms emerging from their holes all at once. When I'd had dinner with Shunsuke, I had spotted Rin'ichi standing several feet away, rather than the other waiter who was in charge of our table. But why? Rin'ichi had been holding a silver tray, yet he looked to me as if he were standing there naked. Come to think of it, Yōji Tomoda, too, was there—a glass of beer in his hand, naked. It was the same with Eikichi and Shunsuke.

Children were running around, raising dust from the pavement. I saw a roller coaster silhouetted against the distant sky. It must have been moving slowly, but from where I stood it looked like it was standing still. I walked, drinking 7UP from a bottle. How did I appear in men's eyes? I wondered. I didn't have a "look" to label me with a certain job, to show I was a wife, or a mother. The sky was pale blue and flat as a photograph. I went toward the amusement park, looking for a man I wanted to have sex with. If I found one, I wanted to do it on the spot. If I caught a man looking at me, wouldn't that mean that he wanted to have sex with me, too? Rin'ichi must have come with such an intention, but my interest in having sex with him had left me before we began a physical relationship. My humiliation passed through him without touching him.

I sat on a bench by a large pond near the center of the amusement park. A drake was gliding on the water in front of me, and a child was throwing bread. There was, as always, a parent nearby, and when the child uttered a word or two, the parent responded. The drake was leaving silently. If mankind did not reproduce we'd get to the end rather quickly, and that would be good, I thought. But the moment I entertained this thought, a shiver of fear came over me; I thought people might see through me. I crouched on the bench, trying to shut out the inquiring eyes of passerby.

I saw an oden shop, which was covered in front with a reed screen. "What time do you close?" I asked a young man, seventeen or eighteen perhaps, who brought me a beer. He gazed at me intently for a moment and said that the shop closed at five. His eyes smiled faintly. Déjà vu, I thought: I've witnessed this scene before; I've been a part of a scene just like this. Although he was tall, the waiter could have been as young as fourteen or fifteen. And yet his male splendor was shining in his eyes as he looked at me.

"We close at five, isn't that right?" he asked someone as he went to the back of the shop. He sounded guileless. "A customer's asking," he said as he disappeared into the back room. Then I heard a low male laugh seeping out that room.

I'm going to sit down on the bench outside and wait until five, I thought. He'll come out of that room sooner or later. He can't die in there.

I am repeating the same behavior, I said to myself, as I stood in the warm wind that swirled dust around me. I had patiently waited for Izumi Motofuji in a dry, cold wind. I would wait exactly as I had before and then I would make love to this young man who would soon come out of that shop. There were some taxis waiting outside the amusement park entrance. I would lead the young man into one of those taxis, like a kidnapper, and take him somewhere. Between the shop and the taxis was only about a hundred feet. I could get him to the car without difficulty. I would say something that would interest him. While I walked with him, I would take his hand or hold his arm, acting like it was natural for me to do so. The shorter the process of getting to sex, the better.

Rin'ichi had wanted to enjoy not the intercourse itself, but the ritual surrounding it, an affair. Izumi Motofuji, age seventeen, had taken a taxi with me to my house; he'd left immediately after having sex. And he had gone forever. His face had been blank. He had twisted his lips stubbornly as if saying he would never confess under torture. He won't ever tell, I thought, remembering his expression. I believed he wouldn't give in easily. A gentle accomplice to a small crime, that's what he'd been. He hadn't asked why I was interested in him. He came to my house with his school bag on his shoulder. When he took off his black school uniform, a plastic box full of English vocabulary cards fell from the pocket. He hadn't even asked my name. The intercourse had ended very quickly, but I had felt a physical connection with him. Izumi's sex organ had entered my body. Excited, it functioned as if it had a separate life. Izumi hadn't seemed to be aware of the possibility that his penis was there to excite the woman and give her pleasure, that he could pierce the woman and her pleasure together like a skewer for barbecuing chicken and onions.

What withers away after repeated sex that goes on and on like the rainy season is enthusiasm, but that isn't all; the relationship itself dies. Pleasure seekers often refuse to acknowledge the point at which the height of pleasure reaches a plateau. With their bodies, they risk the extinction of their sense of self, and yet their bodies also assist this same self as it tries to crawl out of its extinction. When one holds tightly to a sense of self during sexual pleasure, one's partner becomes a mere physical object. Such relationships soon give way to disillusionment. Two people who lie side by side after orgasm are merely two bodies, breathing hard, emptied out, powerless and incapable of anything, like large rotted fish washed up on a shore. Those who go after pleasure are forcing out their bodily fluid. I'm not that type of pleasure seeker.

People were leaving the amusement park. The shop was still open, and I could see the young man moving around in the shop. He seemed to be cleaning up before closing. He wore a short white apron, like a chef's apron. Would he come out at five o'clock? Would he say the same things as Rin'ichi had? Or would he, like Izumi Motofuji, come with me shamelessly?

A man who looked twenty-seven or twenty-eight sat on the bench across from me. He was smoking a cigarette and staring at the pond. He wore pale trousers and a thin, light-green jacket, suitable attire for a holiday outing. A lone woman was a rare sight in this recreation park, where most of the visitors were with families, and occasionally in pairs. It was also unusual to see a man alone. The man in the light-green jacket appeared to be an ordinary white-collar worker. He looked tired and seemed to be resting on the bench. He was smoking a cigarette. I was attracted to his ordinariness.

"Does the park close at five, do you know?" I asked when he looked toward me.

"Since it's a holiday today I think they close at six. That thing over there is still moving," he said, pointing at the Ferris wheel.

"I see. But I don't think they'll let me on now."

"I think they will. I bet they'll operate it for even one passenger."

The large reed screen in front of the shop had been removed now, and a middle-aged man was closing the glass doors at the back. I couldn't see the young man in the white apron. But he should have been coming out any moment. He had no idea that he'd attracted a woman, and the other men in the shop probably didn't think he was particularly attractive to women. Even among children, some will stand out as sexual beings in the eyes of adults of the opposite sex. Women who look quite ordinary in other women's eyes are sometimes attractive to men. It's the same with men. This mystery will never be solved.

"It's five already, isn't it?" I asked the man in the light-green jacket.

"What? Oh, yes," he said, looking at his watch.

"Why don't we ride on that thing over there?" I said, keeping my eyes on the shop.

"What?" He turned his head to look at me.

"Do you want to ride it and then go somewhere?" I said again.

"That wheel?" He stood up.

"Yes, ride it and then go somewhere far. . . ."

The man was about to leave, ignoring me, but he came back and stared at me.

"I think we'll be able to see everything from there, all the people. And then, we can go somewhere far from here and . . ." I trailed off, looking up the man. He looked away as if trying to avoid a light glaring in his eyes. Then he looked at the ground like a child who didn't know what to say.

At that moment I saw a boy, four or five years old, running toward us.

"Why don't we go somewhere?" I repeated.

"What do you mean by that? What are you doing here, anyway?"

"Daddy!" the child was nearing us, still running.

"What I mean is that we should go somewhere and have a good time."

"You're crazy, aren't you? This is where kids have fun." The man raised his voice and several people walking with their children stopped. The man raised his voice even more. "You're insane, trying to pick up a man at a place like this. Something's wrong with you."

Now people were staring at us and beginning to crowd around us.

"Daddy," the child called and ran to the man, who, still talking loudly, picked up his son. Then he put the child down and hid him behind his back, as if to protect him from me.

"This is a place for children to have fun," he repeated. "So don't you say anything weird. I'll call the police if necessary."

The man was standing with his feet slightly apart, shielding his son. He looked like a mother protecting her child against an enemy. The number of spectators was increasing.

"Let's go, Daddy, Mom wants you to come," said the child, pulling the man's hand.

I sat there stiffly, both hands gripping the bench. I might have looked like a person with a terrible stomach ache. From an opening in the wall of people that surrounded me I stealthily watched the oden shop. Parents and children stared at me; I heard voices from behind the wall of people, asking what was happening. The young father left, holding his son's hand and repeating words of reassurance: "It's all right." Other people began moving on.

Absent-mindedly, I tried to remember what I'd said to the man. He'd taken my words "have a good time" as an attempt to lure him into a sexual encounter. I felt like a person who, after realizing he has been a victim of extortion, still can't help being impressed by the skill with which the scheme was pulled off. When I said "have a good time," I meant having sex. But I didn't mean to "allure" him. And what did he mean by saying to his child, "It's all right"?

The oden shop was closed now, but no one came out. At the back of the shop was a high stone wall, so even if the young man had left from the rear he would still have to come around to the front, where I was watching. I couldn't have missed him. A middle-aged man had gone toward the back door earlier; he must have gone inside. I'd seen a few men going into the shop, but none had come out. I heard a loudspeaker announcing that the park was closing at six. I saw someone pulling a brown curtain across the glass door of the shop. Several long tables and small plastic chairs that had been outside were all gone now. Without those tables and chairs and the reed screen, the shop looked naked. Someone had been cooking oden in back, but no one had come out yet. It was a small, shabby establishment with reed screens on three sides.

There have to be several men in that shop, I kept thinking. That young man who looked seventeen or eighteen and another fellow were waiters, and it seemed there were two or three more in the back room of the shop. Another man went in. He wore a gray shirt, like those worn by the men who worked in the flower garden. Now many people were walking toward the gate but I sat on the bench in front of the oden shop, watching. There were less than five feet between me and the shop. I couldn't have missed. . . .

Two more men in gray shirts went into the shop, this time through the front glass door. A gray shirt seemed to be the uniform of the park employees.

A man in a gray shirt came up to me and told me that the park was closing. There was no one around except me. I stood up and pretended to walk toward the gate, but when the man had gone, I sat on the bench again. The man who'd told me the park was closing also went inside the shop. Then, a few minutes afterward, another four or five men went in; they paid no attention to me. Yet no one had come out of the shop. The back of the shop was a high wall of rocks over which tree branches hung heavily.

Even while the man with the child was loudly protesting my conduct, I'd kept a watch on the shop through the cracks in the wall of spectators. I hadn't seen that young man come out of the shop. I was no longer thinking of him, however. Instead, I gazed at the shop, the cheaply assembled building. As I watched the building intently, it seemed to swell. Since more men had gone inside, it had expanded. Now, two more went toward the back door. It was getting dark, the twilight setting like mist. Two men in gray shirts came toward me, pulling a large metal trash can. There was no doubt now that the shirt was a workmen's uniform. They saw me but didn't tell me to leave.

How many had gone into the shop? I'd lost count. Although it was now dark, there was no light inside. But I kept watching the shop from the bench by the pond. I had lost interest in the young man— my interest was now focused on the small shop where they sold oden. The small, cottagelike building had swelled up with so many men inside. I was not interested in those men. I simply found it amazing that so many men could fit inside. Another group of men went in but now it was impossible to tell whether they wore gray uniforms. There were at least ten. Then, another black shadow appeared from the direction of the big wheel and disappeared into the shop. I wondered if there might be a tunnel connecting the back door to somewhere outside. Otherwise it was a complete mystery. Lights went on here and there in the park, and a lamp near the bench where I sat formed a circle of bright light around me. People could see me well now. The shop just stood there, still dark inside. In the darkness outside, it was swelling. From that building they should be able to see me well. But no one was coming out to tell me to leave.

Rope-Bound

■

JOHN A. DAY

*H*er shift had been minutes from ending when Charlie walked into Buddy's All Night Café on Route 57. You got used to pickup lines from lonely truckers when you worked the night shift, but something different about Charlie attracted her.

From the minute he strode into the café his eyes locked on Amy and tracked her as she served dinners and refilled drinks. He ordered black coffee and a piece of apple pie. The pie, he said, was sweet, but not as sweet as her. It was a hokey line, but when he said it, staring intently into her eyes, it had seemed real, not contrived; so when her shift ended and he asked her to join him for dinner, she accepted.

Charlie led her to a faded red '78 Chevy pickup. When she tugged on the passenger's door, it wouldn't open. Charlie grinned. "Sorry 'bout that," he apologized. "The door's stuck. I've been meaning to fix it but never got around to it."

He opened the driver's door. She slid across the bench seat. Charlie ground the ignition until the truck started, then shifted into first and spun out onto Route 57, heading away from town.

"Where are we going?" Amy asked. Depending on which direction you drove on the highway, Buddy's All Night Café was either the first restaurant in twenty miles or the last. "What's out this way?"

Charlie grinned slyly, a wicked I've-got-a-secret smirk that said plainer than words that he wanted more than dinner. What he wanted and what he would get were two different things. She didn't know anything about this guy; didn't really care to. She had just wanted to get away from the diner and her apartment for a while. Her eyes flicked to him, then back. A few kisses would be easy enough, he was handsome when he wasn't leering. If he wanted more than that she had mad money in her purse and a can of Mace.

"Sorry I didn't tell you before," he said. "I've got to drop something at a friend's. It's a life-or-death situation. Then we can go on our little date. Don't worry, we won't be delayed much."

The wind from the open window displaced the air that had grown stale and flat while he charmed her in the diner. August in Texas, even hours after the sun dropped below the horizon, stole life with heat. The gusts played with his hair—thick, black, and curly, styled longer in the back and short on the top like the younger, newer country stars.

He glanced at her and smirked. She liked his smile less each time she saw it, becoming uncomfortably aware of the growing distance from town. The cab was quiet except for the rush of wind and the song of passing traffic; he didn't seem to want to talk, and if she opened her mouth she knew she would reveal her nervousness by blathering on and on. He wore a blue work shirt open at the collar to reveal a thick mash of black hair, jeans, a leather belt with a fist-sized silver buckle, and black boots scrapped and roughened by long wear. A faded blue nylon garter, edged with white lace, dangled from the rearview mirror. She hoped it hadn't been from his wedding, although it wouldn't be the first time she had dated a married man. A glass rosary and silver cross swung from the mirror, surprising her since he hadn't seemed to her the religious type.

She worried at a hangnail. When he had said dinner, she had been thinking of a burger and coffee. What if he wanted something fancy? She wouldn't go by her apartment to change. Not with this guy. Not yet. Maybe not ever.

Solitary lights, scattered on the flat horizon, spoke of lonely farmhouses. She felt lost in all that emptiness. Where the hell were they going? The Mace in her purse suddenly seemed poor protection. It was a long walk back to the diner if things went wrong.

"I think we should turn around," she said.

He grinned again. "Don't worry, honey, we're almost there. Everything'll be all right. I promise."

He turned right onto black asphalt. After the lights of the highway, the sky startled her with an inky blackness she hadn't seen since a child; every star a visible pinprick. The moon was an orange sliver on the horizon. Oaks and elms, humping dark shapes on a black background, divided the fields. Rusting barbed-wire fences bound the road on both sides.

Every few seconds he checked the rearview mirror, as if watching for someone. It made her nervous. As if sensing her fears, he grinned again. Definitely a leer this time, she thought. He made no attempt to hide it.

He turned onto a road so ancient and ill-used the asphalt had returned to chunks of black rock and white gravel. He slowed the truck and turned off the motor. It pinged as it cooled.

"We're there, darling. Now you can get what you've been waiting for."

He edged across the seat and pressed her against the passenger door. She struggled with his hands, which seemed to be in eight places at once, then slapped him. He cursed. Enough of this jerk! She was walking back, whether it was one mile or eighty. She scrabbled at the door release. Her hands found a hole in the door paneling and inside—the remains of the gear. The bastard had removed the door handle so she couldn't get out. He grabbed her again, mashing her against the door, squeezing the breath from her lungs while smearing kisses across her cheeks.

"Ug . . . get off me! Let me go!" She scratched him furiously, long nails leaving parallel streaks of blood across his cheek. When he grinned again, there was nothing of joy in it, only darkness and hate. His eyes were bitter pills. He drew back his hand and slapped her.

"I can play it rough," he said. "In fact, I prefer it that way."

He struck aside her guarding arms and snapped her head into the truck door. Her mouth flooded with a bitter, copper taste. While she was stunned, he flipped her over, pulled a section of rope from under the seat, and tied her hands behind her. She bucked, kicked, screamed, and wept into the plastic seat. His hand slipped under her skirt. He stroked her, then hooked the waistband of her panties and pantyhose and slid them slowly down—over her hips, down her thighs, past her knees into a pile at her ankles. He spun her onto her back, pressing hot, sweaty lips on hers while fumbling at his belt.

"Wait," she said with a gasp, trying a smile, abandoning it as it weakly failed, and licked nervous lips, tasting lipstick and his sweat. Her mind flicked over everything she knew about rapists. The cops were split on the subject. Some said to fight, others said to give in and ride it out. Easy for them, they couldn't be raped. Funny all the dark streets she had walked, nervous, fearing an attacker from every dark alley, from every passing male, her hand ready on the can of Mace attached to her keychain, her lips ready with a shout. Now it had happened and she was stupidly unprepared. The can of Mace might as well be on the moon for all it would do for her.

If, however, she got him out of the truck long enough for her to get back in—

"Wait. I want to do it, but not here. Not in these tight quarters. Let's do it outside, under the stars."

He hesitated, gave her a distrusting look, obviously divided between raping her in the cab or in the road. She smiled again; it felt plastic on her face. He nodded and opened the driver's door. She struggled to sit up. He reached into the cab and she fleetingly thought he would release her. The delicate hope lit her brain like lightning, but he snagged her ankles and yanked her out of the cab. Her head struck the runner, then the pavement, as he hauled her out of the cab. Sparks whirlpooled before her eyes as he dragged her across the rocks to behind the truck. He dropped her onto the asphalt and fumbled at his belt.

Her head felt loose and wobbly. Pain jingled down her scraped back and arms. He loomed above her, silhouetted against the stars, his pants and underwear about his ankles, his breath rushed with desire. A primitive reflex screamed in the back of her brain, the gibbering ape raging and afraid—but cunning from outfighting or outrunning every predator to live, to mate, to produce a chain of survivors from the first primitive ape to her. Reflex told her what to do. She kicked with every ounce of frustration and fear at the crux of his legs. He howled and collapsed, retching.

She struggled to her feet.

Charlie choked with dry heaves. The ape gibbered louder in her head, moving from hindbrain to fore, the reflex changing from fight to flight. The open fields beckoned, a place to run, to hide. To draw him away from the truck. She kicked off her shoes and the lingerie wrapped about her heels and dove through the barbed-wire fence into the field.

She ran through waist-high weeds; her eyes focused on the dark line of trees, on the promised safety of the woods. Her arms, trapped behind her, canted her balance; several times she barely caught herself from falling. Her chest heaved. She drove on when she felt she couldn't run any more, despite lungs that felt loaded with hot needles. Too terrified to stop, she ran on. Charlie might catch her.

The ground had been plowed once, when cotton was king—long enough ago that oaks had sprung up and grown taller than a house. The hills and burrows of the cotton rows remained hidden under weeds. Amy's foot caught in a burrow and she tumbled. Her neck whipped as she struck the earth; vertebrae popped. She stifled a gasp.

Got to keep moving. Can't stop. Her legs moved but refused to lift her. Her heart pumped blood in overdrive, building pressure until she felt her brain would explode. Her lungs failed her when she needed them most. There wasn't enough air. Lord!—she didn't care if Charlie found her, if only she could rest a little while longer.

When her shift ended, she had heard on the diner radio that it was still 85 after a high of 102 that afternoon. She panted and wished she could wipe the stinging sweat out of her eyes. Her father once said that the body sweated to cool itself. Something called evaporative cooling, he had said, like the water-cooled fan on their front porch. Water dripped on mossy panels around a barrel fan; the fan sucked the moisture off the wet panels and fed it into the house. Coming home on summer's days, she would stand in the breeze of the fan, letting the cool air lift her sticky blouse off her skin and push her hair away from her face in feathery wings. The water-cooled fan was the closest thing to an air conditioner in those days.

She didn't think her sweating cooled her much tonight; the hot and humid air pressed against her. *What I wouldn't give for a fan or a bit of breeze.* She rested her head in the dry, shattered undergrass and crumbling soil. Every movement coated her skin with a batter of dirt and grass. She didn't care.

A gentle breeze rustled the weeds, a sound like a blue taffeta dress she had once worn. Cicadas hummed, crickets strummed, and a bullfrog sang low and deep. A long gash on her thigh, sticky with dirt and blood, throbbed painfully. Her shoulders ached from the unnatural position forced by her bound wrists. The rope scraped her skin—already raw and bloody.

She twisted to examine the knot. A sharp jab in her neck brought a gasp to her lips. She twisted again slower and traced the path of the rough hemp around her wrists. She couldn't see where it began or ended. The bastard had done a good job. *Have to find something sharp. Cut myself free.*

Amy fumbled grass stalks and moist soil, scurrying insects—and who knew what—searching for a sharp stone or stick. Nothing. She slumped in defeat, her breasts rising and falling with exertion.

A stick snapped in the grass nearby. She stilled her panting and listened. Nothing. Wait—was that a snippet of song? He was singing? Careful to not rustle the tall grass, she brought her eyes level with the tops of the weeds. Charlie was perhaps a hundred feet south, between her and the truck, a blob against the skyline. Something white flashed in his left hand. He brought it up to his face and sniffed with relish. She couldn't quite see what he clutched in his other hand, but feared it was a gun.

"You can't hide from me, little darlin'. I know where you are! I can smell you!" He shouted. His head traversed like a bloodhound sniffing a trail. She froze, even her heart seemed to hesitate, so strong was her wish to be silent, to wish him to pass by.

Involuntarily she ducked as he seemed to stare at her. The grass rustled and waved.

"There you are! Wahoo!" He raised his right hand and fired a shot. She shrieked and scrambled, running in a blind panic toward the woods. His feet thumped behind her. A second shot blasted out.

She broke from the open fields into the trees and the darkness became absolute. Branches thumped her, limbs snagged her hair and scratched her face. She raced, unheeding, until a limb thick as her arm smacked into her throat. She spun on her neck, then smashed to the ground. She gagged and choked, breathless, but struggled to her knees. Got to get away. Got to keep moving!

Her arms were numb. She staggered like a drunk. Crunching leaves shouted her position with each ragged step. Unexpectedly, the ground dropped away. Her foot wavered for a minute in the air, then landed roughly, sliding, in thickly piled leaves. She tumbled uncontrollably, became airborne for a shocking second, then splashed into black waters.

She was directionless, any way might be right or left, up or down. She kicked frantically, spraying water. Her head struck murky bottom and she gagged on rancid mud. Amy twisted, kicked the creek bottom and lunged, gasping, to the surface.

The creekbank, two feet over her head, had been sharply undercut by the flowing water. She examined it with defeat. *I can't get out that way.* She trudged downstream, following the gentle flow of water. Her feet sank a few inches into sticky muck before hitting a firmer surface.

She tried not to think of crawdads and snakes.

As a young girl, she had fished for crawdads with her brother along the muddy banks of creeks like this one, tying raw bacon to a string and lowering the bait into the turbid water of a crawdad hole. After a few minutes, a tug would pull up a surprised crawdad, its claw clamped obsessively on the greasy meat. Crawdads didn't have enough sense to know a trap when it snuck up and landed in their claws and didn't know to let go when pulled out of their hole, so she had to shake the string until the claw slipped loose. Once free from the lure of the bacon, the crawdad would seem to wake from a trance and, embarrassed at being caught by such an old trick, would scuttle backward for his hole, pushing with his one large claw, his tail curled under him. Some people ate crawdads, she had heard, but not her brother or her. Crawdaddies were filthy creatures good only for catching repeatedly with the same dumb trick until the bacon, waterlogged and pinched thin, fell off the string into the hole and the crawdad won after all.

The last trip, they had been walking down the sandy bottom of a mostly dry creek when they surprised a nest of water moccasins. The deadly black snakes coiled and whipped in a puddle at their feet. Father heard their screams and ran with his shotgun. The shotgun had vaporized the snake heads. Their flesh splayed out like a celery garnish, spraying blood. Their bodies had twisted and flopped for long seconds after they should, by all rights, have been long dead. She had been both fascinated and repulsed—by the deadly snakes, by blood and death itself, and by her father's strength and courage. Even dead, they frightened her as if their bodies would infect her with their blood or as if their venom oozed into and poisoned the soil where the five black snakes had slept and dreamed their evil snake dreams of sharp, poisonous teeth and little-girl ankles. She had wondered if the soil would die from snake poisoning and if the venom could seep through the ground, through her Keds, and into her flesh. She scrubbed her legs that night until they were raw, to wash away the snake venom.

So she tried not to think of snakes.

The creekbank rose and fell, sometimes waist-deep, sometimes below her knees. Finally it flattened and she climbed out. Her snaggled hair clung to her face, mud streaked her uniform, and water glistened on her legs. She wondered if the water had loosened the rope enough for her to slip free.

She struggled against her bonds, twisting one wrist away from the other. Her arms rotated within the rope but wouldn't pull free.

Amy squatted and curved her back to bring her wrists over her hips. A twinge shivered up her spine. She persevered, straining to draw her arms below her hips. It was like trying to push an egg into a soda bottle, but the mud helped to grease her thighs and after a few minutes of grunting effort, her arms slipped past her hips. She straightened with relief. Now it only remained to remove her legs from the loop of her arms. She hunched, digging her legs against her breasts, thrusting until her breath pinched out in short gasps. First one foot slid from the circle of her arms, then the other. She flopped into the leaves, exhausted, not caring whether she lived or died, whether Charlie found her or not.

She almost drowsed, all energy spent. The moon had moved above the horizon and lit the woods in silver light and sharpened shadows. For the first time the trees were distinct entities, not amorphous blobs, but boles sharp and distinct with thrashing limbs and blades that alternately blotted and revealed the stars. The leaves hissed, the stream gurgled, and something—something just across the creek— hummed. Hurriedly, she brushed leaves onto her legs and dress and ducked behind the poor protection of a shrub just as Charlie stepped out from behind a tree.

He strode through the dark woods, as if on his way down a well-lit boulevard to buy a pack of cigarettes at the corner 7-Eleven, the gun gripped in his right hand. He had pulled a white baglike cloth with two large, saggy eyeholes in front, over his head. He hummed as he walked, occasionally breaking into words, and sniffed as he swung his head back and forth.

"Hm-mm. Hm-mm. Follow that girl, pick her up, give her that magic touch. Hm-mm. Hm-mm. Follow that girl, pick her up, give her that magic touch. Hm-mm. Hm-mm."

Thirty or forty feet away, he dropped to the ground and sniffed, then edged closer to the water. Did he think he could smell her? Did he think he was a bloodhound? The man's insane, she thought. She froze as he came to the water's edge. He stared at her suddenly—she knew she was hidden; she had to be!—but he seemed to look straight into her eyes. Behind the mask, his eyes were large and white; the bag and eyeholes made him resemble some kind of bizarre human/panda transplant. She itched to jump up madly and dash until her last breath. Only her will kept her silent and still.

He stared across the water at her. He began to chuckle, a bubbling, watery sound like a brook breaking over rocks, rising gradually into a horrible laugh that sounded like the ignition of an old Ford, grinding and trying to start on the coldest night of winter.

"I see you, girl!" he yelled. "Not with my eyes. I can smell you! You're in those bushes and you're thinking if you just lay low I'll pass on by! Charlie, he can't possibly see me. Well, you're right, girl! That's real smart! Only thing is, I know you're there. And I'm coming to get you. So you better run, girl, run!"

He threw back his head and howled.

Her body snapped upright without a thought, leaves scattering from her like feathers, and she bolted. His laughter followed her.

"Run, girl, run! Run! Hide! It don't matter. Where you gonna run to? We're all alone out here and I can follow you wherever you go! Sooner or later you're gonna tire, then I got you! And, oh, how sweet you'll be! Sweeter than pie!"

She snapped a glance behind. He crouched, unmoving, as if giving her a head start. She forced leaden legs to pump, to leave the shadows of the trees and cross the open field. In her heart, swamped in the vapors of fear, burned a little spark of hope. The truck was in front of her and he was behind her. If she ran hard enough, long enough . . .

The adrenaline burst didn't last; her speed lagged. She collapsed at the fence, spasms cramping her stomach, heaving, all energy spent. Sweat was sticky on her face. Her lungs sucked in giant gasps as she fought panic. *He won't stay at the creek; he'll pass through the woods*, she guessed, *where I can't see him until he comes to the road. If only I could get out of this damn rope!*

She gripped the rope with her teeth, sucking bracken water as she tore at the knot. Water swelled the fiber, binding the loops as tightly as if set in concrete. She spat out mud and grass and studied the distance to the truck.

The half moon, a full hand's span above the shadowy horizon, lit the fields. The road was a black tongue between grassy fields. The windshield of the truck reflected moonbeams. He'd see her the minute she stepped onto the road. She'd be as obvious as a whore in a church. Not that she had any choice. If she remained by the fence she would be raped, then shot by that bastard. Or shot, then raped. She sucked in a quivering lip and slid between the barbed wires into the road.

Rocks bit into her bare feet. The black asphalt was eerily like a moonscape, an old black-and-white broadcast from the moon: the black, rocky soil, the barren light on empty land, and the feeling of exposure. No space suit protected her from vacuum, none needed, yet she felt at any moment there would be a puncture and her life would bleed out of her. She bolted for the truck.

The door squealed as she scrambled inside. The interior flooded with light, dazzling her after so long in the dark, and she slammed the door, then was blind again while her eyes adjusted. Her hands searched the ignition for the keys. Nothing. The bastard had taken them! She ground her teeth in frustration. Maybe he had dropped them. She bent to search the floor.

The windshield exploded. She didn't hear the gunshot, but glass showered over her and she screamed. She remained hunched, trembling, hearing shoes thud up the road and heavy breathing.

Somewhere in the cab was a can of Mace. Her fingers fumbled over sharp shards of glass. *Damn!* Her purse was open; the contents spilled over the floor. She knelt to make the search easier, not caring as glass bit into her knees. Her doubled hands scrabbled through the purse's contents.

The door opened.

Charlie stood in the light. The mask hid his smile, but she knew he leered. His eyes crinkled with laughter.

"Well, well, well!" he said, all jolly. "Here we are again. You did all that running around and what did it get you? Hot, tired, wet, and beaten. You look a mess."

His eyes stroked her mud-coated legs, her tangled hair, her blood-streaked face. He shook his head. "You should have just let me have my way. Things would have gone a lot easier and you would have enjoyed it a lot more. Now, as it is, I don't know if you're going to enjoy it that much."

He laid the gun on the roof of the truck and ducked into the cab. She realized for the first time that he had made a mask of her panties: the waist to the back of his head, legholes for eyeholes, and the crotch of her panties across the bridge of his nose. She felt violated, like he had already had his way with her. As he leered at her again, she swung her arms up—and sprayed Mace. He shrieked and fell out of the cab, clawing at his eyes. The spray, in the close interior of the cab, gassed her, too. She gagged, tears streaming from her eyes, and scrambled out of the truck. She struggled against nausea and rubbed her eyes on her uniform until she saw again through watery, blinking eyes.

She snatched the gun from the roof. Charlie rolled, moaning, scrubbing his face in the Johnson grass. His eyes had swollen to mere slits. She held her arms rigid, pointing, the gun at the apex.

"Give me the keys, Charlie."

"Or you'll what? Shoot me?" He grinned. She wanted to wipe that grin in the dirt. She wanted to pull the trigger again and again so no woman would ever have to see it again. He pulled the keys out of his pocket and jingled them, taunting her. "You haven't got the nerve."

She reached for the keys. "Toss them on the ground in front of me, then step back."

He grinned and flipped them away. They sparkled in the light from the cab, then disappeared into the darkness of the field. She cursed.

"You crazy bastard! What did you do that for? Now we're both stuck!"

He shook his head, stood up. "No. You're stuck. I'll just hitchhike on the highway or steal another truck." He stepped closer. "But what are you going to do? You can't survive like me. You aren't tough. You don't have the balls to survive. You've got to be tough or you'll get taken. Again."

He shuffled forward. Her arms quavered.

"Stop or I'll shoot!" she cried. He laughed and moved closer. The gun bucked in her hands, surprising her by the remarkable kick that shook her hands and arms, even to the shoulders when she squeezed the trigger. The gun flamed. He cried out.

A spot appeared on his shoulder, then spread, darkening a region first the size of a quarter, then the size of a fist. His face faded to white with shock, then rage flooded his face.

"You bitch! You slut!" He shouted and stepped inside her arms. He struck her. The gun flew from her hands and slid under the truck as she spun with the force of the blow. He slapped her again, knocking her back against the truck. He bent, grabbed her ankles, and yanked. Her feet shot up and she landed roughly on the asphalt. He undid the silver buckle on his belt, whipped it off, threw it to the ground.

"That's it! No more Mace! No more guns! You've got nowhere to run and I'm going to give it to you—hard!"

He thrust her legs apart. She twisted, groping with both hands for a rock, a stick, anything. He unzipped his pants and grunted, lowering himself into position, pinning her against the truck. Her hands touched his disgarded belt. In desperation, she spun, whipping it full force into his face.

The silver buckle bit his eye. Blood spurted. He slapped both hands to his eye and bleated like a wounded puppy. She rolled under the truck, groping for the gun. His cries changed to curses.

"My eye! You ruined my eye, you bitch! I'm going to kill you!"

The gun was silhouetted against the ground. She fought to grab it as he seized her ankle. She kicked him and stretched, longer, tighter, knowing this was her last chance.

Her outstretched fingers touched the gun as he yanked her back. She clutched it and spun around.

He snarled like an animal. His face was smeared with blood and scarlet with rage. One eye was red and puffy; the other, a crimson explosion. He didn't seem human to her.

"I'm going to kill you. Kill you!" he promised, wrenching her from the undercarriage. She thrust the gun in his face; he ignored it, swept up in an animalistic rage.

She squeezed the trigger. Once. Twice. The shots echoed between the pavement and the steel undercarriage. She didn't flinch.

When his hands had been still on her ankles for a time, she kicked them viciously away and rolled out from under the truck. She staggered over to the open door and sat, within the comforting light, on the runner. The moon shone on empty fields, the grass waved in dark shadows, moved by an easterly breeze. The distant highway moaned. The moon had risen more than a head above the horizon. *How quickly does the moon move? How long have I been running, struggling?* It seemed a lifetime. It seemed like another person who had been trusting enough to ride with a stranger.

She regarded the body wedged under the rear wheel, the body half in, half out, and still as death. Like a snake, some things are so dangerous, you have to take out a gun and blow off their heads.

She folded her head into her rope-bound hands and began to cry.

Women's Stories

■

JANE YOLEN

There are two fathers I do not understand:
the one at the bridge,
devil's bargain still warm on his mouth,
kissing his daughter first, saying:
"Do I have a husband for you";
and Abraham, with his traitor's hand,
leading Isaac up the hill to God.

These are not women's stories.
Even before I birthed my three,
and the one bled out before its time,
and the one encysted in the tube,
even before that I would have thrust the knife
in my own breast, before God;
I would have swallowed the kiss,
gone back to the beast myself.

Job's wife has her own story.
Lot's pillar of salt cried tears
indistinguishable from her eyes.

Who invented a glass slipper
never had to dance.

Do not try to climb my hair.
Do not circle me with a hedge of thorns.
My stories are not your stories.
We women go out into the desert together,
or not at all.

How-to Books & Other Absurdities

■

ERICA JONG

Distrusting advice—
there is no one she wants to be
but herself—
although sometimes
she wishes
herself dead.

Who can tell her how to live?
Ms. Lonelyhearts—
with her heap of red letters?
Doctor X—
with his couch shaped
like a coffin?
Mr. Sex—
gimlet-eyed
cock-of-the-walk,
with his cakewalks & tangos,
his mangoes & bitter persimmons,
his helium balloons
bursting on branches

& his condoms
that glow in the dark?

No.
She turns her back.
Mistakes: she will make them
herself.
Love: she will choose,
like the rest of us,
badly.
Death: it will come
when it will come.

& Life: not reasoned or easy
but at least
her own.

Heat

■

NANCY HOLDER

*I*t is so easy to blame others, and Genevieve did, but perhaps she had cause. Her husband when he began his affair with her was most attentive, most ardent, and, most importantly, most available.

But as soon as their names were on the marriage license, all signs of wooing ceased: no more flowers, no more expensive gifts, and very few passionate hours.

Very few: Having tamed the mistress, having made a wife of her, he had lost interest.

She should have anticipated it, perhaps even accepted it as an ironic, although just, punishment. But she was so used to his adoration that it had never occurred to her that anything could happen to change it. In her naïveté she had believed that his offer of marriage was a culmination, a triumph, the prize.

Now, these hot, sultry nights of a Tokyo summer, when the illuminated Tokyo Tower so resembled the Eiffel Tower that tears sprang to her eyes, she lay alone in bed watching the beautiful soft-core pornography of her native France on laser disc and touched herself, pretending her hands and fingers were his.

As illicit lovers, they had often watched such movies, both aroused by the perfection of the bodies as they writhed and clung together. He had been fascinated to discover that she, too, found pleasure in the beautiful breasts and hips of the women. Most women did, she informed him. They had been trained to from birth—witness the dozens of fashion magazines, the advertisements, the preponderance of closeups in movies and on TV. Their softly lit, airbrushed bodies as men took them in various positions sent her into a dreamlike state of receptivity that drove him wild.

They had coupled in the corporate apartment in Harajuku, in hot springs resorts on Hokkaido, in a charming inn at the southern tip of the Izu Peninsula—the golden tip, the dark pink tip at sunset, dipping into pearl drops of ocean foam as the water eternally tantalized the shore.

He had bought her pearls, and a Mercedes, and fabulous underthings that he would put on her very slowly, and rip off her with his teeth.

Now, he "worked late." Now, he "had to entertain clients."

It occurred to her that he had probably found himself a new mistress.

She opened her legs to her lonely fingers and imagined herself confronting him, making a tremendous scene. But his wife—his former wife—had done that, and had it helped her win the battle?

But Hiroyo had lost the moment Kenji had lain eyes on Genevieve. Attached to the French consulate, Genevieve had helped him with some import documents; as thanks, so he said, he had asked her to have dinner. It was the beginning, and it was glorious.

Poor Hiroyo. Now Genevieve recalled their lunch, the defeated general laying down arms before the victor. Genevieve had almost tried to apologize:

"I'm so sorry, Owasawa-san, but he's so perfect. I couldn't refuse him."

Hiroyo had picked daintily at her luncheon omelette, the garnishes of strawberries. "I think living as a wife will go more easily for you, Debeau-san, if you do not think of my husband as perfect." She picked up her coffee cup and held it in both hands. "No man is perfect." She sipped. "They are heartless."

Poor Hiroyo.

Poor Hiroyo, indeed. An earthquake of a divorce settlement, and word was that she had moved in with a man two-thirds her age who was willing to slice open his bowels for her.

Genevieve rolled over on her stomach. Sweat trickled between her breasts. Her silk and lace nightgown twisted around her buttocks; she rotated her hips against the satin pillow positioned there, just so. She let the bodice of the gown pull taut against her nipples as the fabric soaked up the moisture. The thick, wet summer air saturated the flesh of her buttocks. She was hot, and wanting. She wanted him, his thick muscles and his tight chest and his exquisite penis. He knew how to move with her, in her; he knew what to do, and when. He was the finest lover she had never known, and she had assumed, perhaps foolishly, that it was because he was with her. Skill born of desire, and love.

The door to their penthouse opened.

She caught her breath and listened to the familiar jingle of his keys. He was home.

She began to pull her gown over her bottom, but wives did that. Mistresses made sure to put on their highest high heels, to daub a bit of perfume along the Delta of the Nile, awaiting the inundation.

She lay as she was, panting a little.

He went into the kitchen and poured himself a drink. She heard the splash of liquor and the tinkle of ice cubes.

She waited.

After a time she began to dose.

When she awakened and heard the TV, a slow anger burned through her. *How dare he?* The anger built. She moved herself against the pillow. The satin caressed her sex, the shell-pink folds and spirals of pleasure, and she moved against it harder as her mind turned red. Unthinking bastard.

She moved harder.

Pig.

Harder.

Harder.

Harder.

The small of her back rippled and tingled. Eddies swirled in her abdomen, her loins, her thighs. Her nipples were erect.

Arrogant *Jap.*

The pleasure began to ascend toward ecstasy. Her breath came in gasps, barely came at all. She gripped the headboard. She would slap him if he came in. She would throw something at him.

She saw his face spiderwebbed with blood. She saw a bruise on his check.

With a tiny shout deep in her throat, she climaxed.

It was not a large orgasm, not her best or deepest, but it was release.

Some minutes later, Kenji came into the room. His suit jacket was slung over his arm, his white shirt unbuttoned three buttons, his tie loosened. His hair was damp from the heat. He was the most incredible man, broad-shouldered and muscular, his hips narrow, his thighs large and well defined. His cheekbones were astonishing. She couldn't believe she had called him a Jap.

"I was awake when you came home," she said.

"Then why didn't you come to me?" he asked. Of course. A Japanese wife would have had dinner and a hot bath waiting. Summer or winter, they loved their hot baths.

Uneasiness washed over her, and though he began to undress slowly, seducing her, she felt absolutely no passion. Nothing stirred within her, and she was astounded: This was Kenji! This was the lover supreme! He smiled his lazy smile and let his pants drop to the floor, followed by his underwear. He was enormous. His balls were full and heavy. The mere sight of his erect penis usually made her very wet. Now she stared and felt nothing.

Her lack of interest was not because she had recently played with herself. She could come again and again. When they had first gotten together, Kenji had marveled at her capacity, her appetite. He was thrilled that she was nearly insatiable.

Now he approached the bed and stood over her. She made herself smile and open her arms. Like a cat, he began to climb onto the mattress, slinking up and over her. He pulled down her bodice and touched and caressed her breasts, one and then the other, pinched the nipples.

She could only think that she should have made him something to eat.

He kissed her. She opened her mouth and let him slide his tongue in, allowing him to explore before she touched his tongue in return. It was the way he liked it.

She should have made him a bath.

He nudged her legs apart and entered her in a long, sliding motion that filled her.

When he had come home, she should have gotten up and greeted him.

He thrust hard; she was still moist from having masturbated. Otherwise, the movement would have hurt her.

Bastard, she thought fiercely. Bastard for not making sure she was ready. And since when did her life revolve around someone else's? In Japan it was a man's world, but she was not Japanese. If he'd wanted a simpering slave he should have stayed married to Hiroyo. He was a thoughtless jerk. He was just like—

Heat overtook her. Her nerves overloaded, her pleasure centers, and suddenly she was clinging to him, thrusting with his rhythm, crying out. He murmured to her in Japanese, calling her his little fox because there were no words of endearment in his native tongue. She hated it; he knew she did because she had asked him not to ever call her that again. And he had promised, after she told him about the Belgian woman in Paris who had said those same words in German, and Genevieve, not realizing the sexual import of the term, had politely said, *"Ja?"* and the woman had raped her in an alley with the end of an umbrella.

How could he say that to her? He had held her while she cried. Insensitive boor!

She came, hard, and he followed after. She wanted to scratch out his eyes. Instead, spent, she collapsed into the mattress and lay still as he fell against her.

In the distance, an ambulance *bee-booed* through the Tokyo dawn. Summer heat, summer fires. Luckily the traffic slackened in the wee hours after the hostess bars and Pachinko parlors closed down. She remembered a spring night in Shinjuku when they had gotten their fortunes told. For her, something blasé: good fortune and conjugal felicity. For him, something odd: Beware a hot wind. How they had laughed at the absurdity.

Kenji, her Kenji. He loved her. She snuggled into his embrace and told herself she was imagining things. Everything was all right. Exhausted, she began to drift. She would never be able to move again, speak, open her eyes. She had never felt so wonderfully drained in her life.

"Make me some tea," he said.

"Oh, Kenji," she protested.

"I'm thirsty." He waited.

She clamped her jaw. He wasn't even asking. He was demanding. Anger surged again.

And with it . . .

. . . desire.

She opened her eyes wide. Allowed the anger to build. Desire built, too.

She looked at him and he nudged her impatiently.

It was all she could do to keep from smacking him.

And sucking him.

Unsteadily she rose from the bed, not because she wanted to obey him but because she needed to think. His seed spilled from her body and she found herself wanting more. Needing more.

"First," she said, and put her leg on the bed.

"First, tea." He smiled at her expectantly.

Her anger grew.

She walked from the bedroom into the living room, lay on the couch, and brought herself to another climax.

Then she got up and dutifully made him tea, trembling all the while.

He did not have a mistress after all.

So Genevieve invited Arja, a statuesque Finnish girl, to their next dinner party. Arja wore a very revealing black satin dress. Genevieve seated her next to Kenji. He ogled her all night, not bothering to hide it. Genevieve was furious.

In the kitchen, on the pretense of preparing espresso, Genevieve brought herself to climax.

Kenji offered to drive Arja home.

Genevieve came three times, and twice more when Kenji finally came home, smelling of the other woman's perfume, of her sex.

It was true, then. She had proven it: Her anger at him made her desire for him all the more intense.

Think of the ecstasy if she could come to hate him.

She had lunch with Arja, a complex woman who was obviously wrestling with her conscience and her sense of triumph at the same time. She wore a large ring Genevieve made a point of admiring; Arja colored and murmured something about it being new, from a friend, but the smile couldn't quite stay from her lips. Genevieve was even angrier with Kenji that he would find such a bitch alluring. How dare he? How *dare* he?

That night she met him naked at the door and pulled off his clothes. She asked, hissing at him, "You're hungry? You want something to eat?" and dragged his head between her legs. He was thrilled. His pleasure made her rage. She came and came; seething, thinking about hurting him in some way, about the knives in the kitchen. About . . .

. . . stabbing, her own form of penetration. . . .

She was shocked; she pushed him away and walked to the panorama windows of the penthouse living room, whipping open the drapes and looking down on the vast jewel box of the skyline. Kenji's seed sparkled on her thighs like diamonds; heat rose from the streets, twenty-four stories below.

He came up behind her and cupped her breasts. She clenched her fists as she began to pant. He kissed the side of her neck and whispered, "I have to go away tomorrow. I have to go to Osaka for two days."

With her. Genevieve moved her legs apart so that he could slide his fingers into her. She was sick; she was insane. This had all begun because she missed his companionship and attention, and now she was deliberately courting the absences so that she could get off. She was destroying her love for him for sexual pleasure. But was it not his fault? If he weren't so thoughtless and faithless, would all of this have come about?

"Bastard," she said hotly, but under her breath. Every part of her was hot. Very, very hot.

Would she hate him if she pushed him through the window? If she was left with her remorse and her grief, would she be able to sustain a cold, dark fury?

It seemed that steam sizzled off her body. It would be easy. The windows were actually two horizontal pieces of glass one opened and closed with latches. They were flimsy and she had already asked the manager to replace them.

"I'll need a suitcase for the morning," he went on.

Hate was the opposite of love, they said, but at some point, would it not dissipate? Would she then be left with nothing?

"Kenji," she whispered, turning around, trying at the last to save him. "Kenji, I want a divorce."

He looked startled. Saying nothing, he took a step back from her. She stared at his perfect brown skin, his almond eyes. His sexy, pouting mouth. Would she would hate him for leaving her more than she would hate him for dying?

He inclined his head and said, "I'll give her up."

She almost smiled. "There will be others."

"No."

"Yes." She opened her arms to him. "There must be others for you, Mr. Fox." If he lived. And she must hear of them, all of them, and be bitter, and angry, and rich.

For she realized at last that Hiroyo, Kenji's first wife, was correct: No man was perfect. No man.

And there were hundreds of men in Tokyo who could incite her to heights of hot, delirious anger.

Hundreds.

If not thousands.

The sweat rolled off her.

"On occasion," she whispered to him, "we must fuck."

"*Nan desuka?*" he asked in Japanese, bewildered. *What?*

But maybe not. What had the Shinjuku fortune teller told him? *Beware a hot wind.*

As the old story went: *Which shall it be, the lady or the tiger?*

"Now open the window, Kenji. It's sweltering in here."

He moved. She began to pant. She was so hot.

So very hot.

The Wife's Story

■

URSULA K. LE GUIN

*H*e was a good husband, a good father. I don't understand it. I don't believe in it. I don't believe that it happened. I saw it happen but it isn't true. It can't be. He was always gentle. If you'd have seen him playing with the children, anybody who saw him with the children would have known that there wasn't any bad in him, not one mean bone. When I first met him he was still living with his mother, over near Spring Lake, and I used to see them together, the mother and the sons, and think that any young fellow that was that nice with his family must be one worth knowing. Then one time when I was walking in the woods I met him by himself coming back from a hunting trip. He hadn't got any game at all, not so much as a field mouse, but he wasn't cast down about it. He was just larking along enjoying the morning air. That's one of the things I first loved about him. He didn't take things hard, he didn't grouch and whine when things didn't go his way. So we got to talking that day. And I guess things moved right along after that, because pretty soon he was over here pretty near all the time. And my sister said—see, my parents had moved out the year before and gone south, leaving us the place—my sister said, kind of teasing but serious, "Well! If he's going to be here every day and half the night, I guess there isn't room for me!" And she moved out—just down the way. We've always been real close, her and me. That's the sort of thing doesn't ever change. I couldn't ever have got through this bad time without my sis.

Well, so he come to live here. And all I can say is, it was the happy year of my life. He was just purely good to me. A hard worker and never lazy, and so big and fine-looking. Everybody looked up to him, you know, young as he was. Lodge meeting nights, more and more often they had him to lead the singing. He had such a beautiful voice, and he'd lead off strong, and the others following and joining in, high voices and low. It brings the shivers on me now to think of it, hearing it, nights when I'd stayed home from meeting when the children was babies—the singing coming up through the trees there, and the moonlight, summer nights, the full moon shining. I'll never hear anything so beautiful. I'll never know a joy like that again.

It was the moon, that's what they say. It's the moon's fault, and the blood. It was in his father's blood. I never knew his father, and now I wonder what become of him. He was from up Whitewater way, and had no kin around here. I always thought he went back there, but now I don't know. There was some talk about him, tales, that come out after what happened to my husband. It's something runs in the blood, they say, and it may never come out, but if it does, it's the change of the moon that does it. Always it happens in the dark of the moon. When everybody's home and asleep. Something comes over the one that's got the curse in his blood, they say, and he gets up because he can't sleep, and goes out into the glaring sun, and goes off all alone—drawn to find those like him.

And it may be so, because my husband would do that. I'd half rouse and say, "Where you going to?" and he'd say, "Oh, hunting, be back this evening," and it wasn't like him, even his voice was different. But I'd be so sleepy, and not wanting to wake the kids, and he was so good and responsible, it was no call of mine to go asking "Why?" and "Where?" and all like that.

So it happened that way maybe three times or four. He'd come back late, and worn out, and pretty near cross for one so sweet-tempered— not wanting to talk about it. I figured everybody got to bust out now and then, and nagging never helped anything. But it did begin to worry me. Not so much that he went, but that he come back so tired and strange. Even, he smelled strange. It made my hair stand up on end. I could not endure it and I said, "What is that—those smells on you? All over you!" And he said, "I don't know," real short, and made like he was sleeping. But he went down when he thought I wasn't noticing, and washed and washed himself. But those smells stayed in his hair, and in our bed, for days.

And then the awful thing. I don't find it easy to tell about this. I want to cry when I have to bring it to my mind. Our youngest, the little one, my baby, she turned from her father. Just overnight. He come in and she got scared-looking, stiff, with her eyes wide, and then she begun to cry and try to hide behind me. She didn't yet talk plain but she was saying over and over, "Make it go away! Make it go away!"

The look in his eyes, just for one moment, when he heard that. That's what I don't want ever to remember. That's what I can't forget. The look in his eyes looking at his own child.

I said to the child, "Shame on you, what's got into you!"—scolding, but keeping her right up close to me at the same time, because I was frightened too. Frightened to shaking.

He looked away then and said something like, "Guess she just waked up dreaming," and passed it off that way. Or tried to. And so did I. And I got real mad with my baby when she kept on acting crazy scared of her own dad. But she couldn't help it and I couldn't change it.

He kept away that whole day. Because he knew, I guess. It was just beginning dark of the moon.

It was hot and close inside, and dark, and we'd all been asleep some while, when something woke me up. He wasn't there beside me. I heard a little stir in the passage, when I listened. So I got up, because I could bear it no longer. I went out into the passage, and it was light there, hard sunlight coming in from the door. And I saw him standing just outside, in the tall grass by the entrance. His head was hanging. Presently he sat down, like he felt weary, and looked down at his feet. I held still, inside, and watched—I didn't know what for.

And I saw what he saw. I saw the changing. In his feet, it was, first. They got long, each foot got longer, stretching out, the toes stretching out and the foot getting long, and fleshy, and white. And no hair on them.

The hair begun to come away all over his body. It was like his hair fried away in the sunlight and was gone. He was white all over, then, like a worm's skin. And he turned his face. It was changing while I looked. It got flatter and flatter, the mouth flat and wide, and the teeth grinning flat and dull, and the nose just a knob of flesh with nostril holes, and the ears gone, and the eyes gone blue—blue, with white rims around the blue—staring at me out of that flat, soft, white face.

He stood up then on two legs.

I saw him, I had to see him, my own dear love, turned into the hateful one.

I couldn't move, but as I crouched there in the passage staring out into the day I was trembling and shaking with a growl that burst out into a crazy, awful howling. A grief howl and a terror howl and a calling howl. And the others heard it, even sleeping, and woke up.

It stared and peered, that thing my husband had turned into, and shoved its face up to the entrance of our house. I was still bound by mortal fear, but behind me the children had waked up, and the baby was whimpering. The mother anger come into me then, and I snarled and crept forward.

The man thing looked around. It had no gun, like the ones from the man places do. But it picked up a heavy fallen tree branch in its long white foot, and shoved the end of that down into our house, at me. I snapped the end of it in my teeth and started to force my way out, because I knew the man would kill our children if it could. But my sister was already coming. I saw her running at the man with her head low and her mane high and her eyes yellow as the winter sun. It turned on her and raised up that branch to hit her. But I come out of the doorway, mad with the mother anger, and the others all were coming answering my call, the whole pack gathering, there in that blind glare and heat of the sun at noon.

The man looked around at us and yelled out loud, and brandished the branch it held. Then it broke and ran, heading for the cleared fields and plowlands, down the mountainside. It ran, on two legs, leaping and weaving, and we followed it.

I was last, because love still bound the anger and the fear in me. I was running when I saw them pull it down. My sister's teeth were in its throat. I got there and it was dead. The others were drawing back from the kill, because of the taste of the blood, and the smell. The younger ones were cowering and some crying, and my sister rubbed her mouth against her forelegs over and over to get rid of the taste. I went up close because I thought if the thing was dead the spell, the curse must be done, and my husband could come back—alive, or even dead, if I could only see him, my true love, in his true form, beautiful. But only the dead man lay there white and bloody. We drew back and back from it, and turned and ran, back up into the hills, back to the woods of the shadows and the twilight and the blessed dark.

Bits and Pieces

■

LISA TUTTLE

*O*n the morning after Ralph left her, Fay found a foot in her bed.

It was Ralph's foot, but how could he have left it behind? What did it mean? She sat on the edge of the bed holding it in her hand, examining it. It was a long, pale, narrow, rather elegant foot. At the top, where you would expect it to grow into an ankle the foot ended in a slight, skin-covered concavity. There was no sign of blood or severed flesh or bone or scar tissue, nor were there any corns or bunions, overlong nails or dirt. Ralph was a man who looked after his feet.

Lying there in her hand it felt as alive as a motionless foot ever feels; impossible as it seemed, she believed it was real. Ralph wasn't a practical joker, and yet—a foot wasn't something you left behind without noticing. She wondered how he was managing to get around on just one foot. Was it a message? Some obscure consolation for her feeling that, losing him, she had lost a piece of herself?

He had made it clear he no longer wanted to be involved with her. His good-bye had sounded final. But maybe he would get in touch when he realized she still had something of his. Although she knew she ought to be trying to forget him, she felt oddly grateful for this unexpected gift. She wrapped the foot in a silk scarf and put it in the dresser's bottom drawer, to keep for him.

Two days later, tidying the bedroom, she found his other foot under the bed. She had to check the drawer to make sure it wasn't the same one, gone wandering. But it was still there, one right foot, and she was holding the left one. She wrapped the two of them together in the white silk scarf and put them away.

Time passed and Ralph did not get in touch. Fay knew from friends that he was still around, and as she never heard any suggestion that he was now crippled, she began to wonder if the feet had been some sort of hallucination. She kept meaning to look in the bottom drawer, but somehow she kept forgetting.

The relationship with Ralph, while it lasted, had been a serious, deeply meaningful one for them both, she thought; she knew from the start there was no hope of that with Freddy. Fay was a responsible person who believed the act of sex should be accompanied by love and a certain degree of commitment; she detested the very idea of "casual sex"—but she'd been six months without a man in her bed, and Freddy was irresistible.

He was warm and cuddly and friendly, the perfect teddy bear. Within minutes of meeting him she was thinking about sleeping with him—although it was the comfort and cosiness of bed he brought to mind rather than passion. As passive as a teddy bear, he would let himself be pursued. She met him with friends in a pub, and he offered to walk her home. Outside her door he hugged her. There was no kissing or groping; he just wrapped her in a warm, friendly embrace, where she clung to him longer and tighter than friendship required.

"Mmmm," he said, appreciatively, smiling down at her, his eyes button-bright, "I could do this all night."

"What a good idea," she said.

After they had made love she decided he was less a teddy bear than a cat. Like a cat in the sensual way he moved and rubbed his body against hers and responded to her touch: She could almost hear him purr. Other catlike qualities, apparent after she had known him a little longer, were less appealing. Like a cat he was self-centered, basically lazy, and although she continued to enjoy him in bed, she did wish sometimes he would pay more attention to *her* pleasure instead of assuming that his was enough for them both. He seemed to expect her to be pleased no matter what time he turned up for dinner, even if he fell asleep in front of the fire immediately after. And, like many cats, he had more than one home.

Finding out about his other home—hearing that other woman's tear-clogged voice down the phone—decided her to end it. It wasn't— or so she told him—that she wanted to have him all to herself. But she wouldn't be responsible for another woman's sorrow.

He understood her feelings. He was wrong, and she was right. He was remorseful, apologetic, and quite incapable of changing. But he would miss her very much. He gave her a friendly hug before they parted, but once they started hugging it was hard to stop, and they tumbled into bed again.

That had to be the last time. She knew she could be firmer with him on the phone than in person, so she told him he was not to visit unless she first invited him. Sadly, he agreed.

And that was that. Going back into the bedroom she saw the duvet rucked up as if there was someone still in the bed. It made her shiver. If she hadn't just seen him out the door, and closed it behind him she might have thought . . . Determined to put an end to such mournful nonsense she flung the duvet aside, and there he was.

Well, part of him.

Lying on the bed was a headless, neckless, armless, legless, torso. Or at least the back side of one. As with Ralph's feet there was nothing unpleasant about it, no blood or gaping wounds. If you could ignore the sheer impossibility of it, there was nothing wrong with Freddy's back at all. It looked just like the body she had been embracing a few minutes before, and felt . . .

Tentatively, she reached out and touched it. It was warm and smooth, with the firm, elastic give of live flesh. She could not resist stroking it the way she knew he liked, teasing with her nails to make the skin prickle into goose bumps, running her fingers all the way from the top of the spine to the base, and over the curve of the buttocks where the body ended.

She drew her hand back, shocked. What *was* this? It seemed so much like Freddy, but how could it be when she had seen him, minutes before, walking out the door, fully equipped with all his body parts? Was it possible that there was nothing, now, but air filling out his jumper and jeans?

She sat down, took hold of the torso where the shoulders ended in smooth, fleshy hollows, and heaved it over. The chest was as she remembered, babyishly pink nipples peeking out of a scumble of ginger hair, but below the flat stomach only more flatness. His genitals were missing, as utterly and completely gone as if they had never been thought of. Her stomach twisted with shock and horror although, a moment later, she had to ask herself why that particular lack should matter so much more than the absence of his head—which she had accepted remarkably calmly. After all, this wasn't the real Freddy, only some sort of partial memory of his body inexplicably made flesh.

She went over to the dresser and crouched before the bottom drawer. Yes, they were still there. They didn't appear to have decayed or faded or changed in any way. Letting the silk scarf fall away she gazed at the naked feet and realized that she felt differently about Ralph. She had been unhappy when he left, but she had also been, without admitting it even to herself, furiously angry with him. And the anger had passed. The bitterness was gone, and she felt only affection now as she caressed his feet and remembered the good times. Eventually, with a sigh that mingled fondness and regret, she wrapped them up and put them away. Then she returned to her current problem: what to do with the part Freddy had left behind.

For a moment she thought of leaving it in the bed. He'd always been *so* nice to sleep with . . . But no. She had to finish what she had begun; she couldn't continue sleeping with part of Freddy all the time when all of Freddy part of the time had not been enough for her. She would never be able to get on with her life, she would never dare bring anyone new home with her.

It would have to go in the wardrobe. The only other option was the hall closet, which was cold and smelled slightly of damp. So, wrapping it in her best silken dressing gown, securing it with a tie around the waist, she stored Freddy's torso in the wardrobe behind her clothes.

Freddy phoned the next week. He didn't mention missing anything but her, and she almost told him about finding his torso in her bed. But how could she? If she told him, he'd insist on coming over to see it, and if he came over she'd be back to having an affair with him. That wasn't what she was after, was it? She hesitated, and then asked if he was still living with Matilda.

"Oh, more or less," he said. "Yes."

So she didn't tell him. She tried to forget him, and hoped to meet someone else, someone who would occupy the man-sized empty space in her life.

Meanwhile, Freddy continued to phone her once a week—friendly calls, because he wanted to stay friends. After a while she realized, from comments he let drop, that he was seeing another woman; that once again he had two homes. As always, she resisted the temptation she felt to invite him over, but she felt wretchedly lonely that evening.

For the first time since she had stored it away, she took out his body. Trembling a little, ashamed of herself, she took it to bed. She so wanted someone to hold. The body felt just like Freddy, warm and solid and smooth in the same way; it even smelled like him, although now with a faint overlay of her own perfume from her clothes. She held it for a while, but the lack of arms and head was too peculiar. She found that if she lay with her back against his and tucked her legs up so she couldn't feel his missing legs, it was almost like being in bed with Freddy.

She slept well that night, better than she had for weeks. "My teddy bear," she murmured as she packed him away again in the morning. It was like having a secret weapon. The comfort of a warm body in bed with her at night relaxed her, and made her more self-confident. She no longer felt any need to invite Freddy over, and when he called it was easy to talk to him without getting more involved, as if they'd always been just friends. And now that she wasn't looking, there seemed to be more men around.

One of them, Paul, who worked for the same company in a different department, asked her out. Lately she had kept running into him, and he seemed to have a lot of business that took him to her part of the building, but it didn't register on her that this was no coincidence until he asked if she was doing anything that Saturday night. After that, his interest in her seemed so obvious that she couldn't imagine why she hadn't noticed earlier.

The most likely reason she hadn't noticed was that she didn't care. She felt instinctively that he wasn't her type; they had little in common. But his unexpected interest flattered her, and made him seem more attractive, and so she agreed to go out with him.

It was a mistake, she thought, uneasily, when Saturday night came around and Paul took her to a very expensive restaurant. He was not unintelligent, certainly not bad-looking, but there was something a little too glossy and humorless about him. He was interested in money, and cars, and computers—and her. He dressed well, and he knew the right things to say, but she imagined he had learned them out of a book. He was awfully single-minded, and seemed intent on seduction, which made her nervous, and she spent too much of the evening trying to think of some way of getting out of inviting him in for coffee when he took her home. It was no good; when the time came, he invited himself in.

She knew it wasn't fair to make comparisons, but Paul was the complete opposite of Freddy. Where Freddy sat back and waited calmly to be stroked, Paul kept edging closer, trying to crawl into her lap. And his hands were everywhere. From the very start of the evening he had stood and walked too close to her, and she didn't like the way he had of touching her, as if casually making a point, staking a physical claim to her.

For the next hour she fended him off. It was a wordless battle that neither of them would admit to. When he left, she lacked the energy to refuse a return match the following weekend.

They went to the theater, and afterward to his place—he said he wanted to show her his computer. She expected another battle, but he was a perfect gentleman. Feeling safer, she agreed to a third date, and then drank too much; the drink loosened her inhibitions, she was too tired to resist his persistent pressure, and finally took him into her bed.

The sex was not entirely a success—for her, anyway—but it would doubtless get better as they got to know each other, she thought, and she was just allowing herself a few modest fantasies about the future, concentrating on the things she thought she liked about him, when he said he had to go.

The man who had been hotly all over her was suddenly distant and cool, almost rude in his haste to leave. She tried to find excuses for him, but when he had gone, and she discovered his hands were still in her bed, she knew he did not mean to return.

The hands were nestling beneath a pillow like a couple of soft-shelled crabs. She shuddered at the sight of them; shouted and threw her shoes at them. The left hand twitched when struck, but otherwise they didn't move.

How dare he leave his hands! She didn't *want* anything to remember him by! She certainly hadn't been in love with him.

Fay looked around for something else to throw, and then felt ashamed of herself. Paul was a creep, but it wasn't fair to take it out on his hands. They hadn't hurt her; they had done their best to give her pleasure—they might have succeeded if she'd liked their owner more.

But she didn't like their owner—she had to admit she wasn't really sorry he wouldn't be back—so why was she stuck with his hands? She could hardly give them back. She could already guess how he would avoid her at work, and she wasn't about to add to his inflated ego by pursuing him. But it didn't seem possible to throw them out, either.

She found a shoe box to put them in—she didn't bother about wrapping them—and then put the box away out of sight on the highest shelf of the kitchen cupboard, among the cracked plates, odd saucers, and empty jars that she'd kept because they might someday be useful.

The hands made her think a little differently about what had happened. She had been in love with Ralph and also, for all her attempts to rationalize her feelings, with Freddy—she hadn't wanted either of them to go. It made a kind of sense for her to fantasize that they'd left bits of themselves behind, but that didn't apply to her feelings for Paul. She absolutely refused to believe that her subconscious was responsible for the hands in the kitchen cupboard.

So if not her subconscious, then what? Was it the bed? She stood in the bedroom and looked at it, trying to perceive some sorcery in the brand-name mattress or the pine frame. She had bought the bed for Ralph, really; he had complained so about the futon she had when they met, declaring that it was not only too short, but also bad for his back. He had told her that pine beds were good and also cheap, and although she didn't agree with his assessment of the price, she had bought one. It was the most expensive thing she owned. Was it also haunted?

She could test it; invite friends to stay . . . Would any man who made love in this bed leave a part of himself behind, or only those who made love to her? Only for the last time? But how did it know? How could it, before she herself knew a relationship was over? What if she lured Paul back—would some other body part appear when he left? Or would the hands disappear?

Once she had thought of this, she knew she had to find out. She tried to forget the idea but could not. Days passed, and Paul did not get in touch—he avoided her at work, as she had guessed he would—and she told herself to let him go. Good riddance. To pursue him would be humiliating. It wasn't even as if she were in love with him, after all.

She told herself not to be a fool, but chance and business kept taking her to his part of the building. When forced to acknowledge her his voice was polite and he did not stand too close; he spoke as if they'd never met outside working hours; as if he'd never really noticed her as a woman. She saw him, an hour later, leaning confidentially over one of the newer secretaries, his hand touching her hip.

She felt a stab of jealous frustration. No wonder she couldn't attract his attention; he had already moved on to fresh prey.

Another week went by, but she would not accept defeat. She phoned him up and invited him to dinner. He said his weekends were awfully busy just now. She suggested a week night. He hesitated—surprised by her persistence? Contemptuous? Flattered?—and then said he was involved with someone, actually. Despising herself, Fay said lightly that of course she understood. She said that in fact she herself was involved in a long-standing relationship, but her fellow had been abroad for the past few months, and she got bored and lonely in the evenings. She'd enjoyed herself so much with Paul that she had hoped they'd be able to get together again sometime; that was all.

That changed the temperature. He said he was afraid he couldn't manage dinner, but if she liked, he could drop by later one evening—maybe tomorrow, around ten?

He was on her as soon as he was through the door. She tried to fend him off with offers of drink, but he didn't seem to hear. His hands were everywhere, grabbing, fondling, probing, as undeniably real as they'd ever been.

"Wait, wait," she said, laughing but not amused. "Can't we . . . talk?"

He paused, holding her around the waist, and looked down at her. He was bigger than she remembered. "We could have talked on the phone."

"I know, but . . ."

"Is there something we need to talk about?"

"Well, no, nothing specific, but . . ."

"Did you invite me over here to talk? Did I misunderstand?"

"No."

"All right." His mouth came down, wet and devouring, on hers, and she gave in.

But not on the couch, she thought, a few minutes later. "Bed," she gasped, breaking away. "In the bedroom."

"Good idea."

But it no longer seemed like a good idea to her. As she watched him strip off his clothes she thought this was probably the worst idea she'd ever had. She didn't want him in her bed again; she didn't want sex with him. How could she have thought, for even a minute, that she could have sex for such a cold-blooded, ulterior motive?

"I thought you were in a hurry," he said. "Get your clothes off." Naked, he reached for her.

She backed away. "I'm sorry, I shouldn't have called you, I'm sorry—"

"Don't apologize. It's very sexy when a woman knows what she wants and asks for it." He'd unbuttoned her blouse and unhooked her bra earlier, and now he tried to remove them. She tried to stop him, and he pinioned her wrists.

"This is a mistake, I don't want this, you have to go."

"Like hell."

"I'm sorry, Paul, but I mean it."

He smiled humorlessly. "You mean you want me to force you."

"No!"

He pushed her down on the bed, got her skirt off despite her struggles, then ripped her tights.

"Stop it!"

"I wouldn't have thought you liked this sort of thing," he mused.

"I don't, I'm telling the truth, I don't want to have sex, I want you to leave." Her voice wobbled all over the place. "Look, I'm sorry, I'm really sorry, but I can't, not now." Tears leaked out of her eyes. "Please. You don't understand. This isn't a game." She was completely naked now and he was naked on top of her.

"This *is* a game," he said calmly. "And I do understand. You've been chasing me for weeks. I know what you want. A minute ago, you were begging me to take you to bed. Now you're embarrassed. You want me to force you. I don't want to force you, but if I have to, I will."

"No."

"It's up to you," he said. "You can give, or I can take. That simple."

She had never thought rape could be that simple. She bit one of the arms that held her down. He slapped her hard.

"I told you," he said. "You can give, or I can take. It's that simple. It's your choice."

Frightened by his strength, seeing no choice at all, she gave in.

Afterward, she was not surprised when she discovered what he had left in her bed. What else should it be? It was just what she deserved.

It was ugly, yet there was something oddly appealing in the sight of it nestling in a fold of the duvet; she was reminded of her teenage passion for collecting beanbag creatures. She used to line them up across her bed. This could have been one of them: maybe a squashy elephant's head with a fat nose. She went on staring at it for a long time, lying on her side on the bed, emotionally numbed and physically exhausted, unable either to get up or to go to sleep. She told herself she should get rid of it, that she could take her aggressions out on it, cut it up, at least throw it, and the pair of hands, out with the rest of her unwanted garbage. But it was hard to connect this beanbag creature with Paul and what he had done to her. She realized she had scarcely more than glimpsed his genitals; no wonder she couldn't believe this floppy creature could have had anything to do with her rape. The longer she looked at it, the less she could believe it was that horrible man's. It, too, had been abused by him. And it wasn't his now, it was hers. Okay, Paul had been the catalyst, somehow, but this set of genitalia had been born from the bed and her own desire; it was an entirely new thing.

Eventually she fell asleep, still gazing at it. When she opened her eyes in the morning it was like seeing an old friend. She wouldn't get rid of it. She put it in a pillowcase and stashed the parcel among the scarves, shawls, and sweaters on the shelf at the top of the wardrobe.

She decided to put the past behind her. She didn't think about Paul or Ralph or even Freddy. Although most nights she slept with Freddy's body, that was a decision made on the same basis, and with no more emotion, as whether she slept with the duvet or the electric blanket. Freddy's body wasn't Freddy's anymore; it was hers.

The only men in her life now were friends. She wasn't looking for romance, and she seldom thought about sex. If she wanted male companionship there was Christopher, a platonic friend from school, or Marcus, her next-door neighbor, or Freddy. They still talked on the phone frequently, and very occasionally met in town for a drink or a meal, but she had never invited him over since their breakup, so it was a shock one evening to answer the door and discover him standing outside.

He looked sheepish. "I'm sorry," he said. "I know I should have called first, but I couldn't find a working phone, and . . . I hope you don't mind. I need somebody to talk to. Matilda's thrown me out."

And not only Matilda, but also the latest other woman. He poured out his woes, and she made dinner, and they drank wine and talked for hours.

"Do you have somewhere to stay?" she asked at last.

"I could go to my sister's. I stay there a lot anyway. She's got a spare room—I've even got my own key. But—" He gave her his old look, desirous but undemanding. "Actually, Fay, I was hoping I could stay with you tonight."

She discovered he was still irresistible.

Her last thought before she fell asleep was how strange it was to sleep with someone who had arms and legs.

In the morning she woke enough to feel him kiss her, but she didn't realize it was a kiss good-bye, for she could still feel his legs entwined with her own.

But the rest of him was gone, and probably for good this time, she discovered when she woke up completely. For a man with such a smooth-skinned body he had extremely hairy legs, she thought, sitting on the bed and staring at the unattached limbs. And for a woman who had just been used and left again, she felt awfully cheerful.

She got Ralph's feet out of the drawer—thinking how much thinner and more elegant they were than Freddy's—and, giggling to herself, pressed the right foot to the bottom of the right leg, just to see how it looked.

It looked as if it was growing there and always had been. When she tried to pull it away, it wouldn't come. She couldn't even see a join. Anyone else might have thought it was perfectly natural; it probably only looked odd to her because she knew it wasn't. When she did the same thing with the left foot and left leg, the same thing happened.

So then, feeling daring, she took Freddy's torso out of the wardrobe and laid it down on the bed just above the legs. She pushed the legs up close, so they looked as if they were growing out of the torso—and then they were. She sat it up, finding that it was as flexible and responsive as a real, live person, not at all a dead weight, and she sat on the edge of the bed beside it and looked down at its empty lap.

"Don't go away; I have just the thing for Sir," she said.

The genitals were really the wrong size and skin tone for Freddy's long, pale body, but they nestled gratefully into his crotch, obviously happy in their new home.

The body was happy, too. There was new life in it—not Freddy's, not Paul's, not Ralph's, but a new being created out of their old parts. She wasn't imagining it. Not propped up, it was sitting beside her, holding itself up, alert and waiting. When she leaned closer she could feel a heart beating within the chest, sending the blood coursing through a network of veins and arteries. She reached out to stroke the little elephant head slumbering between the legs, and as she touched it, it stirred and sat up.

She was sexually excited, too, and, at the same time, horrified. There had to be something wrong with her to want to have sex with this incomplete collection of body parts. All right, it wasn't dead, so at least what she felt wasn't necrophilia, but what was it? A man without arms was merely disabled, but was a man without a head a man at all? Whatever had happened to her belief in the importance of relationship? They couldn't even communicate, except by touch, and then only at her initiative. All he could do was respond to her will. She thought of Paul's hands, how she had been groped, forced, slapped, and held down by them, and was just as glad they remained unattached, safely removed to the kitchen cupboard. Safe sex, she thought, and giggled. In response to the vibration, the body listed a little in her direction.

She got off the bed and moved away, then stood and watched it swaying indecisively. She felt a little sorry for it, being so utterly dependent on her, and that cooled her ardor. It wasn't right, she couldn't use it as a kind of live sex aid—not as it was. She was going to have to find it a head, or forget about it.

She wrapped the body in a sheet to keep the dust off and stored it under the bed. She couldn't sleep with it anymore. In its headless state it was too disturbing. "Don't worry," she said, although it couldn't hear her. "This isn't forever."

She started her headhunt. She knew it might take some time, but she was going to be careful; she didn't want another bad experience. It wouldn't be worth it. Something good had come out of the Paul experience, but heads—or faces, anyway—were so much harder to depersonalize. If it looked like Freddy or Paul in the face, she knew she would respond to it as Freddy or Paul, and what was the point of that? She wanted to find someone new, someone she didn't know, but also someone she liked; someone she could find attractive, go to bed with, and be parted from without the traumas of love or hate. She hoped it wasn't an impossible paradox.

She asked friends for introductions, she signed up for classes, joined clubs, went to parties, talked to men in supermarkets and on buses, answered personal ads. And then Marcus dropped by one evening, and asked if she wanted to go to a movie with him.

They had seen a lot of movies and shared a fair number of pizzas over the past two years, but although she liked him, she knew very little about him. She didn't even know for sure that he was heterosexual. She occasionally saw him with other women, but the relationships seemed to be platonic. Because he was younger than she was, delicate-looking and with a penchant for what she thought of as "arty" clothes, because he didn't talk about sex and had never touched her, the idea of having sex with him had never crossed her mind. Now, seeing his clean-shaven, rather pretty face as if for the first time, it did.

"What a good idea," she said.

After the movie, after the pizza and a lot of wine, after he'd said he probably should be going, Fay put her hand on his leg and suggested he stay. He seemed keen enough—if surprised—but after she got him into bed he quickly lost his erection and nothing either of them did made any difference.

"It's not your fault," he said anxiously. It had not occurred to her that it could be. "Oh, God, this is awful," he went on. "If you only knew how I've dreamed of this . . . only I never thought, never dared to hope, that you could want me too, and now . . . you're so wonderful, and kind, and beautiful, and you deserve so much, and you must think I'm completely useless."

"I think it's probably the wine," she said. "We both had too much to drink. Maybe you should go on home . . . I think we'd both sleep better in our own beds, alone."

"Oh, God, you don't hate me, do you? You will give me another chance, won't you, Fay? Please?"

"Don't worry about it. Yes, Marcus, yes, of course I will. Now, good night."

She found nothing in her bed afterward; she hadn't expected to. But neither did she expect the flowers that arrived the next day, and the day after that.

He took her out to dinner on Friday night—not pizza this time—and afterward, in her house, in her bed, they did what they had come together to do. She fell asleep, supremely satisfied, in his arms. In the morning he was eager to make love again, and Fay might have been interested—he had proved himself to be a very tender and skillful lover—but she was too impatient. She had only wanted him for one thing, and the sooner he left her, the sooner she would get it.

"I think you'd better go, Marcus. Let's not drag this out," she said.

"What do you mean?"

"I mean this was a mistake, we shouldn't have made love, we're really just friends who had too much to drink, so . . ."

He looked pale, even against the pale linen. "But I love you."

There was a time when such a statement, in such circumstances, would have made her happy, but the Fay who had loved, and expected to be loved in return, by the men she took to bed, seemed like another person now.

"But I don't love you."

"Then why did you—"

"Look, I don't want to argue. I don't want to say something that might hurt you. I want us to be friends, that's all, the way we used to be." She got up, since he still hadn't moved, and put on her robe.

"Are you saying you never want to see me again?"

She looked down at him. He really did have a nice face, and the pain that was on it now—that she had put there—made her look away hastily in shame. "Of course I do. You've been a good neighbor and a good friend. I hope we can go on being that. Only . . ." She tried to remember what someone had said to her once, was it Ralph? "Only I can't be what you want me to be. I still care about you, of course. But I don't love you in that way. So we'd better part. You'll see it's for the best, in time. You'll find someone else."

"You mean you will."

Startled, she looked back at him. Wasn't that what she had said to Ralph? She couldn't think how to answer him. But Marcus was out of bed, getting dressed, and didn't seem to expect an answer.

"I'll go," he said. "Because you ask me to. But I meant what I said. I love you. You know where I live. If you want me . . . if you change your mind . . ."

"Yes, of course. Good-bye, Marcus, I'm sorry."

She walked him to the door, saw him out, and locked the door behind him. Now! She scurried back to the bedroom, but halted in the doorway as she had a sudden, nasty thought. What if it hadn't worked? What if, instead of a pretty face, she found, say, another pair of feet in her bed?

Then I'll do it again, she decided, and again and again until I get my man.

She stepped forward, grasped the edge of the duvet, and threw it aside with a conjurer's flourish.

There was nothing on the bare expanse of pale blue sheet; nothing but a few stray pubic hairs.

She picked up the pillows, each in turn, and shook them. She shook out the duvet, unfastening the cover to make sure there was nothing inside. She peered beneath the bed and poked around the sheet-wrapped body, even pulled the bed away from the wall, in case something had caught behind the headboard. Finally she crawled across the bed on her belly, nose to the sheet, examining every inch.

Nothing. He had left nothing.

But why? How?

They left parts because they weren't willing to give all. The bed preserved bits and pieces of men who wanted only pieces of her time, pieces of her body, for which they could pay only with pieces of their own.

Marcus wanted more than that. He wanted, and offered, everything. But she had refused him, so now she had nothing.

No, not nothing. She crouched down and pulled the sheet-wrapped form from beneath the bed, unwrapped it, and reassured herself that the headless, armless body was still warm, still alive, still male, still hers. She felt the comforting stir of sexual desire in her own body as she aroused it in his, and she vowed she would not be defeated.

It would take thought and careful planning, but surely she could make one more lover leave her?

She spent the morning making preparations, and at about lunchtime she phoned Marcus and asked him to come over that evening.

"Did you really mean it when you said you loved me?"

"Yes."

"Because I want to ask you to do something for me, and I don't think you will."

"Fay, anything, what is it?"

"I'll have to tell you in person."

"I'll come over now."

She fell into his arms when he came in, and kissed him passionately. She felt his body respond, and when she looked at his face she saw the hurt had gone and a wondering joy replaced it.

"Let's go in the bedroom," she said. "I'm going to tell you everything; I'm going to tell you the truth about what I want, and you won't like it, I know."

"How can you know? How can you possibly know?" He stroked her back, smiling at her.

"Because it's not normal. It's a sexual thing."

"Try me."

They were in the bedroom now. She drew a deep breath. "Can I tie you to the bed?"

"Well." He laughed a little. "I've never done that before, but I don't see anything wrong with it. If it makes you happy."

"Can I do it?"

"Yes, why not."

"Now, I mean." Shielding the bedside cabinet with her body, she pulled out the ropes she had put there earlier. "Lie down."

He did as she said. "You don't want me to undress first?"

She shook her head, busily tying him to the bedposts.

'And what do I do now?' He strained upward against the ropes, demonstrating how little he was capable of doing.

"Now you give me your head."

"What?"

"Other men have given me other parts; I want your head."

It was obvious he didn't know what she meant. She tried to remember how she had planned to explain; what, exactly, she wanted him to do. Should she show him the body under the bed? Would he understand then?

"Your head," she said again, and then she remembered the words. "It's simple. You can give it to me, or I can take it. It's your choice."

He still stared at her as if it wasn't simple at all. She got the knife out of the bedside cabinet and held it so he could see. "You give, or I take. It's your choice."

Rabbit Hole

■

JANE YOLEN

*T*he rabbit hole had been there from the first, though everything else had changed.

"Especially me," thought Alice, smoothing down her skirt and tucking the shirtwaist back in. She straightened the diamond ring on her left hand, which had a tendency to slip around now that she had lost so much weight. It was certainly going to be more difficult falling down the hole at eighty than it had been at eight. For one thing, the speed would no longer be exhilarating. She knew better now. For another, she feared her legs might not be up to the landing, especially after the operation on her hip.

Still, she wanted a bit of magic back in her life before she died and the doctor, bless him, thought she might go at any time. "Consider that you have had more than your share of years already," he had said. He'd never been a tactful man, though she appreciated his bluntness in this particular instance.

So she had sneaked away from her grandniece, set as a keeper over her, and still a bit unsteady with the cane, had come back to the meadow where it had all begun.

The tree her sister Edith and she had been reading under when that first adventure started had long been felled after a lightning strike. Council houses now took up most of the open space: tan-faced two-story buildings alike as cereal boxes. But the rabbit hole was still there, as she had known it would be, in the middle of the little green park set aside for pensioners. She opened the gate and checked around. No one else was in the park, which pleased her. It would have been difficult explaining just exactly what it was she planned to do.

Closing the gate behind her, she went over to the hole and sat down beside it. It was a smallish hole, ringed round with spikey brown grass. The grass was wet with dew but she didn't mind. If the trip down the hole didn't kill her outright, magic would dry off her skirts. *Either way . . .* she thought *. . . either way . . .*

She wondered if she should wait for the rabbit, but he was at least as old as she. If rabbits even lived that long. She should have looked that up before coming. Her late husband, Reggie, had been a biologist manqué and she knew for certain that several volumes on rabbits could be found in his vast library, a great many of them, she was sure, in French. He loved reading French. It was his only odd habit. But the white rabbit might just be late; it had always been late before. As a child she had thought that both an annoying and an endearing quality. Now she simply suspected the rabbit had had a mistress somewhere for, as she recalled, he always had a disheveled and uncomfortable look whenever they met, as if just rumpling out of bed and embarrassed lest anyone know. Especially a child. She'd certainly seen that look on any number of faces at the endless house parties she and Reggie had gone to when they were first married.

She didn't think she had time enough now to waste waiting for the rabbit to show up, though as a child she'd a necessary long patience. Those had been the days of posing endlessly for artists and amateur photographers, which took a great deal of time. She'd learned to play games in her head, cruel games some of them had been. And silly. As often as not the men she posed for were the main characters in the games, but in such odd and often bestial incarnations: griffins, mock turtles, great fuzzy-footed caterpillars. And rabbits. What *hadn't* she imagined! Mr. Dodgson hadn't been the only one who wanted her for a model, though she never understood why. She'd been quite plain as a child, with a straight-haired simplicity her mother insisted upon. That awful fringe across her forehead; those eyebrows, pronounced and arched. A good characteristic in a woman but awful, she thought consideringly, in a child. In all the photographs she seemed to be staring out insolently, as if daring the photographer to take a good picture. *What could Mr. Dodgson have been thinking?*

And then there'd been that terrible painter, Sir William Blake Richmond, for whom she'd spent hours kneeling by Lorina's side in the Llandudno sands for a portrait Father never even hung in the house. Though years later, she recalled suddenly, Lorina—who'd really never had very much art sense—displayed it without apology in her sunny apartment. *The Ghastlies,* Father had called that painting, remarking how awful his beautiful girls looked in it. And they really had: stiff and uncharming. Like old ladies, really, not young girls. The sand had hurt her knee, the sun had been too hot, and Sir William an utter fool. They'd nicknamed him "Poormond" as a joke. It was her art tutor's idea, actually—Mr. Ruskin. *A poor nickname and a poor joke as well,* she thought.

Leaning over, she peered down into the hole and thought she saw the beginnings of the shelving that lined the sides, though the first time she'd dropped down the hole it had gone—she seemed to remember dimly—straight like a tunnel for some time. *Marmelade,* she thought suddenly. That had been on the shelves. The good old-fashioned hand-made orange stuff that her governess, Miss Prickett, had insisted on, not the manufactured kind you get in the stores today. She could almost taste it, the wonderful bits of candied rind that stuck between your teeth. *Of course, that was when I had all my own.*

She sat a bit longer remembering the maps and pictures hung upon pegs that had been scattered between the shelves; and the books— had there been books or was she misremembering? And then, when she was almost afraid of actually doing it, she lowered herself feet first into the suddenly expanding hole.

And fell.

Down, down, down.

As if accommodating to her age, the hole let her fall slowly, majestically, turning over only once or twice on the way. *A queen,* she thought, *would fall this way.* Though she had no title, much as Reggie had longed to be on the Honors List. And then she remembered that in Wonderland she *was* a queen. With that thought there was a sudden deliberate heaviness atop her head. It took all the strength she could muster to reach up as she fell, but she just managed. Sure enough, a crown, bulky and solid, was sitting upon her head.

She fell slowly enough that she could adjust her glasses to see onto the shelves, and so that her skirts never ruffled more than a quarter inch above her knees. They were good knees, or at least handsome knees, still. She'd many compliments on them over the years. Reggie, of course, had adored them. She often wondered if that was why she had married him, all those compliments. He'd stopped them once they were safely wed. The crown prince himself—and Dickie Mountbatten, too—had remarked on her knees and her ankles, too. Of course that was when knees and ankles had been in fashion. It was all breast and thigh now. *Like,* she thought, *grocery chickens.* She giggled, thinking of herself on a store shelf, in among the poultry. As if responding to her giddy mood, the crown sat more heavily on her head.

"Oh, dear," she said aloud. "We are *not* to be amused." The giggles stopped.

As she continued falling, she named the things on the shelves to herself: several marmelade jars; a picnic basket from Fortnum and Mason; a tartan lap robe like the one her nanny used to wrap around her on country weekends; a set of ivory fish tile counters; a velvet box with a mourning brooch in which a lock of hair as pale as that of her own dear dead boys' was twisted under glass; a miniature portrait of the late queen she was sure she'd last seen at a house party at Scone, back in the days before it had become a tourist attraction.

She had not finished with the namings, when she landed, softly, upon a mound of dry leaves and found herself in a lovely garden full of flowers: both a cultivated rose bed and arbor, and a herb garden in the shape of a Celtic knot. It reminded her of her own lovely garden at Cuffnells, the small one that was hers, not the larger-than-life arboretum that Reggie had planted, with its Orientals, redwoods, and Douglas pine. Poor lost Cuffnells. Poor dead Reggie. Poor gone everybody. She shook her head vigorously. She would *not* let herself get lost in the past, making it somehow better and lovelier than it was. She'd never liked that in old people when she was young, and she wasn't about to countenance it in herself now. The past was a lot like Wonderland: treacherous and marvelous and dull in equal measure. Survival was all that mattered—and she was a survivor. *Of course, in the end,* she thought, *there is no such thing as survival. And just as well. What a clutter the world would be if none of us ever died.*

She took a deep breath and looked around the garden. Once, the flowers had spoken to her but they were silent now. She stood up slowly, the hip giving her trouble again, and waved her cane at them, expecting no answer and receiving none. Then she walked through the garden gate and into Wonderland proper.

"Proper!" she said aloud and gave a small laugh. Proper was one thing Wonderland had never been. Nor was she, though from the outside it must have looked it. But she could still play all those games in her head. Griffins and mock turtles and caterpillars. And rabbits. Men all seemed to fall so easily into those categories. She brushed off her skirt, which was suddenly short and green, like her old school uniform.

"Curioser and curioser," she remarked to no one in particular. She liked the feel of the words in her mouth. They were comfortable, easy.

There was a path that almost seemed to unroll before her. *A bit,* she thought, *like the new path to the Isis from Tom Quad, which Father had had dug.* She was not at all surprised when she spied a young man coming toward her in white flannel trousers, striped jacket, a straw hat, and a pair of ghastly black shoes, the kind men had worn before tennis shoes had been invented. She thought tennis shoes were aces. The young man glanced at his pocket watch, then up at her, looking terribly familiar.

"No time," he said. "No time." He stuttered slightly on the *n.*

"Why, Mr. Dodgson," she said, looking up at him through a fringe of dark hair and holding out a ringless hand. "Why, of course there's plenty of time."

And there was.

Iphigenia

■

NANCY A. COLLINS

*P*eople are always asking me if I like my job or not. Sometimes I wish those reporters and TV people would ask me
other things. I get tired of saying the same old stuff over
and over again but I always smile and say yes. That's my job.

I don't really mind the reporters asking me things and stuff but I
wish one of them would think of something new! Being famous is not
what I thought it would be back when they started the contest. I
thought being famous was when you got to be on TV and in the paper.
I didn't think it could be boring. I was just a little kid back then. The
president always laughs when I say that, but he looks sad even when
he is smiling. He looks sad a lot. I follow him around all the time,
that's why I know. That he looks sad, I mean. That's my job.

I'm famous. Everybody knows who I am. I am not bragging or telling
lies. I've been on the covers of all kinds of magazines since I got my
job. *Time. U.S. News & World Report. Newsweek.* Even *Weekly Reader*! It
was kind of neat, seeing pictures of me with the president and Dr.
Ballard. I was even on TV! I bet Marjorie was really mad when she
saw me on CNN! Marjorie thinks she's hot snot because her dad
bought her that pony but she's really cold boogers.

I get to go to Camp David a lot. It's okay but it isn't as fun as Camp

Tallyho when I went with Aunt Mimi and got to play with other kids and they gave me a neat T-shirt. I also get to go to all these weird countries with the president. It's part of my job. That's better than some stupid pony!

Even though I'm famous and everybody in the world knows who I am (I got a birthday present from the queen! She sent me this really neat doll that used to belong to her grandmother. It's real old, so Mama doesn't let me play with it too much, but that's okay, I guess.) I try not to let it make me stuck up like Marjorie. Mama says I shouldn't get a big head. She's right. I'm real lucky they let her visit me on weekends. At first they said they couldn't let her come and see me but Dr. Ballard made them change their minds. He said it was important that I needed to feel safe. He said other people might not understand taking a kid away from her mom and dad and making her live in the White House for so long. I don't know how he talked them into it, but I'm glad Mama is here on Saturday and Sunday.

Dr. Ballard is a nice man. He's almost as nice as the president. Dr. Ballard spends a lot of time with me and making sure I don't get weird. He looks after me when Mama isn't here. He's the one who came up with this idea. He's real smart. Some people say he's a monster, but they don't know anything. They think it's all a trick, that I don't know what my job is really about. They think that because I'm a kid I don't know anything. They must think kids are real stupid. Dr. Ballard says they're just scared and I should feel sorry for them. Dr. Ballard says that I'm a living symbol of life—not just here in the U.S.A. but all over the world. My job is to remind the President of that when things get bad.

I understand a lot about symbols. I understand them a lot better than when I first got into the contest. A lot of people were against the contest, but then something happened someplace that made them change their minds.

A bunch of doctors with white coats and clipboards came to our school and gave us a bunch of tests and took our pictures. None of us minded because it got us out of class for the day. I was the only kid picked from my school. Mama took me to the testing center in another city, and I took some more tests and I talked to more people in white coats. There were other kids at the testing center too. Most of them were my age, which was okay, I guess, although there were a couple of big kids, too. The big kids didn't pass the second test for some reason.

That's where I met Dr. Ballard. He was different from the other doctors. He didn't wear a white coat. He wore a baggy old sweater and a pair of jeans. He smiled a lot, but his eyes were sad. Just like the president. He talked to me about my pets and what I did good in at school and who my friends were, and Marjorie and her dumb pony. The kind of stuff you talk to your grandma and grandpa about.

Then Dr. Ballard told me about the job. He explained how I was the only kid in the whole U.S.A. who passed the tests. He said that the president and I have something called "empathic resonance," which means that the president likes me a lot. He told me all the things I would have to do, but he also told me I had to volunteer. No one could make me take the job. Not him, not Mama, not even the president! He told me that if I took the job I could quit when the president quit his job. I'd get lots of money and the government would pay for my school when I grew up.

He said another kid would take over my job someday, but I would always be the most important, because I would be the first. I would be in the history book just like George Washington and Thomas Jefferson and kids in school would have to know my name on tests! He told me I should think about it before saying yes or no.

I was just a dumb little kid back then. I didn't know about symbols and how people pay more attention to them than to things that are real. But even if I'd known, I'd have still said yes in the end. I like the president.

Being a little kid is scary. You don't know the rules of the game that grown-ups play. Sometimes they act like they don't want you to know. Even if you did know they wouldn't pay any attention to you anyhow. But I know about The Bomb. All kids know about it.

The first time I heard about The Bomb I got scared and had bad dreams. Then I found out that grown-ups were scared of it too and how they don't always understand the rules either. That scared me a lot, but when I talked to Dr. Ballard about it he said sometimes grown-ups aren't as smart as you think. He said sometimes they get stuck and kids have to help them.

So I made up my own mind. Not Mama, not Dr. Ballard, and not the president—no matter what the newspapers say. I did it because I owe it to all the little kids in the world, not because I would be famous and get in the history books. Dr. Ballard says I'm a living symbol that says "I want to grow up." If I do well at my job, then all the other countries will have kids just like me. That's why I've written all of these essays for Dr. Ballard. Because it's history. Writing is okay but I wish I could go outside and play.

I've had my job two years now. That means I get to retire soon. The scar from where they opened me up to put in the codes doesn't hurt anymore, but it's still there. Sometimes the reporters ask me if I can feel the metal thing inside me near my heart. I tell them no, but sometimes I can feel it. Or I think I can. I talked with Dr. Ballard about it and he thinks it's in my head. I told him no, it's in my chest. That made him laugh. I almost never see him laugh for real anymore.

I wonder how it will feel when they take the briefcase off my wrist. It doesn't really bother me. It isn't heavy at all and the handcuff doesn't bug me anymore, like it did at first. It did take me a long time to get used to carrying it around everywhere I went, but now I don't really notice it. I don't think about what's inside it.

I only got to see the knife the day Dr. Ballard put it inside the briefcase and locked it and gave the key to the president.

A lot of things are happening now. The president keeps going to meetings with the generals from the Pentagon. I have to sit on a chair near the president where they can see me. I spend most of the time coloring or working in my workbook. I don't understand what the generals say most of the time and it's boring. Mainly I don't like the way they look at me. Dr. Ballard says they just don't want me hanging around. Maybe they think I am a spy or something. That is so dumb! The way they look at me makes me feel real funny, though. When I look back at them, they pretend they weren't staring at me and they get embarrassed. Sometimes they look at me with this real mean look. Like Marjorie, only worse.

I like the president. I always have. He's a nice man. He's got a granddaughter the same age as me. We even get to play together in the Rose Garden when she comes to visit him. When his dog Tinkerbell has puppies, he said I can have one! He wants me to grow up, he says. I wish his eyes weren't so sad. I hope Mama will let me keep it.

Werewomen

■

URSULA K. LE GUIN

I want to go moonwalking
on it or under it I don't care
I just want to go moonwalking
alone.
    Women in their sixties
don't go to the moon,
    women in the cities
don't go out alone.
    But I want O listen what I want
is to be not afraid.
Listen what I need is freedom.
    Women in their sixties
think about dying,
    women in the cities
think about dying,
    all kinds of women
think about lying,
think about lying alone.
    But listen there's a moon out there
and I don't want sex and I don't want death

and I don't want what you think I want,
only to be a free woman.
    What is that, a free woman,
    a young free woman,
    an old free woman?
    Asking for the moon.
Women in their sixties
    have no moon.
Women in the cities
    howl at the moon.
All kinds of women
talk about walking alone.
When the moon is full
listen how they howl,
listen how they howl together.

Talking to the Dead

■

SYLVIA WATANABE

We spoke of her in whispers as Aunty Talking to the Dead, the half-Hawaiian kahuna lady. But whenever there was a death in the village, she was the first to be sent for; the priest came second. For it was she who understood the wholeness of things—the significance of directions and colors. Prayers to appease the hungry ghosts. Elixirs for grief. Most times, she'd be out on her front porch, already waiting—her boy, Clinton, standing behind with her basket of spells—when the messenger arrived. People said she could smell a death from clear on the other side of the island, even as the dying person breathed his last. And if she fixed her eyes on you and named a day, you were already as good as six feet under.

I went to work as her apprentice when I was eighteen. That was in '48, the year Clinton graduated from mortician school on the GI bill. It was the talk for weeks—how he'd returned to open the Paradise Mortuary in the heart of the village and had brought the scientific spirit of free enterprise to the doorstep of the hereafter. I remember the advertisements for the Grand Opening, promising to modernize the funeral trade with Lifelike Artistic Techniques and Stringent Standards of Sanitation. The old woman, who had waited out the war for her son's return, stoically took his defection in stride and began looking for someone else to help out with her business.

At the time, I didn't have many prospects—more schooling didn't interest me, and my mother's attempts at marrying me off inevitably failed when I stood to shake hands with a prospective bridegroom and ended up towering a foot above him. "It would be bad enough if she just looked like a horse," I heard one of them complain, "but she's as big as one, too."

My mother dressed me in navy blue, on the theory that dark colors make things look less conspicuous. "Yuri, sit down," she'd hiss, tugging at my skirt as the decisive moment approached. I'd nod, sip my tea, smile through the introductions and small talk, till the time came for sealing the bargain with handshakes. Then, nothing on earth could keep me from getting to my feet. The go-between finally suggested that I consider taking up a trade. "After all, marriage isn't for everyone," she said. My mother said that that was a fact that remained to be proven, but meanwhile it wouldn't hurt if I took in sewing or learned to cut hair. I made up my mind to apprentice myself to Aunty Talking to the Dead.

The old woman's house was on the hill behind the village, just off the road to Chicken Fight Camp. She lived in an old plantation worker's bungalow with peeling green and white paint and a large, well-tended garden—mostly of flowering bushes and strong-smelling herbs.

"Aren't you a big one," a voice behind me said.

I started, then turned. It was the first time I had ever seen her up close.

"Hello, uh, Mrs. Dead," I stammered.

She was little, way under five feet, and wrinkled. Everything about her seemed the same color—her skin, her lips, her dress. Everything was just a slightly different shade of the same brown-gray, except her hair, which was absolutely white, and her tiny eyes, which glinted like metal. For a minute those eyes looked me up and down.

"Here," she said finally, thrusting an empty rice sack into my hands. "For collecting salt." Then she started down the road to the beach.

In the next few months we walked every inch of the hills and beaches around the village, and then some. I struggled behind, laden with strips of bark and leafy twigs, while Aunty marched three steps ahead, chanting. "This is *a'ali'i* to bring sleep—it must be dried in the shade on a hot day. This is *noni* for the heart, and *awa* for every kind of grief. This is *uhaloa* with the deep roots. If you are like that, death cannot easily take you."

"This is where you gather salt to preserve a corpse," I hear her still. "This is where you cut to insert the salt." Her words marked the places on my body, one by one.

That whole first year, not a day passed when I didn't think of quitting. I tried to figure out a way of moving back home without making it seem like I was admitting anything.

"You know what people are saying, don't you?" my mother said, lifting the lid of the bamboo steamer and setting a tray of freshly steamed meat buns on the already crowded table before me. It was one of my few visits since my apprenticeship, through I'd never been more than a couple of miles away, and she had stayed up the whole night before, cooking. She'd prepared a canned ham with yellow sweet potatoes, wing beans with pork, sweet and sour mustard cabbage, fresh raw yellowfin, pickled eggplant, and rice with red beans. I had not seen so much food since the night she tried to persuade Uncle Mongoose not to volunteer for the army. He went anyway, and on the last day of training, just before he was to be shipped to Italy, he shot himself in the head while cleaning his gun. "I always knew that boy would come to no good," was all Mama said when she heard the news.

"What do you mean you can't eat another bite?" she fussed now. "Look at you, nothing but a bag of bones."

The truth was, there didn't seem to be much of a future in my apprenticeship. In eleven and a half months I had memorized most of the minor rituals of mourning and learned to identify a couple of dozen herbs and all their medicinal uses, but I had not seen, much less gotten to practice on, a single honest-to-goodness corpse. "People live longer these days," Aunty claimed.

But I knew it was because everyone, even from villages across the bay, had begun taking their business to the Paradise Mortuary. The single event that had established Clinton's monopoly was the untimely death of old Mrs. Parmeter, the plantation owner's mother-in-law, who'd choked on a fishbone in the salmon mousse during a fund raising luncheon for Famine Relief. Clinton had been chosen to be in charge of the funeral. After that, he'd taken to wearing three-piece suits, as a symbol of his new respectability, and was nominated as a Republican candidate for the village council.

"So, what are people saying?" I asked, finally pushing my plate away.

This was the cue that Mama had been waiting for. "They're saying that That Woman has gotten herself a pet donkey, though that's not the word they're using, of course." She paused dramatically; the implication was clear.

I began remembering things about living in my mother's house. The navy-blue dresses. The humiliating weekly tea ceremony lessons at the Buddhist temple.

"Give up this foolishness," she wheedled. "Mrs. Koyama tells me the Barber Shop Lady is looking for help."

"I think I'll stay right where I am," I said.

My mother fell silent. Then she jabbed a meat bun with her serving fork and lifted it onto my plate. "Here, have another helping," she said.

A few weeks later Aunty and I were called outside the village to perform a laying out. It was early afternoon when Sheriff Kanoi came by to tell us that the body of Mustard Hayashi, the eldest of the Hayashi boys, had just been pulled from an irrigation ditch by a team of field workers. He had apparently fallen in the night before, stone drunk, on his way home from the La Hula Rhumba Bar and Grill.

I began hurrying around, assembling Aunty's tools and potions, and checking that everything was in working order, but the old woman didn't turn a hair; she just sat calmly rocking back and forth and puffing on her skinny, long-stemmed pipe.

"Yuri, you stop that rattling around back there," she snapped, then turned to the sheriff. "My son Clinton could probably handle this. Why don't you ask him?"

Sheriff Kanoi hesitated before replying, "This looks like a tough case that's going to need some real expertise."

Aunty stopped rocking. "That's true, it was a bad death," she mused.

"Very bad," the sheriff agreed.

"The spirit is going to require some talking to," she continued. "You know, so it doesn't linger."

"And the family asked especially for you," he added.

No doubt because they didn't have any other choice, I thought. That morning, I'd run into Chinky Malloy, the assistant mortician at the Paradise, so I happened to know that Clinton was at a morticians' conference in Los Angeles and wouldn't be back for several days. But I didn't say a word.

When we arrived at the Hayashis', Mustard's body was lying on the green Formica table in the kitchen. It was the only room in the house with a door that faced north. Aunty claimed that a proper laying out required a room with a north-facing door, so the spirit could find its way home to the land of the dead without getting lost.

Mustard's mother was leaning over his corpse, wailing, and her husband stood behind her, looking white-faced, and absently patting her on the back. The tiny kitchen was jammed with sobbing, nose-blowing mourners, and the air was thick with the smells of grief—perspiration, ladies' cologne, the previous night's cooking, and the faintest whiff of putrefying flesh. Aunty gripped me by the wrist and pushed her way to the front. The air pressed close, like someone's hot, wet breath on my face. My head reeled, and the room broke apart into dots of color. From far away I heard somebody say, "It's Aunty Talking to the Dead."

"Make room, make room," another voice called.

I looked down at Mustard, lying on the table in front of me, his eyes half open in that swollen, purple face. The smell was much stronger close up, and there were flies everywhere.

"We'll have to get rid of some of this bloat," Aunty said, thrusting a metal object into my hand.

People were leaving the room.

She went around to the other side of the table. "I'll start here," she said. "You work over there. Do just like I told you."

I nodded. This was the long-awaited moment. My moment. But it was already the beginning of the end. My knees buckled, and everything went dark.

Aunty performed the laying out alone and never mentioned the episode again. But it was the talk of the village for weeks—how Yuri Shimabukuro, assistant to Aunty Talking to the Dead, passed out under the Hayashis' kitchen table and had to be tended by the grief-stricken mother of the dead boy.

My mother took to catching the bus to the plantation store three villages away whenever she needed to stock up on necessaries. "You're my daughter—how could I *not* be on your side?" was the way she put it, but the air buzzed with her unspoken recriminations. And whenever I went into the village, I was aware of the sly laughter behind my back, and Chinky Malloy smirking at me from behind the shutters of the Paradise Mortuary.

"She's giving the business a bad name," Clinton said, carefully removing his jacket and draping it across the back of the rickety wooden chair. He dusted the seat, looked at his hand with distaste before wiping it off on his handkerchief, then drew up the legs of his trousers, and sat.

Aunty retrieved her pipe from the smoking tray next to her rocker and filled the tiny brass bowl from a pouch of Bull Durham. "I'm glad you found time to drop by," she said. "You still going out with that skinny white girl?"

"You mean Marsha?" Clinton sounded defensive. "Sure, I see her sometimes. But I didn't come here to talk about that." He glanced over at where I was sitting on the sofa. "You think we could have some privacy?"

Aunty lit her pipe and puffed. "Yuri's my right-hand girl. Couldn't do without her."

"The Hayashis probably have their own opinion about that."

Aunty dismissed his insinuation with a wave of her hand. "There's no pleasing some people," she said. "Yuri's just young; she'll learn." She reached over and patted me on the knee, then looked him straight in the face. "Like we all did."

Clinton turned red. "Damn it, Mama," he sputtered, "this is no time to bring up the past. What counts is now, and right now your right-hand girl is turning you into a laughingstock!" His voice became soft, persuasive. "Look, you've worked hard all your life, and you deserve to retire. Now that my business is taking off, I can help you out. You know I'm only thinking about you."

"About the election to village council, you mean." I couldn't help it; the words just burst out of my mouth.

Aunty said, "You considering going into politics, son?"

"Mama, wake up!" Clinton hollered, like he'd wanted to all along.

"You can talk to the dead till you're blue in the face, but *ain't no one listening*. The old ghosts have had it. You either get on the wheel of progress or you get run over."

For a long time after he left, Aunty sat in her rocking chair next to the window, rocking and smoking, without saying a word, just rocking and smoking, as the afternoon shadows spread beneath the trees and turned to night.

Then she began to sing—quietly, at first, but very sure. She sang the naming chants and the healing chants. She sang the stones, and trees, and stars back into their rightful places. Louder and louder she sang, making whole what had been broken.

Everything changed for me after Clinton's visit. I stopped going into the village and began spending all my time with Aunty Talking to the Dead. I followed her everywhere, carried her loads without complaint, memorized remedies, and mixed potions till my head spun and I went near blind. I wanted to know what *she* knew; I wanted to make what had happened at the Hayashis' go away. Not just in other people's minds. Not just because I'd become a laughingstock, like Clinton said. But because I knew that I had to redeem myself for that one thing, or my moment—the single instant of glory for which I had lived my entire life—would be snatched beyond my reach forever.

Meanwhile, there were other layings out. The kitemaker who hanged himself. The crippled boy from Chicken Fight Camp. The vagrant. The blind man. The blind man's dog.

"Do like I told you," Aunty would say before each one, Then, "Give it time," when it was done.

But it was like living the same nightmare over and over—just one look at a body and I was done for. For twenty-five years, people in the village joked about my "indisposition." Last fall, my mother's funeral was held at the paradise Mortuary. While the service was going on, I stood outside on the cement walk for a long time, but I never made it through the door. Little by little, I'd begun to give up hope that my moment would ever arrive.

Then, a week ago, Aunty caught a chill, gathering *awa* in the rain. The chill developed into a fever, and for the first time since I'd known her, she took to her bed. I nursed her with the remedies she'd taught me—sweat baths; eucalyptus steam; tea made from *ko'oko'olau*—but the fever worsened. Her breathing became labored, and she grew weaker. My few hours of sleep were filled with bad dreams. Finally, aware of my betrayal, I walked to a house up the road and telephoned for an ambulance.

"I'm sorry, Aunty," I kept saying as the flashing red light swept across the porch. The attendants had her on a stretcher and were carrying her out the front door.

She reached up and grasped my arm, her grip still strong. "You'll do okay, Yuri," the old woman whispered hoarsely. "Clinton used to get so scared, he messed his pants." She chuckled, then began to cough. One of the attendants put an oxygen mask over her face.

"Hush," he said. "There'll be plenty of time for talking later."

On the day of Aunty's wake, the entrance to the Paradise Mortuary was blocked. Workmen had dug up the front walk and carted the old concrete tiles away. They'd left a mound of gravel on the grass, stacked some bags of concrete next to it, and covered the bags with black tarps. There was an empty wheelbarrow parked to one side of the gravel mound. The entire front lawn had been roped off and a sign had been put up that said, "Please follow the arrows around to the back. We are making improvements in Paradise. The Management."

My stomach was beginning to play tricks, and I was feeling shaky. The old panic was mingled with an uneasiness that had not left me ever since I'd decided to call the ambulance. I kept thinking that it had been useless to call it since she'd gone and died anyway. Or maybe I had waited too long. I almost turned back, but I thought of what Aunty had told me about Clinton and pressed ahead. Numbly, I followed the two women in front of me.

"So, old Aunty Talking to the Dead has finally passed on," one of them, whom I recognized as Emi McAllister, said. She was with Pearlie Woo. Both were old classmates of mine.

I was having difficulty seeing—it was getting dark, and my head was spinning so.

"How old do you suppose she was?" Pearlie asked.

"Gosh, even when we were kids it seemed like she was at least a hundred," Emi said.

Pearlie laughed. " 'The Undead,' my brother used to call her."

"When we misbehaved," Emi said, "our mother always threatened to abandon us on the hill where Aunty lived. Mama would be beating us with a wooden spoon and hollering, 'This is gonna seem like nothing then.' "

Aunty had been laid out in a room near the center of the mortuary. The heavy, wine-colored drapes had been drawn across the windows and all the wall lamps turned very low, so it was darker indoors than it had been outside. Pearlie and Emi moved off into the front row. I headed for the back.

There were about thirty of us at the viewing, mostly from the old days—those who had grown up on stories about Aunty, or who remembered her from before the Paradise Mortuary. People got up and began filing past the casket. For a moment I felt dizzy again, but I glanced over at Clinton, looking prosperous and self-assured, accepting condolences, and I got into line.

The room was air-conditioned and smelled of floor disinfectant and roses. Soft music came from speakers mounted on the walls. I drew nearer and nearer to the casket. Now there were four people ahead. Now three. I looked down at my feet, and I thought I would faint.

Then Pearlie Woo shrieked, "Her eyes!" People behind me began to murmur. "What—whose eyes?" Emi demanded. Pearlie pointed to the body in the casket. Emi cried, "My God, they're open!"

My heart turned to ice.

"What?" voices behind me were asking. "What about her eyes?"

"She said they're open," someone said.

"Aunty Talking to the Dead's eyes are open," someone else said.

Now Clinton was hurrying over.

"That's because she's not dead," still another voice added.

Clinton looked into the coffin, and his face went white. He turned quickly around and waved to his assistants across the room.

"I've heard about cases like this," someone was saying. "It's because she's looking for someone."

"I've heard that too! The old woman is trying to tell us something."

I was the only one there who knew. Aunty was talking to *me*. I clasped my hands together, hard, but they wouldn't stop shaking.

People began leaving the line. Others pressed in, trying to get a better look at the body, but a couple of Clinton's assistants had stationed themselves in front of the coffin, preventing anyone from getting too close. They had shut the lid, and Chinky Malloy was directing people out of the room.

"I'd like to take this opportunity to thank you all for coming here this evening," Clinton was saying. "I hope you will join us at the reception down the hall."

While everyone was eating, I stole back into the parlor and quietly—ever so quietly—went up to the casket, lifted the lid, and looked in.

At first I thought they had switched bodies on me and exchanged Aunty for some powdered and painted old grandmother, all pink and white, in a pink dress, and clutching a white rose to her chest. But there they were. Open. Aunty's eyes staring up at me.

Then I knew. This was *it*: my moment had arrived. Aunty Talking to the Dead had come awake to bear me witness.

I walked through the deserted front rooms of the mortuary and out the front door. It was night. I got the wheelbarrow, loaded it with one of the tarps covering the bags of cement, and wheeled it back to the room where Aunty was. It squeaked terribly, and I stopped often to make sure no one had heard. From the back of the building came the clink of glassware and the buzz of voices. I had to work quickly—people would be leaving soon.

But this was the hardest part. Small as she was, it was very hard to lift her out of the coffin. She was horribly heavy, and unyielding as a bag of cement. I finally got her out and wrapped her in the tarp. I loaded her in the tray of the wheelbarrow—most of her, anyway; there was nothing I could do about her feet sticking out the front end. Then I wheeled her out of the mortuary, across the village square, and up the road, home.

Now, in the dark, the old woman is singing.

I have washed her with my own hands and worked the salt into the hollows of her body. I have dressed her in white and laid her in flowers.

Aunty, here are the beads you like to wear. Your favorite cakes. A quilt to keep away the chill. Here is *noni* for the heart and *awa* for every kind of grief.

Down the road a dog howls, and the sound of hammering echoes through the still air. "Looks like a burying tomorrow," the sleepers murmur, turning in their warm beds.

I bind the sandals to her feet and put the torch to the pyre.

The sky turns to light. The smoke climbs. Her ashes scatter, filling the wind.

And she sings, she sings, she sings.

Lost Girls

■

PAT CADIGAN

Well, I tried to tell him there was going to be trouble. I really did. I really thought that as the female who had been closest to him the longest, I'd have had some major influence, that he would listen. But it's the same old story—it's just about impossible to get anyone to take you seriously when you're only a few inches high and covered with fairy dust. And you're cursed with tinkling bells for a voice. After all that, the frivolous name is practically anticlimax.

Can't say I haven't contributed to my own predicament, though. For time out of mind, I've played the role of the party girl with gusto. I was, after all, the one who always got everybody high—literally. You wanted to fly, I was the girl to see, I had the stuff.

Still am. You can't help what you are, after all. But, as I maintained to Peter, you can help what you do with it.

"We're doing just fine, Tink," he said, folding his arms behind his head and watching the clouds sail by. He was picking out shapes in them—ships, castles, dragons, two-headed teddy bears, the usual for around here. The clouds always do that, float across the sky in shapes you could pick out, except on the few occasions that called for a corker of a thunderstorm. "We're doing better than ever. We're giving all those children a childhood. Childhood's getting scarcer all the time. They have to start school now when they're barely out of their prams—they don't even have prams anymore, not the way we used to know them. And by the time I come to take them away on adventures, they can read and count and write, they can name the days of the week and the months of the year, and their heads are filled with the most peculiar notions!

"For instance," he said quickly, sitting up and letting a really good cloud that looked like a giant porcupine playing a pipe organ break up unnamed, "for instance, that little one that kept trying to tell me the Indians weren't Indians, they were—" he made a face. Couldn't remember, of course. Peter's memory is the size of a hazelnut, and not a very big hazelnut. But then, it has to be, he wouldn't be who and what he is if he had any kind of memory. He's the Original Lost Boy, after all, and so he's perpetually at square one, every hurt is like the first hurt, every joy like the first, and so on and so forth. But when the occasion called for it, he could summon up a little recollection, about something extraordinary bad, or extraordinary good, or just extraordinarily extraordinary. This would stay with him for a little while, until some other extraordinary thing came along to replace it.

"Native Americans," I said. I always remember. Being a fairy, my memory is not subject to the constraints of eternal childhood.

"Who are?" he said.

"Indians, Peter. Indians. The little boy told you that Indians should really be called Native Americans." I wasn't impatient, just bored.

"Oh. Yes. Native Americans, Indians—heavens, Tink, what are 'Americans'? The Indians are the Indians, they've always been the Indians."

No use to explain to Peter about that, that the people he called Indians bore about as much resemblance to the real thing as I did. Some of them could have been Sioux or Comanche or Mohawk, but the rest of them were a mix of nationalities and ethnic groups. Peter had a child's blindness to that kind of difference between people, endearing and beautiful in one way, totally insensitive in another. "Gay, innocent, and heartless," remember?

Tiger Lily and I had covered that subject a few times in the course of our many late-night talks. When Peter thought I was safely shut up in my little house-within-the-house, I would fly off into the night, over the mountains and the valleys and lagoon to her teepee. She was the only other female on the island who would understand. Yes, we set aside our differences a long, long time ago, though Peter doesn't know it. As the source of the problem, he just wouldn't get it, he'd feel betrayed, even though he never understood why we were in conflict in the first place, and never will!

How's that for an obtuse male? I ask you!

"He's a child," Lil said, rolling her eyes. "The idea that there'd be something about people that had nothing to do with him or his ideas just never occurs to him. If you tried to tell him even just a little bit about what really happened to the people called Indians—why, it would be like speaking High Church Latin to him, he'd understand it about as well. He's got just enough information and misinformation in more or less equal parts to offend anyone except a very young child."

"That would have to be a very, very young child," I reminded her.

But mostly what we discussed was what we called the Female Predicament. All sorts of children came to the island with Peter, children of every culture, every color, every faith. The only difference Peter recognized was gender.

Boy! (If you'll pardon the expression.)

Tiger Lily and I laid most of the blame squarely on Wendy. Perhaps that's not really fair, but she did start the whole Mother business.

I knew she was trouble the second I laid eyes on her in the nursery that night—the second Peter laid eyes on her! Forgot his shadow, right! What galls me is that I didn't see through that one immediately. But after all, I'm a fairy—we handle things differently, it's all magic with us. I should have known, though, I'd been around Peter long enough and even if he had lived in Never-Never Land since falling out of his pram in Kensington Gardens, he'd always be more human boy when it came right down to it.

Which suggests, naturally, that even he wasn't really aware of what he was doing when he "forgot" his stupid shadow and then had to go back for it. But with all the signs there, I should have been able to read them, I shouldn't have had to get locked in a damned drawer before I figured out what was going on! Was I mad when he let me out! And was she surprised when she saw me. Tried to kiss up to me right away, too, talking about how beautiful I was and acting all enchanted to see a real live fairy and all that rot. But the look in her eyes wasn't wide, innocent wonder. Her eyes weren't quite wide enough; in fact they were narrowed ever so slightly. It wasn't wonder there but wariness and territoriality and jealousy.

Jealous of a fairy only a few inches high—talk about mixing information and misinformation! Right away she started trying to one-up me. Oh, I can sew, and I can do the spring cleaning, and I'll be your mother, and blah-blah-blah. And I got sucked right into it, I can't deny that. I got pissy about the fairy dust. Okay, shame on me. But in the end, they flew, all of them, they flew away to Never-Never Land and had all those adventures.

Okay, okay, the thing with the arrow was awful, too. But come on, this is Never-Never Land we're talking about, I knew she couldn't actually be killed . . . not killed-killed, not killed dead. It's like a roller coaster, a great scare but nothing permanent. I wanted to scare the living daylights out of her, I wanted to scare her so bad she could fly all the way back to the nursery just by screaming.

Now I shudder to think that I could do such a thing to another female, even if it was Wendy. Do you see how crazy it made me? And in such a short period of time! Awful. Just awful! But she played it for all it was worth and then some—her great hovering-on-the-brink-of-death scene. Name me someone else who got a whole house built for herself that way. So it wasn't much of a house, we all continued to live in the underground place—the symbolism was enough to seal our fates. By attacking her, I had managed to cement her position.

She had second thoughts about it after a while, when it was too late really to do anything about it. If she hadn't started the whole mother business, she'd have been treated like a lost boy with a dirty face and her own bow and arrow. She wasn't the first girl who had made it to Never-Never Land, though there hadn't been many in the past. Peter automatically gravitated to boys, though occasionally one or two of them had sisters who came along, as if caught in the backwash. Canny little things kept a low profile, did everything the boys did, obeyed Peter's orders, and didn't say much. I checked on them later, and I must say it was interesting the way things turned out for them—the little Sanger girl, for instance.

Looking at it from that angle, you would think that the first female to assert herself as a female rather than just one of the boys could have brought some significant changes to Never-Never Land and thence to the world. But as soon as we get one, what does she do but perpetuate the same old roles? Well, it was all she knew. Being female has never saved anyone from a limited imagination. But perhaps it might have been different if she'd been a single parent, and not insisted that Peter be the father. That would have made the position of mother something altogether different, she might have come into her own as a heroic figure. But that was part of all she knew—mother and father, and from her point of view, Peter was the logical choice for father, even leaving the way she felt about him out of it. And when you consider her emotions—well, there was no one on the island to advise her that just because you love a male doesn't mean that you should have a family with him. Would she have listened if there had been?

To be fair, I don't suppose I'd have wanted to be the single mother of that bunch, either. But with Peter as the father, she might as well have been. Peter the father with the roving eye! And dumb enough to talk to Wendy about it! Gosh, Wendy, I don't know what Tiger Lily wants to be to me, but I don't think it's a mother. Woo! Did she give him hell about that! And poor Lil—she got sucked into the game just as I did. Peter and the boys had rescued her from the pirates hundreds and hundreds of times, it was part of the great tradition that makes Never-Never Land what it is. It wasn't that Peter nearly died on the rock—he always nearly died. Hook's bite, the rising tide, Peter speaking what he believes will be his last words about dying being an awfully big adventure—this is fantasy childhood drama.

She changed everything. I saw it at the celebration at the Indian camp later, the way she looked at Lil. It was the same way she had looked at me in the nursery. Lil obviously didn't know what was happening exactly, but she reacted to Wendy the way she would have to anyone hunting on Indian land without permission, and she knew instinctively that she had to win something of Peter's heart if she ever wanted to be rescued from the pirates again.

I think that was the bitterest pill for her—up until then, winning something of Peter's heart wasn't even an issue. If Peter had even just been showing signs of growing up (impossible, of course, but just for the sake of example), she'd have let him go. But that wasn't the problem.

In my more unkind moments, I've thought that was why Wendy got herself captured by the pirates. Of course, everybody got captured by the pirates—that was part of the tradition—but this time, it wasn't just Hook and his men capturing all of Peter's men. This time, Hook and Peter's family, the children and their mother. It put a whole different spin on the rescue, especially after that little scene she played with the boys in the underground house.

Another blatant attempt to force Peter's hand is what that was, telling that story about mothers pining away for their children, reminding the boys. Not the first time she'd told the story; I knew sooner or later Peter would listen to it and it would get to him. Did she really, truly believe deep down that she would be able to pull Peter away from Never-Never Land? If so, the joke was on her—she got everyone except Peter.

And the looks on those boys' faces as they prepared to leave Never-Never Land forever—is it any wonder I tried to kill myself?

I know, everyone thinks it's my noblest moment, saving Peter from drinking Hook's poison. But I didn't have to drink it myself to do that. Every other time I always just flew into the room and knocked the glass from his hands. But that time, I was in despair. I felt Peter's loss even more deeply than he did. I loved those boys, too, after all, they were a big part of my life as well. The way she manipulated their feelings, playing them like blooming violins, for goodness sake! What a nightmare! I felt that was worse poison than what Hook put in Peter's "medicine" (another of Wendy's little innovations, as if anyone ever got sick that way here!). So I squared my shoulders, preened my wings, and said, Good-bye, cruel world.

Yes, I really would have died . . . sort of. As Peter has explained to countless children, real death comes for one of my kind whenever a child says I don't believe in fairies. The poison would have killed me as well, just because of the treatment Peter had decided on—leaving it to children everywhere all over the world to affirm their belief in fairies. Had I expired before Peter could help me, I would simply have been reborn in some other realm that allows the existence of fairies, without memory, without sadness. I was hoping for something Nordic. And then Peter had to interfere.

Had his treatment failed, had there been too few children clapping their hands, there would have been no rebirth for me, just nothingness. Peter felt he had to prove something to both of us—that he still had it, of course, that he was still the most beloved boy of all time, and thus children would clap their hands just because he asked them to. Some see that as Peter's noblest moment, others see it as childhood's noblest moment. The truth is something that is probably best left unsaid in a place like Never-Never Land. You can't have a Never-Never Land without a certain amount of denial.

You know the rest of the story. Did Hook and the pirates really die? Of course not. I found Hook later, washed up on the shore of Mermaid Lagoon with his clothes in rags, cursing a blue streak (most of it sounded like Argh! Argh!) and vowing revenge, if a little confused— he thought he'd lost his hand to the crocodile just then. I kept an eye on him until Smee floated in clinging to a bit of driftwood. If it were not against the rules, I would visit Smee in the middle of the night sometimes and have a few long talks with him, too. I suspect there's a lot of common ground between us, and perhaps the time is coming when I will be able to have a word or two with him.

Everyone weeps over the last meeting between Wendy and Peter in London, myself included. Surprised? Me, too, a little. Of course, I don't just weep over that—I weep for the lost boys who have become bankers and citizens of good standing. How I miss them, Tootles and Slightly and the rest! And I weep for Wendy, too, for her realization of what she lost, which was not Peter. What she lost was much more complex than that.

And then she went and did it anyway—let her own daughter take her place to do Peter's spring cleaning! Oh, that really galled me! I'd have thought that growing up would have made her realize her mistake and instead, she visited it upon her daughter! And her daughter did the same to her daughter—Wendy's granddaughter.

Except by then, things were starting to change.

There was a whole new group of lost boys in Never-Never Land, of course, and Peter's memory didn't admit that there had ever been any others. Though occasionally he slipped and called one of them "Tootles" and was mightily confused at his mistake, since he didn't remember Tootles. The name had just come out of nowhere as far as he was concerned. I never reminded him.

He never slipped with the girls. There would be only one Wendy and though her memory grew dim, it never vanished completely. Odd, but there's no accounting for the vagaries of a mind like Peter's.

What was even more interesting, though, was that from the time Wendy left, there was never more than one girl brought to Never-Never Land, and she was always brought to fill Wendy's old position as quasi-mother. No more did little girls slip in among the gang brought to have adventures with the pirates and the Indians and to vow that they would never grow up, at least for a little while. There was always just the one girl. Wendy's daughter went along with it. But Wendy's granddaughter—ah, she was a different story altogether!

She wasn't completely free of the expectations that had been thrust upon her both here in Never-Never Land and back in the real world. But she questioned a lot, and if she didn't like the answers, she could be quite stubborn. One day, I found Peter and the boys making their own beds; she was off swimming in Mermaid Lagoon. Hook tried to capture her, of course, and Peter and the other boys ran to her rescue. But what do you suppose they found when they got there? Hook running as if for his life while she pelted him with stones and shells and driftwood and anything else she could find to throw! And yelling threats of worse punishment if he ever had the nerve to bother her again.

Poor Hook! He didn't know what hit him. After all, he was a pirate. When he captured her and the boys later, his pirate band was twice the size it usually was, and to this day, I have no idea where he found the extra men. Men, yes. As I said, he was a pirate.

So after they all went home to grow up, I tried to talk to Peter. Next season, I said, just round up a bunch of boys and girls and treat them all like lost boys. The whole point is to have adventures without parents, especially mothers. They'll all like that and if the spring cleaning doesn't get done and the beds don't get made, so what? This is Never-Never Land, for heaven's sake!

But would he listen? Lost boys and a mother, that was the formula, he said; he was Peter Pan, I was just the fairy with the dust. My job was to get them off the ground, he was the one who really taught them how to fly, and he was the leader. Then he reminded me about saving my life the time I drank poison and believe me, I bit my tongue pretty hard to keep from telling him a few hard truths about that.

But then, I'm pretty sure it's against the rules to use the words "su-icide attempt" in Never-Never Land anyway. Certain amount of de-nial, remember? So he went and got Wendy's great-granddaughter, and that's when the, uh, dirt really hit the fan (only Hook is allowed profanity, and he never gets worse than "damn"; I got away with "ass" just because it really is another word for donkey).

Wendy's great-granddaughter got the picture the minute her feet touched down on the island. Oooh! You never saw such a fuss! Mother?! I'll give you Mother! I didn't fly straight on till morning to clean up after a bunch of boys, now bring on those pirates! Where's that Hook? I'll tear him limb from limb! Where are the Indians? I want to beat the tom-tom and go on the warpath! Where's the fairy? I want to fly some more!

Peter, of course, tried to argue with her. From the time he alighted at her window to the time they took off into the night, he never once said "spring cleaning" or "Mother" or anything like it—by then he was taking a lot for granted. He shouldn't have been, you know that, I know that, I think even some of the long-term boys knew that. But Peter—well, that's the perennial boy for you. Things had changed back there in the world. It didn't mean there had to be any kind of major changes in Never-Never Land, except for the genders of the children involved. If he'd just been able to go with that particular flow, eventually he would never have known the difference between having adventures with just all boys and having adventures with a mixed band of boys and girls.

Perhaps that was too mature a viewpoint for the kind of boy he was. And perhaps an invisible line had been crossed when Wendy had played mother . . . the denial for the need of a mother had been erased, you see, and there was no going back. And poor Peter just couldn't read just his perception of what a mother was. Mothers didn't fight pirates, they didn't go on the warpath with the Indians, they didn't have their own bows and arrows.

Ho, ho, ho. What I could have told him about that from my visits to the real world! Yes, I visited there more often after Wendy's grand-daughter. I knew I had some catching up to do.

And yes, I did find Wendy on one of those visits. She was a very old woman by then. I found her in Kensington Gardens, and what do you suppose she was doing? Letting children out of their prams! Yes! And only girl-children! Oh, I know they don't call them prams anymore, but you know what I mean. No one really knew what she was doing, and none of the children ever got far before their mothers caught them again. She was dotty, I decided, as I lured her to a secluded area and revealed myself.

"Hallo, Tink," she said. "Do you still hate me?"

"I never really hated you," I told her. "But you must realize now that what you did wasn't right."

She gave a sigh that shook her body alarmingly. Just a bundle of sticks now, our Wendy. I was glad Peter wasn't here. "Of course I understand," she said. "Why do you think I'm letting the little girls loose? They're entitled to a childhood full of adventures and excitement, not just training for an adulthood of nothing but limitations." She laughed sadly. "Yes, Tink, I've learned—that's part of growing up, you see, to learn some of your lessons too late! I'm trying to make amends. But it's hard. People watch their children so much more closely than they used to, I don't think a child's been lost to the fairies here in over thirty years! And there are so few of them, they're all shut up tight in day-care centers and schools! Peter is lucky to get to any of them at all, boys or girls." She paused, looking alarmed. "Does he still get to them, Tink? Or has the worst happened?"

Obviously she hadn't seen her granddaughter lately, which made me feel very sad for her indeed. I was about to tell her all about that when a police officer came along, rendering me invisible. All she found was a dotty old woman talking to some hydrangea bushes, and she led her away, still talking. That made me feel very, very sad. Poor Wendy, a stereotype to the end. I never found her again after that, so I never got a chance to tell her what happened with her great-granddaughter.

You can see it coming, can't you? Anybody can, except Peter and some of the more obtuse boys. She rebelled completely, of course. The first night in the underground house, she crept up to my chamber, took some fairy dust, and flew out into the darkness. She was back the next morning with her own band and, needless to say, they were all girls.

They set up camp in Mermaid Lagoon and waited for the pirates to attack. Hook, who had been burned before and hadn't forgotten it, held off and had a few halfhearted skirmishes with Peter and his band instead. The girls got tired of waiting and, in a brilliant midnight raid, attacked the Jolly Roger and took it over, forcing all the pirates to walk the plank. They sailed around in it for weeks until they lost interest and went ashore. Hook and his men saved it from going aground, refitted it, and declared war.

What excitement! What action! Sometimes the girls would win, sometimes the pirates would beat them back. But even when the pirates won, they knew they'd been in a fight, I can tell you! Hook lived in mortal fear that the lost girls and the lost boys would join forces and completely overwhelm him and his men.

Do I have to tell you this never happened?

Peter and his boys had a very disappointing season; it rained every other day and they ended up hanging around the underground house bored out of their minds, so much so that some of the new boys started talking about something called videogames and television. That was when Peter had tried to tell me we were doing fine, providing childhoods for those who would otherwise have been forced to unfortunate precocity.

While on the other side of the island, the girls had made a treaty with the Indians and were whooping it up like mad. When it finally occurred to Peter that he hadn't seen Tiger Lily in many, many moons, his dismay was terrible to behold. And when he crept up to the Indian village and found Wendy's granddaughter and Tiger Lily smoking the peace pipe together and leading the dance around the fire without him, I thought he would die of heartbreak.

He could not get over that one, of course, and it was what drove him to ask her for a meeting. I carried the message to her, naturally.

"Well, well," she said to me. "So His Nibs has finally decided to parley, eh? What do you say, girls? Shall I talk with our boy Pan, or shall we attack the pirates again?"

They all voted for the pirates, but she was just being difficult. She agreed to meet him in Mermaid Lagoon.

It didn't go well. Peter swaggered up to her and said brightly, "Well, time to go home and grow up. The boys are ready. How about you?"

She poked him in the chest with her finger. "You can keep that stuff, pal. Not all the boys go home and grow up, You don't go home and grow up. So who says we have to? Maybe some of my girls want to, and if they do, I won't stop them. But me, I like it here. I'm planning to stay a good time, maybe forever and ever. I like showing Hook who's boss. I like dancing around the campfire with Tiger Lily and the rest of the Indians. And I like flying."

Peter gave me a dirty look. He knew I'd been supplying her as well as him. But what could I do? If you're a child in Never-Never Land, you get the dust, it's the law. The pirates could have it if they wanted it, but it won't work for them because they can't think good thoughts, and the Indians have their own way of life.

They argued and argued, but Peter couldn't get her to budge. In the end, some of the boys left, but not one of the girls. And when Peter went out to collect some more children the next season, he couldn't find one girl to be mother. They'd all gone with her.

She stayed, and stayed, and stayed, until it was obvious that she was never going to leave the island. No one knew what to call her— Pammy Pan? Patty Pan? Petra Pan? She settled on Ellspeth—heaven knows why, I don't. And for a long, long time, it was lost boys with Peter, and lost girls with Ellspeth, and never the twain would meet.

And then, of course, it happened. The morning dawned when there were both girls and boys with Ellspeth, and only boys with Peter.

"Nothing I could do, Tink," Ellspeth told me. "I'd been taking their sisters away for years, and the sisters had been telling them stories and they wanted in on the fun. Sure, I said no at first. Then I realized how unfair it was. After all, Peter's been doing just that very thing with the girls—that's how I got started in the first place. It's ridiculous to have the boys with only boys and the girls with only girls, that's not how anyone lives. Oh, the pirates are all male but they're pirates, you don't expect pirates to be enlightened." I had a feeling the pirates' day was coming, too, but they weren't my concern, they could take care of themselves. "Couldn't you just combine the bands?" I said. "Lost girls and lost boys together?"

"Only if I or one of the other girls'll be the mother," Ellspeth said grimly. "And we won't do it. We won't. If Peter can be stubborn, we can be just as stubborn."

And there it sits—Peter on one side of the island with his little band, and Ellspeth on her side with her somewhat larger band. What's really sad is that Peter's band gets smaller every year. Going with Ellspeth has so much more to offer. She gets all the good fights with the pirates and all the good parties with the Indians, and she has even usurped Peter's drowning scene on the rock.

Peter mopes around and cuts himself whittling a lot. Occasionally, a boy goes over to Ellspeth and then it rains for a week on Peter's side.

I guess what it is really is that eternal childhood is—well, not a lie, exactly, but a half-truth. At some point, perhaps the very point at which a child is ready for Never-Never Land, childhood is actually a choice more than a condition. Ellspeth chose. Peter could choose, too, but so far, he won't. I think because he's so afraid that doing such a thing will mean he's growing up, and it won't mean any such thing at all. And there's the whole difference between childhood and childish.

I shouldn't try to be an expert because I am, after all, a fairy and as I said, it's all magic with fairies, magic and no worries, unless you drink poison. And believe me, I'm not stupid enough to try that twice. Not with the way things are today!

Sometimes I wonder, though, what would happen. If my life depended on somebody's faith . . . whose faith would save me? Is Peter's still strong enough? Does he still believe that all those little children out there in the dark believe? After all that's happened, I like to think that's still so. I like to think that's what keeps Peter the eternal boy that he is and that someday, he'll go over to the other side of the island and hail Ellspeth as his ally and friend, forget this silly mother business once and for all. It's not like he's got anything to lose!

Then he'll really be himself again, he'll go back to being brave Peter Pan, the boy who won't grow up, instead of poor Peter, the boy that the children hardly ever fly with anymore.

Psychofemmes

■

MELISSA MIA HALL

Karen

"Are you crazy?—don't do this—please, I'm begging you, sweetheart—don't do this . . ."

The man, already soaked in sweat, pees in his pants and the stink of urine and BO makes the already stale air in the storeroom thicker and more horrible to bear. His executioner twitches her nose like Samantha, a TV character on the old sitcom *Bewitched*, but nothing happens. TV magic is just that, TV magic caught in random airwaves after being played with by a bunch of showbiz folk, amateur illusionists. This is real. The stench gets worse. He no longer looks like a successful accountant. Her patience finally pops like a chewing gum bubble.

"I don't think I'm crazy, at least not the last time I looked," she says, calmly pulling the trigger. "Are you crazy?"

He doesn't say much, since he is dead.

Her aim has been magnificent, ending the nightmare with a perfect bullet hole to the heart. All those weeks practicing at the range have paid off. No longer will the bastard be conducting the criminal business he ran alongside his legit C.P.A. services, making kiddie porn.

The last seedy epic starred her now deceased daughter, Alison. The weight of the cassette bumps her hip where it nestles in the pocket of her Donna Karan jacket like a defanged rattlesnake.

She has not erased this last piece of evidence, although often she has longed to destroy it. It could be just an example of self-punishment. Karen has no intention of ever viewing it again, not the way she does the home movies of happier times. The school concerts Alison soloed in as a talented singer and dancer. The family holidays. Alison's father, still alive, not a middle-aged victim of heart disease. Alison, still alive, not a suicide at fifteen. Her dream to be an actress coincided too neatly with Mom's new boyfriend's plan to put her to work in cheesy blue videos.

Her mom's boyfriend—the thought tickles down her throat like curdled milk she can't spit out. She let the animal, even encouraged the animal to enter their normal lives. At least he has now been returned to the cosmic zoo, hopefully the one in the hotter regions.

A tentative knock on the door signals the time to leave has arrived. "Hurry . . ." the whisper from her sister jolts her out of her despondent and futile reverie. Karen Perkins carefully subtracts any detail of her presence and takes the service elevator to the parking garage. She walks past the almost empty slots with the intent of a panther stalking its kill, but the kill has already been completed.

Her sister Jill meets her in the all-night coffee shop on the corner where several hospital workers just getting off the late shift congregate. Jill lifts her mug of double espresso. "To justice . . ."

Karen slides into the booth and glances at the cappuccino waiting for her. "Did you order me a BLT?"

"Sure did." She has to use the rest room. With a weary nod, she leaves Jill. The gun is still in her purse, wrapped in a scarf, alongside many other articles. Made of dark brown Italian leather, sturdy, but sleek, the bag also holds many other things. The heat of the gun seems to radiate through the bands of woven leather. At any minute she thinks a cop will burst through the rest room to arrest her. She has just killed a man; well, maybe "man" is the wrong term for that worm.

She washes her face and scrubs her hands furiously. Doesn't she smell? She squirts massive amounts of DIVA on her wrists and then combs her long, blond hair. She finds a barrette in the bottom of her suit pocket and clips her hair back neatly. She reapplies her lipstick and mascara.

The light in the rest room isn't so good. She leans closer to the mirror and notices one eyelid seems a little droopy. She is only thirty-two but she feels like sixty-two. She bugs her eyes wide and wonders how on earth she can live with what she has just done.

Veronica Esmeralda Luna, from the group, comes in. "You okay?"

"Are you checking up on me?"

"You completed the assignment. You're a psychofemme, no doubt about it." She hands her the plane ticket and the traveler's checks without a smile or a handshake, just a cool stare that gives Karen a shiver. Veronica never smiles.

"Okay."

"You got the job done—now get on with your life. We cannot tolerate injustice. It's not about power, it's about being whole, not a fragment, doing what's right for you and not because someone tells you it is."

The bathroom seems to shrink. Karen can hardly breathe.

"Good luck." Veronica takes Karen's bag, fishes out the gun and slips it into her attaché case. "Did the silencer work out—did you notice any possible problem spots during the assignment that we need to be aware of?"

"No."

"Fine." Veronica gives her a nod, unlocks the rest room door, and vanishes. Karen splashes some more cold water on her face and leaves.

The BLT waits for her. Her sister tries to smile but her lips keeps slipping back into a worried wrinkle. "I had them do you another cappaccino because I drank yours."

Karen eats part of the sandwich and ingests the caffeine. She has to stay awake.

"I'll miss you."

"You can come and visit after I get settled."

"I will."

"With Sissy dead I just don't have much of a life here."

"I know." Her sister lowers her gaze and tears her napkin into tiny pieces. "So, was it bad?"

"Yeah."

"Were you scared?"

Karen can't answer her. A waitress watches them with a little too much attention. "Say, I've gotta run. Would love to stay and talk, but duty calls."

"Later . . ." Jill manages, knocking back tears Karen is sure will fall all the way back to her home in Arlington.

Jill

Her husband thinks Jill is a member of a book review club that is an offshoot from the Junior League or a continuing ed. class at the local university. He has no idea what they do or what they are doing.

"What's on the agenda tonight—a Sandra Brown romance or a naughty Stephen King book?" Brad hollers on his way out to the ball game.

"Neither. Try Margaret Atwood—she's a Canadian feminist writer."

"Cool," he says as he loads their two boys into the Explorer.

Jill waves as they leave the cul-de-sac.

Her neighborhood seems like an oasis of peace. She blinks back tears as she thinks about Karen leaving town as if it is something she does every day.

The club will begin arriving soon. She goes inside to get the table ready. The dogs, Labs that are affectionate if somewhat slobbery and always underfoot, allow her to sweep the faded Oriental rug. They seem to know something is up. She's not crazy about dogs, prefers cats, but the children and Brad really love dogs. She tolerates them. At least they're not wild dogs, really tame, actually—Pete sits quietly in the corner by the patio door and Marsha snuggles beside him, working on a rawhide chew toy.

Jill keeps checking the clock. Everything looks lovely. She lights the candles, not for romantic effect but to mask the faint doggy smell she is always so sensitive about.

The cars begin arriving in the cul-de-sac around seven. Jill welcomes the group with a strained smile. She recognizes some regulars and a few strangers. A disparate crowd—a curious assortment of age, ethnicity, talents, economic worth, and temperament. Jill feels both fear and pride to be among them.

Everyone clusters around the table heavy with food and drink. One woman, who looks especially impoverished and malnourished, takes up a quiet post at the end of the table, eats several helpings without looking up. She sniffs at the eggplant casserole. "Needs more garlic," she says, then finally heads to the sofa, coffee and éclair in hand.

Veronica sips merlot and nibbles on celery dipped in crab dip.

"Karen—" Jill's voice freezes in her throat as Veronica's eyebrows shoot up. You are never supposed to bring up the name of any graduate. Her exploits are never supposed to be discussed. It is over; Karen is over, done with. Through. Still, Jill can't let it go. The sisters had discussed it beforehand, over and over. With tears and pleading, she had resorted to their Christian upbringing. " ' "Vengeance is mine," saith the Lord.' Karen, don't you think, when it all comes down to Judgment Day, he will get his just reward?"

Her sister's pain rang shrilly in her voice. "I can't wait for that. My child is dead. She killed herself over what he did to her—a man I even slept with. Now she's gone, my baby's gone, suicide at fifteen because I didn't believe her, my own daughter, and then, there it was on the TV, playing with blood all over the floor. My baby's blood? She'd timed it so I'd find her when I came in from work. Come on, Jill, you've said it yourself, you'd like to be the one to pull the trigger." Her sister had looked so strong, so full of righteous glory, like an angel with a sword. Jill had pushed away the little voice that said, "Let Jesus handle it." They had gone to church every Sunday, growing up. They had prayed. Jill finds herself praying now. God help me get out of all this.

Veronica's voice startles her back to reality. She has one of those musical throaty voices at once hypnotic and awakening. "Your sister is dead—I am so sorry to hear about it. It was on the news at five P.M."

"What?" Jill feels shock spread throughout her body, numbing it.

"Plane crashed."

"Excuse me?" Jill will not believe her ears. It has to be some sort of cover or hidden message.

"Yes, I imagine it will be hard for you to adjust to the loss. We're all so sorry."

Jill's legs can't support her. The group all stares at her, pairs upon pairs of dead eyes unblinking, dry.

"She was a queen."

"Queen."

"Master of the Game."

"Blessed Demoiselle of Psychofemmedom," Babette says. The almost-super model just in from the Paris collections lifts her wineglass in tribute, then drains the wine in one gulp.

"Was there anything else on the agenda tonight?"

"Leslie's assignment."

Leslie Trenton is in the corner, studying the sculpture of Mother and Child Brad gave Jill for their tenth anniversary. Her dark red hair obscures her expression. One perfectly manicured hand rests on the head of the mother.

"The newspaper publisher."

"Maybe," Veronica says. The impoverished woman, on her second éclair, licks a chocolate smear off her thumb and mutters under her breath. "Excuse me, Hazel. Did you have something to share with us?"

"Gotta happen right away. My source says she's leaving the country for a sabbatical in three days after her elective surgery."

"Good work."

Leslie sits down, watching Veronica with unabashed respect. "The arrangements are all in place?"

"I'll let you know when it's time and also the confirmation of the victim's identity. There could be a last-minute emergency."

Babette raises her hand and waves it like a child.

"What is it?" Veronica says a little impatiently.

"I want my assignment verified. The girls are watching me too closely. They think something is up. If I'm going to do it—I've got to do it soon."

"Something is up."

"I want to do it real bad but the girls don't think he is so bad."

"The girls—the girls—are you all under eighteen, or what?" Jill says, wishing they could get back to Karen.

"Almost—"

"And you are almost as old as Cindy Crawford, Babette—you are not a girl. You are a woman," Jill says suddenly, her head pounding. The impoverished woman suddenly pulls out a platinum diamond-studded cigarette case and proceeds to light up. "Not in my house," Jill snaps.

"What's her problem?" a strange woman with short white hair says with a gasp. She is about seventy, wearing Armani and Ralph Lauren in a haphazard mix. She digs in her Chanel handbag and produces a cigar. "See this, honey? I'll smoke anytime, anywhere I damn well please, and so can Hazel!"

"No, you won't," Jill says.

Veronica shakes her black hair back and groans. "Oh, for heaven's sake, to smoke or not to smoke is not even in the ballpark."

"Excuse me?" the smoker arches a perfectly plucked eyebrow but puts her stogie back in her purse.

"Let's get back to what's really important. Is my sister really dead?" Jill's teeth chatters. Her whole body trembles as if an unseasonable arctic blast had blown through the room.

Hazel puts her cigarette case back into the shabby pocket of her dirty trench coat and produces a small pocketknife. She begins cleaning her fingernails.

Babette fidgets with her short see-through plastic skirt. She reaches into her silver thong and scratches. "I need some sex." She turns to look at Veronica pointedly.

"Not now—you little slut," Veronica says.

"I know—and not ever—I just like to pull your string, like I pull on mine. So sue me. I like pussy."

Babette loves flaunting her lesbianism. Right now Jill just wants her to stop playing with herself and to leave. She wants all of them to leave. She flinches when she thinks she hears Brad's Jeep pull up outside.

"Did you sabotage the plane? Did you kill her and how many innocent people along with her?"

"She's breaking the rules," a quiet woman says softly from her position near the Monet reproduction of water lilies. To Jill she looks like the waitress.

"Karen broke the rules," Babette says. "I don't break rules. I make them and I say that I want my assignment. I want to kill that two-faced jerk who doesn't want lesbians on the cover of *Vogue* or *Elle* or any damn magazine that promotes Miss Perfect GIRLIE GIRL as MS HETERO."

"Shut up," Veronica says, staring at Jill.

"I don't have to."

"We will end our meeting today without following *Robert's Rules of Order*. Jill will soon be deluged with company."

"This is my house and I demand answers."

Veronica just looks at Jill and shakes her head.

"How did she break the rules?" Jill almost screams, one hand digging into Veronica's thin shoulders.

"Don't touch me!" Veronica pushes her away.

Babette laughs. "Yes, don't touch Veronica, don't ever touch Veronica."

The dark woman's brown eyes shine with hatred. "Babette, I am warning you—don't make me lose my temper. I have killed twelve people. Maybe it's time for a lucky thirteen."

The group hushes. For a few moments no one can speak, then one at a time, members get up to leave. As each passes Jill, they make the club's crooked peace sign and say "Good luck," then disappear out the front door.

Veronica is the last to leave.

"I want out," Jill tells her, searching for signs of intelligent life in the face of the club's president. Jill suspects "Veronica" isn't even her name. Intelligence has long ago been replaced by a mask that chills and repels Jill even as it impresses her.

"We don't do that," she says. "You knew that going in. Karen knew that going in. Accidents happen. You give us too much power, Jill. Do you really think the club would kill innocent women and children?"

Jill has to admit that doesn't make much sense.

"A tragic accident, that's all."

"I still want out," Jill says.

"I'm afraid that's just not possible," Veronica says. "Remember: *Mi casa* is my house."

This time it is Brad's Jeep. Jill doesn't want the club president to see him, but it is too late. He brushes by the curvaceous brunette with an appreciative smile. He starts to introduce himself, but Veronica's exit is too quick.

"What's wrong with her?"

"She's in a hurry," Jill says. "She's just always in a hurry."

"Hey—look—is that your mother coming?"

Her mother's Oldsmobile squeals as she parks it haphazardly and runs, crying up the drive. "OH, MY GOD, JILL—I've had some just horrible news . . ."

The dogs begin barking then. It will be an hour before the house has any semblance of calm. Calm, not joy. Jill feels it will be years before she can ever find that again.

Too many secrets corrupt. Revenge corrupts. Evil destroys. All means do not justify the cause. Her head keeps getting larger and thicker with confusion.

Karen can't be dead, she just can't be.

Hazel and Leslie

"I used to be married to a guy who worked for a *Fortune* 500 company. He was a vice president. He gave me diamond bracelets and gold necklaces. One time he gave me a ruby. We were so rich we had platinum toothpicks and towel warmers in every bathroom, not to mention a housekeeper."

"That's right, Hazel. Would you like a Big Mac? I'm making a run."

"No, I ate real good tonight."

"Sure you don't want some French fries?"

"Well, maybe I'd share some." Hazel belches. "But I did eat me more than one chocolate éclair and you wouldn't want me to lose my girlish figure, Isaac."

"No, now that would be just terrible."

"Yes, it would," Hazel says with a laugh. The ER tech gave her back a slap and Hazel belched, as if on cue.

"How do you do that?" he says, escaping between the automatic doors.

Hazel watches him with a grin. Magic.

Everything is magic.

Dr. Leslie Trenton passes Hazel and winks. "What is it this time? An ingrown toenail?"

"Sarcasm gets you zippo, *nada*, nothing." Hazel slips an envelope in the doctor's white coat and whispers in her ear. "Your orders, ma'am." Then she turns and leaves. "I'm going home."

"Don't forget to take a bath," Dr. Trenton calls after her, fumbling in her pocket, a frown slitting her forehead like a badly done suture.

She joined the club by accident, although Veronica always says there are no accidents, after trying to save Lois, a new recruit of the group in the ER, who had finally gotten the courage to divorce her abusive husband. She had died of a cerebral hemorrhage when her ex had surprised her in the parking lot of their former home. Too many blows to the head from a golf club.

Another group member, Nancy, had brought Lois in on the night Leslie was on duty. She had also been her next-door neighbor. "I told her this was going to happen. She kept thinking he would change. Leopards don't change their spots. I told her, you know," the woman kept saying over and over. "This didn't have to happen."

"I know," Leslie said under her breath. "Maybe she was just too scared. Where's the guy?"

"Drunker than the lord. Police should've taken him downtown by now."

"Next of kin?"

"How about a boy, age eight? He's in the waiting room with my husband, Marlon, and my daughter, Sara."

"I wish this stuff wouldn't happen." A policeman approached her, flipping through papers. "Doc? Can I talk to you about—about—"

"Lois Benson," Nancy interrupted. "What—you get so many you can't keep the names straight?"

"Excuse me, are you related to the victim?"

"We all are," Nancy said.

Leslie had been so impressed. When she got the invitation to the first meeting, something had told her to go.

Now she wasn't so certain it had been a good idea. A doctor doesn't get into death. A doctor is supposed to save lives, not take them.

Of course, there's always a first time.

Babette

The Glamour Café in New York City appears deserted. A goofy, rather brainless imitation of the Fashion Café and Planet Hollywood with a dash of McDonald's, it had been opened by a trio of television actresses formerly of a hit sitcom that once been the epitome of Trend. They had made a fortune, become stars almost overnight, authorities upon glamor and style to the twentysomething and whateversomething group who dined on tabloid TV style with the hunger of cats who haven't eaten in days, then when fed, gobble so fast they have to throw up an hour later. Bulimic chic. Babette nurses her gin and tonic and stares at her empty shot glass that had held overpriced tequila.

The Man sits across from her.

"So my contract has been terminated."

"You can make this easy or you can make this hard. Face it, Babette, you had a good run."

The Other Man had done it to her.

"Who made him God? Stop it, don't answer that. I know, the billboards make him God. His fucking empire of designer shops, lines, commercials, perfumes, and farts makes him God. So I mean, what's the big deal? So I wouldn't fuck him? He fucks everyone. Why was my turn down so special?"

The Man looks away politely, ignoring her tirade. He stares at the giant face of the actress with the super hair and big mauve mouth. "She's so Not Important. . . ."

"Don't try to change the subject." Babette's hands shake as she tries to light a cigarette.

"You're not supposed to smoke in here," their chirpy waitress reminds her.

Babette curses and throws the unlit cigarette down. "And now I'm supposed to say I'm not important or it's not important that bastard has so much effing power, he can just do this to me?"

"You did it to yourself. You can't expect to be a role model to teenagers with your stupid attitude. You're selfish, Babette. Who cares who you sleep with? Moms care. Not the kids, certainly, but let's face it, you are not the *Seventeen* cover girl anymore. Hell, you couldn't even make *Sassy,* and *Vogue* thinks you're trashy; *Elle* thinks you are no longer thin enough; and *Playboy* only wants to do a spread because you're so good at showing everyone you don't have to wear panties or bras. Europe's the only place for you. Our agency is no longer representing you but I'm sure someone will like you over there, where they don't understand English so well. Face it, Babs, baby, you just talked too much."

"About him."

"You blew it."

All the money, too. "I was *Clairvoyant*. I made all that money for that stinking perfume."

"I know, go into acting." The man examines his manicure. His cell phone buzzes. "Sorry," he turns his attention to his call, moving away from Babette, speaking quietly.

Babette stares into the painted eyes of the actress reportedly now an alcoholic whore.

The man ends his call and smiles at Babette. "We can still be friends, at least. I can tell Hayley we're square."

Hayley is his boss, her real boss, not this thing. She has to work to recall his name. Clark something. Not Clark Kent. More like Clark Fart. He has pale green eyes and pale white skin with moles on his cheek and a hairless chest he has waxed regularly. She wonders if he has armpit hair and if this also gets removed weekly.

"Just admit it. He's put out the word, hasn't he?"

"God, Babette, you're so *noir*. Things like that just don't happen. Do you think he gives a damn about you? Simply put, your time in the spotlight has passed. Move on. Get a life." Clark strokes the plastic salt shaker in the shape of one of the actresses. "Take acting lessons. . . ."

Very funny. Babette looks down at her manicure, at her pale blue nails. It had seemed a good idea at the time. Now it just seems pathetic.

"Are you screwing him?"

Clark turns red. "Wha-at?"

"The Big Kahuna. I know he does boys and girls. See, that's the thing I don't understand. Why does he have to pick on me?"

"Look, I have a meeting." Clark stands and stares at her icily. "See ya—good luck." He leaves a paper she needs to sign and send back to the agency. She may or may not sign it. She could make things hard.

Or easy. It might be very easy. To do him. Not Clark. The other man. The Emperor of Star, the Showman of Style without Substance, He Who Will Be Obeyed.

The chirpy waitress returns. "Anything else?"

Some tourists have landed. All is right with the world.

"Yeah, some cyanide, if you have it."

"Oh, you models are so funny," she says with a laugh.

Right.

Babette grubs around in her bag for a mirror. She studies her mouth. The bluish-brownish-reddish stain upon her licks suddenly seems totally hideous. She is not going to wait for the club to give her approval for what must be done. There comes a time when you have to break from the pack.

He wanted to do her in the rear. He wanted to hear her say she preferred him to his wife. She just couldn't do it.

She starts to light the cigarette again. The chirpy waitress is busy and doesn't notice. But her hand's shaking too much.

She could do him, all right. A woman could do anything once she really focuses. The actresses beam down from the walls, smiling, always smiling or pouting with just the right finesse, sparkling with glamor. Look what they had done with minimal talent and looks, thanks to Nielsen numbers and smart TV writers and directors and producers and money. Money.

Money talks. Money listens. Advertising. Image.

Clairvoyance. This is the face of the future.

"I see a line that leads to you," she says. Suddenly a line of coke dances in her brain. Nope, she can't afford to do that again. She has to remain *clairvoyantly* clear. On what must be done.

Jill and Hazel

"I just want it to stop," Jill says very softly.

The bag lady doesn't say anything at first, she just sighs and scrambles around in the plastic bag. "Hate these things—always prefer paper, brown paper, but they're too lazy to open them up and bag the groceries in 'em. Have to ask, and they act like it's a special gift. Bottles are too heavy for plastic. Waste paper. They always waste paper because they're lazy. Want to load up your arm with 'em." Hazel remembers how simple the beginning of the club had been. Years ago it had been just a sisterhood of women who wanted to take charge of their lives, to seize their own power, to avenge those who had none. How had it become more of a powerhood than a sisterhood?

She sighs. It began with the first killing. A man who had gotten away with murder. Of his own mother. Hazel's mother. Hazel's brother a murderer. She sighs, wanting to forget. She will forget. Somehow.

"Can't we make it stop? I'm a Christian. Christians don't kill."

"Yes, sometimes they do." The bus stop was still pretty empty, but soon it would fill up. "Let's walk down to Sundance Square and look at the courthouse. I like looking at that thing. Downtown Fort Worth is just so much easier to walk around in than downtown Dallas. President Clinton stopped here, you know, rather than Dallas. Probably the Kennedy thing. Bad karma. But Dallas isn't a bad place, entirely. They have the State Fair. Ever been to the State Fair? I think Big Tex oughta be black once in a while. But then he'd need to be Hispanic, and then Vietnamese. Lots of Orientals here now. Texas is a melting pot. Melting pot. That can be good and that can be bad, I suppose."

"Hazel, killing people is a bad thing. I just don't think it's a good thing. You just shouldn't. ' "Vengeance is mine," saith the Lord.' Jesus didn't approve of it."

"It's a little late in the day to start having a conscience. I don't approve of it either, but sis, it happens, for a very good reason. An eye for an eye, and isn't it better to be organized? To this day my first kill remains 'accidental death' on the books, and he ain't going around burning churches and temples of good God-fearing, God-loving folk any longer, praise God. Jill, he was a very bad man. I can even say it was self-defense. He tried to rape me and . . ." Hazel is lying, of course.

That no-account fool church-burning fool did deserve to die. But the first real kill had been her own brother. Her boyfriend on the police force had found her crying over her mother's inert form, oblivious to dead Jay in the corner, where she whooped him on the side of the head with her mom's iron skillet, still dripping warm bacon grease. Hazel had looked up, crying, ignoring her own knife wounds. "Jay said he wouldn't take no back talk no more. He was going to take the rent money and Mama said no. . . ." Maybe it was justified, righteously so. Jill's whimpering brings her back to the present.

"Look, I want it to stop, for me, at least. Can't I please leave the group? I really think she sabotaged the whole plane Karen was on— I really do. Why would she kill Karen?"

"You know why," Hazel says unhappily.

"No, I don't."

"Maybe Veronica believed she was going to snitch on us. Maybe she even had proof that she had already begun talking to someone at *The Dallas Morning News*. But let me ask you this, little sister: If you leave us, how are we to be sure you wouldn't go to someone about your suspicions? At least Karen was a murderer. You're still a greenhorn. And seriously, now, Veronica wouldn't sabotage a whole plane. It was just a horrible accident."

"If she was going to do that, we'd all get into trouble—so I don't believe Karen was going to tell anyone about us. And why would I want to get myself in trouble? It doesn't make any sense. Besides, Karen would've told me—we never kept secrets from each other. And furthermore, she wouldn't have wanted me to pay for her crime. I just don't trust Veronica."

Hazel smiles her trademark crooked smile. "I wouldn't either, if I were you, child."

"What does that mean?"

"You know, sister, any woman doing my man would be sure enough suspect in my eyes."

Jill turns to look at Hazel slowly, her breath coming and going in ragged little gasps. It feels like someone is squeezing her chest. She could be having a heart attack. Her blood pressure could be going through the roof. She could be dying. "What are you saying?"

"Don't tell me you don't know." She had chosen Veronica to be her successor to the throne. Now it is time to dethrone Veronica, now a liability, a disgrace through bad judgment, ill will, and pure, unadulterated instability. If the center does not hold, chaos always erupts. Hazel sees that Jill might be the right one to take over. The simplicity of her rage appears both holy and organized. That's what the club needs, if it is to endure such tragedy.

Jill touches her bare neck. The short, sassy haircut she'd just gotten earlier that morning suddenly feels too bare and mannish. Her skin feels cold. What she needs is more hair and it is gone, all gone. A wind kicks up. She watches Hazel's plastic bag take to the air like a balloon that has been deflated by the prick of a malicious child. Karen did that once, just to be mean because Jill had gotten the red balloon

Karen wanted, while she got stuck with a boring white one on Valentine's Day.

Hazel takes a bite out of a Ding Dong. She swallows happily and shakes her head. "Damn, you girls slay me. The wives are always the last to know even when it's right there, in front of their face.

"I think I'm ready to stop this routine. I want to go back to being rich. It will be good getting back home to Highland Park. Or maybe I'll go back to my Santa Fe condo or maybe open up the beach house in Malibu. Or the mountains. I could buy a place in Aspen. Or no, Montana, a ranch in Montana or Wyoming. No, it's too cold up there. Europe—haven't been there in a while. France. Rich black women always do well in France. . . ." She wipes her mouth daintily on the sleeve of her jeans jacket.

"Hazel!" Jill's whole body turns to Hazel's, trembling vaguely like a poodle held back by a strong leash. "Hazel, come on, tell me what you know!"

"Tell me what *you* know, sweetie."

"I don't know anything—what you're saying. He wouldn't be unfaithful to me. We have a good marriage. It was like a romance novel, how we met. And he brings me little surprises. Especially Godiva chocolates and sometimes flowers or jewelry. Charms for this sterling silver bracelet—hearts, lots of little hearts—"

"But I bet he never quotes Maya Angelou."

"He doesn't like poetry."

"Honey, he doesn't like you and I bet you get these little surprises after every time he's unfaithful."

"He loves me," Jill whispers.

Hazel coughs and studies her feet in the ugly old nurse's shoes Doc had given her for her masquerade. "Liking should come first. Then when the loving gets harder, the man's more liable to stick around to wait for the tide to come back in."

"What's that?"

"Loving goes in and out like the tides. But if you don't like the ocean you're swimming in, what can I say, baby, but watch what happens when the moon comes out and he's thinking, whoa—'I got to get to the Pacific' when he oughta stick to the Atlantic, if you know what I mean."

Jill doesn't exactly know what she means but she remembers the last charm Brad gave her. The little coyote. She hates coyotes. When she was a little girl, she tried to pet a wild dog that bit her. The emergency room doctor had to give her twelve stitches. Her father had told her, "That's what you get for petting a coyote." How had Brad forgot? After all this time, she still has the scars.

Veronica

His body reminds her of a glove her mother used to keep in the bottom drawer of her antique bureau. It smelled of old moisture, almost a mildew smell but scented lightly with old rose petals and ancient ghost clothes no longer stored there. Nightshirts, long johns, silken underthings no longer in fashion, teddies and slips, hosiery that needs washing. Panties that are not quite clean. Memories of ancient couplings. White-people clothes. It should remind her of her father, the lost bullfighter from Madrid, the one in the storybook her mother gave her when she was six. "This is your father." It was a drawing. He had on fancy clothes, almost girl clothes. He even had a little cape and a funny hat only an old crazy woman would wear.

Carlos. Pedro. Juan. She does not know his name. Her mother was such a liar. She will never know his name.

Veronica once owned a petticoat that her mother said belonged to his mother. Later she found out it came from JCPenney. There are no traces of her heritage. She practically took apart the bureau once, looking for a secret drawer to see if she could find the love letters. Her mother said her father used to write the most beautiful, ardent letters any woman could wish for, in Spanish, never in English. Her mother met her father while she was on vacation in Spain, an innocent young student he deflowered and impregnated but never married. "He killed many bulls, my conquistador."

"Excuse me?"

Veronica's exquisite body turns on the creamy silken sheets. Her lovely head in profile, her dark, shiny hair fanned across the pillowcase fringed with lace shot through with golden thread urges him to touch her. She watches him fondle her right breast, the nipple coming awake. "My father killed bulls."

"My father was as stubborn as an old bull," he says with a laugh.

Veronica tenses. "You shouldn't make fun of your father."

The hand falls in supplication. She grabs it and places it between her legs. "What are we going to do about her?"

"Who?"

"Your wife. She is in the way."

"I'll divorce her."

"And the children?"

"Do you want to have children?"

"Your children?"

"Mine? 'Rica—my 'Rica, you are mine, mine. I love you; I love you . . ." His mouth litters her body with his sloppy kisses and he comes down on her like a devouring angel.

Veronica pretends to care. "We can keep the children but she's in the way, the mother is in the way. She won't give them up without a fight—and today we started a family, I think, I really believe it is so."

He moans, unable to answer. He will do anything for her. She will make sure. Jill is a mess. Karen was a disaster. The whole thing's crashing down on her head. She still recalls the voice in the night on her answering machine. Karen had panicked. Karen had to come clean. No time to plan. She just had to do it. It was messy. Sometimes the voices scream in her head. The headlines dance in her brain, accompanied by that awful song, the one they said originated in Mexico. Sometimes Selena is singing it. Sometimes it is Garth Brooks. But the worst dream is when the passengers of the plane she doomed to death do it, dripping blood and tears. Blood and tears. It is driving her crazy. Psycho. For real. A woman who is crazy.

Jill must get out of the way. She knows. No one must know.

The man's body falls off of her and she thinks of the seed spilled upon her and how they may sprout something inside her. It's not enough that she gets rid of her. She must show her who has the power to create, take charge.

Her father's body created her. Then abandoned her. Veronica rises, stands naked over her lover. Her looks up at her hungrily. "Come back to bed; turn around, let me kiss your ass."

"You must promise to tell her."

He looks suddenly toward the bedroom door slowly opening. "I don't have to."

Veronica smiles, looking over her shoulder at the foolish girl he calls a wife.

Jill's pale white face has no blood in it. Just pain and the powdery blush she probably got in her Lancôme gift bag when she bought the exfoliant that was supposed to make her fake tan look better. Veronica wants to laugh out loud at the streaks on her silly white legs.

Veronica smells her fingers. It's repulsive but she wants to get her point across. "Baby, look, it's not what you think, not exactly. Brad, darling, we are not alone, we have a visitor, I'm afraid." His exhausted penis is exposed. "Cover yourself, Brad, your wife has just joined us. I think we need to have a talk, just the three of us, to set things straight. Don't you?"

He's not even embarrassed or even ashamed, just disgusted. Veronica puts on his white shirt stiff with extra starch. "Brad and I are getting married," she says, "I hope we can still be friends, though. It just happened—we didn't plan it, Jilly."

Jill makes the sign of the cross. She hates anyone to call her Jilly, and today she also hates Veronica. It is a sin to hate.

Veronica's eyes suddenly rest on the crucifix hanging over their bed. It is her turn to feel terrified and hideous. "You didn't say you were Catholic," she splutters, loosing composure for just a second, for just one brief second. Veronica thinks her father was Catholic. Certainly he has been crucified on the cross as long as Jesus.

Jill has left the room, unable to digest the grotesque display, the aftermath of illicit sex.

Veronica rummages through Jill's lingerie drawer, stealing some Dior hose and some fresh panties. She will not clean herself. She needs to be pregnant. She hopes to be pregnant. There's a gun there. The convenience of the gun unnerves her. It is too perfect.

He sits on the side of the bed, head in hand. "It is not what I thought it would be. I shouldn't have let it go this far. I have to make it up to her. What we did was cruel, unspeakable. Did you see her face? Oh, God, how can I live with myself?" The tone in his voice is both insincere and almost humorous.

How can anyone? Veronica finds gloves in Jill's drawer, under a tangle of silken scarves and discarded hair ornaments. They are old-fashioned, probably belonged to Jill's mother or grandmother. Blue as a sky, soft, delicate. She puts them on, smiling at the mother-of-pearl closing. The gun is loaded. She can shoot him. Instead of her. Or herself. She chooses to do neither. Instead she puts the gun into her purse. Then she goes to him, naked with blue gloves on her hands. "Don't worry, darling, I will not leave you," she says, kneeling before him.

It starts all over again. She is almost disappointed he is so weak.

Leslie and Babette

"How did it really happen?"

"How does anything?"

"He just fell in front of the car and I ran over him. The traffic is terrible in New York City. Someone in the back squealed their tires and honked and someone was running down the street, screaming about a purse snatcher or a kid, I don't know. I just hit him. It was an accident. A fortunate one, but an accident nonetheless. He was drunker than the Lord. The autopsy proved that. Higher than a Goodyear blimp on Super Bowl Sunday."

"You had been stalking him, Babette. We all knew you wanted him to be your kill, and now he's dead. Are you telling me it was an accident?"

"The police said it was. Didn't you hear the news report? It's in every magazine and every newspaper and every tabloid show in the nation. It was an accident, I tell you." Babette pulls at the hair on her forehead nervously. Her eyes seem wild, directionless. She will not look at Leslie directly.

Leslie doesn't like her assignment. It is not the one she expected, the publisher in bed with the drug cartel. And the drug in the syringe? She doesn't even know what it is. All she has is an educated suspicion, and this hotel room is not an operating room.

Killing a sister was never part of the agreement. Her stomach aches, and she longs to pop an antacid. She feels nauseous. A doctor doesn't kill people, at least not on purpose. Swallowing down bilge, she forges on bravely. "You need to play by the rules, Babette. If you can't play by the rules you shouldn't be allowed to be in the club."

"The club? Good heavens, Leslie, you sound like you belong to the NFL or something—no, I know—you sound like you're talking about my mother's country club. They had rules. Oh, didn't they. I got